DESERVED

Deserved

ECONOMIC MEMORIES AFTER
THE FALL OF THE IRON CURTAIN

Till Hilmar

Columbia University Press
New York

Columbia University Press
Publishers Since 1893
New York   Chichester, West Sussex
cup.columbia.edu

Copyright © 2023 Columbia University Press
All rights reserved

Library of Congress Cataloging-in-Publication Data
Names: Hilmar, Till, 1985– author.
Title: Deserved : economic memories after the fall of the Iron Curtain / Till Hilmar.
Description: New York, NY : Columbia University Press, [2023] |
Includes bibliographical references and index.
Identifiers: LCCN 2022051741 (print) | LCCN 2022051742 (ebook) |
ISBN 9780231209786 (hardback) | ISBN 9780231209793 (trade paperback) |
ISBN 9780231558112 (ebook)
Subjects: LCSH: Post-communism—Europe, Central. |
Post-communism—Europe, Eastern. | Former communist countries—Economic conditions. |
Former communist countries—Social conditions.
Classification: LCC HC244 .H55 2023 (print) | LCC HC244 (ebook) |
DDC 330.947—dc23/eng/20221104
LC record available at https://lccn.loc.gov/2022051741
LC ebook record available at https://lccn.loc.gov/2022051742

Columbia University Press books are printed on permanent
and durable acid-free paper.
Printed in the United States of America

Cover design: Noah Arlow
Cover image: Colin McPherson/Alamy Stock Photo

CONTENTS

Introduction   1

Chapter One
Historical Trajectories   33

Chapter Two
Remembering Economic Change After 1989   62

Chapter Three
Deserving and Undeserving Others   92

Chapter Four
The Social Experience of the Transformation Period   111

Epilogue
How Right-Wing Populists Capture Deservingness   167

METHODOLOGICAL APPENDIX   173

ACKNOWLEDGMENTS   183

COPYRIGHT ACKNOWLEDGMENTS   187

NOTES   189

BIBLIOGRAPHY   239

INDEX   257

DESERVED

INTRODUCTION

REMEMBERING ECONOMIC PAIN

In 1973, American artist and photographer Allan Sekula presented his exhibition *Aerospace Folktales* at the University of California in San Diego. The show featured a set of photos, an audio track, and a short interview that revolved around the life of an aerospace engineer. The engineer had recently been laid off by a large Lockheed Martin plant in California. "With military contracts cancelled," the engineer recounts to Sekula, "many of our major aerospace companies were forced to lay off quite a number of their professional-technical personnel." He found himself in a situation with "hundreds of people applying for the limited jobs that exist." In his photos and in the conversations, the artist carefully documents the economic pain suffered by the engineer's family: "There is a demoralizing reaction on the part of the individual experiencing unemployment. At first, he might feel very confident that he has something that will impress a potential employer. And as time goes on and he is faced with refusal after refusal, he begins to doubt," the engineer reveals. Yet there can be no doubt about the value of his expertise: "I wish to make one point clear: these people are capable of adapting themselves to many, many different types of jobs. A good scientist and engineer, with his organizing ability, his preciseness, his ability to adapt to different situations, can be of great value in administrative positions and clerical tasks—checking procedures, and assisting in systems analyses."[1]

Then the engineer makes a remarkable suggestion. Drawing a lesson from his disheartening experience, he targets the institutions of society as a whole: "We're faced with a problem today among the welfare agencies where there have been accusations that there's been a misuse of public funds. And granted, there must be a certain percentage of people receiving aid—taxpayers' money—who do not deserve it, who have either lied or have misrepresented facts. And this is a burden upon the taxpayer," he explains to Sekula. The solution, he proposes is to have professional people like him "investigate" these individuals, "to pin down any potential fraud . . . You would be able to give a well-earned salary to these unemployed engineers and scientists, and you would also be able to save a tremendous amount of money."

Aerospace Folktales is a piece of art, yet Sekula also invites us to consider that the engineer himself engages in a form of aesthetic representation of what he had to endure, who is to blame, and what should be done about it, that he deploys a specific cultural language to make sense of economic shock and social shame. It is a language that translates economic pain into a problem of moral deservingness.

We live in a world of multiple crises today: war, climate emergencies, a pandemic, financial crises, and automation in the workplace produce economic dislocation for millions of people at a historically unprecedented pace. These turbulent processes confront individuals with realities that are not of their own choosing. Yet we also live in a world in which people are increasingly prone to think of their economic outcomes— careers, income, wealth, social status—as something that they have generated individually. The meritocratic ideology, in which differences in those achievements are seen as legitimate if they are rooted in effort, skills, or individual performance, is more dominant than ever. Around the world, the fact that social inequalities have dramatically risen over the past decades has not abated this trend. In fact, it has only reinforced it: people who grew up with rising levels of inequality tend to adhere to the principle of meritocracy ever more strongly.[2] This is a world presaged by Sekula's *Aerospace Folktales*, a world in which the *winners* of the game of economic competition can take full credit for what they have; the *losers* seemingly only have themselves to blame.

INTRODUCTION

In this book, I ask: how it is possible that people who underwent disruptive economic change perceive its outcomes in individual terms? A common answer is to say that we live in neoliberal societies that encourage people to put their self-interest first and to disregard others around them. People have become atomized and isolated, the argument goes, and they have unlearned what it means to be part of a community. They have forgotten what we owe each other. Yet something is not quite right about this diagnosis. It assumes that we live our lives today in a space that is somehow devoid of morality.

It thereby misses a crucial fact: people are embedded in social relations, and they therefore articulate economic aspirations and experiences as part of a social dynamic. In this book, I draw on in-depth interviews with dozens of people who lived through disruptive economic change. Based on this research, I show that it is precisely the concern of what people owe each other—the moral concern—that drives how many people reason about economic outcomes. They perceive them, I demonstrate, through the lens of moral deservingness, judgments of economic worth that they pass on each other. Those judgments are nurtured in the very social fabric of everyday life. I show that people negotiate ideas of economic deservingness in their social surroundings—so much so, in fact, that they make their social ties dependent on the need for recognition. Recalling episodes of broken friendship ties after 1989, people invoke ideas of deservingness to give account for why interpersonal ruptures happened.

Judgments of deservingness are powerful because they constitute a _cultural language of social inclusion_. They reveal deeper dimensions of the meaning of the economic realm: they are concerned with issues of social recognition, membership, and belonging. People think of their economic outcomes as deserved, and they think of their social ties also as deserved. I set out to demonstrate in this book that this is a dynamic of social memory. Specifically, I show that social inclusion and exclusion is intricately intertwined with how people remember economic change, with the ways in which they narrate, interpret, and share difficult pasts with others. References to the past bind people together, but they can also divide them. Much has been written on the role of memory in politics, nationalism, and ethnic identity, so we may be well aware of this mechanism in these realms. But we are only beginning to grasp its power in relation to work and economics. Fostering understanding of economic memories, both theoretically and empirically, is a core aim of this book.[3]

4

INTRODUCTION

THE RUPTURE OF 1989: LASTING CONSEQUENCES

In this book, I explore the aftermath of a relatively recent large-scale crisis: the shift from state-socialist rule to capitalist market democracy in Central Europe after 1989. This process, which is variously referred to as the postsocialist *transformation* or *transition* in the social science literature, was nothing short of an epic break that turned the lives of hundreds of millions of people upside down. The revolutions of 1989 and the fall of the Berlin Wall were followed by a deep economic recession that was about as dramatic as—and, in some former Soviet societies, lasted even longer than—the Great Depression of the 1920s and 1930s in the United States. Existing labor arrangements were shaken up in the blink of an eye. Large-scale sectoral changes, before all rapid deindustrialization, swiftly upended the world of work. Millions lost their jobs, many slid into poverty, and scores of people migrated somewhere else in the hope of leaving economic despair behind. If socialist states had guaranteed basic economic security for generations, now, all of sudden people had to assume risks individually. Social inequality was growing after 1989, a process palpable in each and everyone's immediate environment of family and friends.

Across the former state-socialist world, the breakdown of state socialism unleashed a set of processes that social scientists call *structural* in nature: society-wide developments that leave individuals with very little space to make autonomous decisions on their own. Instead, the ways people were affected by these changes fundamentally varied by factors that were not of their own choosing: depending on a person's age, gender, ethnicity, location, qualifications, and social connections in 1989, he or she found themselves with very different chances and opportunities to adjust to the new order. All of these conditions decisively shaped people's economic trajectories during the 1990s and beyond. In other words, 1989 wasn't so much about individual choice as it was about a given set of social conditions, preexisting resources, and carved-out trajectories.

This may strike us as a peculiar reading. Isn't the legacy of 1989 something else—don't the fall of the Berlin Wall, the Velvet Revolution, and the Polish roundtable represent the most iconic moments of freedom in recent history? There can be no doubt about it. The changes of 1989–1991 were moments of extraordinary excitement, enthusiasm, and hope across

INTRODUCTION

Europe and the former Soviet Union. Unexpectedly, millions found themselves seemingly in a suspension of time. By the late 1980s, everyone had become accustomed to the political and economic repression of dissident voices, the political distribution of life chances, and the nefariousness of the Communist Party elite. "Throughout the long decades of the 1970s and 1980s", writes Marci Shore, "there were many people who believed that 'it'—communism—would one day come to an end. There were very few, however, who believed that it would come to an end in their lifetime." When the militarized border suddenly came down, it was all a thing of the past. This was the moment that revealed that "everything was forever, until it was no more." It was a liberation from a political system that had no positive vision for the future to offer, a system that instead policed fragments of an ideology that not even its ruling elites believed in anymore using intimidation, oppression, and propaganda.[4]

Fast-forward to today. What image do we gain from these societies? In Central Europe, a lot has been achieved in the three decades after 1989: elections are free (in most cases), the rule of law is formally in place, economic growth has been spectacular in some cases, living standards have risen, and the seeds of civil society have grown. At the same time, there is a pervasive sense of distrust: distrust in elites and in the political institutions of liberal democracy. It has become painfully clear that, today, large swaths of the population in Central Europe harbor sentiments of injustice and feel that they live in deeply corrupt societies. Wide parts of the population are infuriated with the ways a tiny elite managed to concentrate wealth among themselves; in fact, in the eyes of many, wealth is inseparable from corruption. The polarization of *winners* and *losers* of the transformation fuels distrust, as rapidly rising levels of inequality have left people with a strong sense of social dislocation. As Nina Bandelj and Christopher Gibson point out, feelings of hostility are so widespread in the region that, of the ten countries in the world that show the lowest levels of acceptance of migrants among citizens, nine are former socialist societies—only the 2022 Russian attack on Ukraine, when millions of Ukrainians were forced to flee to Poland, has altered these statistics.[5] In some post-Soviet societies—and in Russia today, once again a repressive regime—there is now a significant number of citizens who openly favor authoritarian over democratic rule. Right-wing populist parties have flourished in this environment, proposing nativist and nationalist answers that resonate with the sense of loss nourished by the experiences of the post-1989 period. They are the false prophets of social disintegration.

To understand what happened, we must focus on how people experienced the changes in their everyday lives. For a long time, social scientists have studied the period from a top-down perspective, focusing on elites and elite institutions. This has finally changed. This book is part of a broader effort to reconstruct the ways in which the manifold dimensions of political, economic, and social change were perceived and navigated by the people who, after all, directly had to bear their consequences.

Economies in Turmoil

The quest to understand the consequences of these shifts necessarily begins with economics. Before everything else, the shifts represent a story of loss. The pace of change in the early 1990s was breathtaking, but nowhere across the postsocialist world was it initially a story of growth; instead, it was one of a devaluation of existing economic arrangements. Currencies, firms, savings, and labor all profoundly lost in value. This was not, in fact, an aberration from what policymakers had expected. It was instead the core tenet of the now-infamous policy of shock therapy: the idea that, for a market economy to emerge, one had to move fast and break all things that represented the old, state-socialist economic order. In order to purify the region from its socialist economic baggage, political and economic experts quickly agreed on what was to be done. After the demise of state socialism, international financial institutions recommended a uniform package of macroeconomic stabilization to be implemented across the region. Elaborated by the International Monetary Fund, the World Bank, and the European Bank for Reconstruction and Development, it came to be known as the Washington Consensus. The power of these institutions over domestic policy decisions in the early 1990s can hardly be overstated: very few states—such as Turkmenistan and Belarus—resisted the pressure to adjust in the spirit of the reform agenda.[6] Policymakers' overarching goal was to install a market logic of supply and demand. Prices, formerly fixed by socialist states, needed to be liberalized. State subsidies, which before 1989 made most everyday goods and services in food, housing, transportation, and health care affordable, were to be radically reduced or removed. The state was to retreat from society.

INTRODUCTION

Inflation

For ordinary citizens, the immediate effect of these reforms was that prices shot up. High levels of inflation diminished people's savings and the value of firms. In the early 1990s, in Poland, for instance, prices for medicine were suddenly so high that many elderly people could no longer afford prescription drugs. Wages, on the other hand, did not increase. Many could barely generate sufficient income to make ends meet in the first years after the revolutions. In many cases, real wages declined and didn't return to their 1989 levels until around the turn of the century. Weak consumer spending in turn resulted in lower levels of productivity. *joblessness*

What kind of economic reality was emerging for working people? Across the region, the workforce was dramatically downsized. If Communist Party elites had wanted more people to participate in the workforce, the new political and economic rulers wanted less. In the first decade after 1989, the total number of employees declined by 25 percent in Hungary, by around 15 percent in the Czech Republic and Slovakia, and by around 8 percent in Poland.[7] Millions left the labor force, often in early retirement. Joblessness was particularly acute for those working in agriculture or industry, the sectors of the economy that were now in steep decline. Industrial production dwindled by between 30 percent and 50 percent compared to its 1989 levels in the first three years after the system change—East Germany, which experienced a whopping 75 percent reduction in industrial output, was hit particularly hard. People's former workplaces disappeared from one day to the next. Job loss was a different reality depending on where one lived. In Poland, around 13.5 percent of the population was unemployed in 1992; in East Germany, a staggering 30 percent were affected in some parts of the country by the mid-1990s.[8] In the Czech Republic, by contrast, unemployment levels remained relatively low throughout the 1990s.

The very idea of shock therapy was predicated on the notion that the transition to a market economy would necessarily have to be painful. How long and how deep this pain would run was a question that no one seemed to care to answer. Further into the 1990s, policymakers remained committed to this agenda. It did not make a difference whether a rightist or leftist government was in power, and power did actually change hands, which was widely regarded as an indicator that democratic consolidation was underway. Shock therapy reforms were implemented in any case. In fact, leftist governments, perpetually in fear of being deemed *backward* and associated with the old Communist Party elites, proved to be even more zealous in pursuing privatization schemes than rightist parties in power.[9] The political consensus was that labor had to become cheaper. And it was, indeed, very cheap: labor costs were only 7 percent of the European Union average at the 1990 exchange rate, with the exception of East Germany, which adapted the West German currency that year.[10] Except for East Germany, it took a long time for wages to rise. Only at the turn of the century did real incomes finally grow in most Eastern European countries. And except for the relatively successful Visegrad economies—Poland, Czechia, Slovakia, and Hungary—the situation was particularly dire. In a comparative overview, anthropologist Kristen Ghodsee and political scientist Mitchell Orenstein note that, from twenty-eight postsocialist societies, it took the average country around seventeen years to return to 1989 levels of economic production—and some countries in the particularly hard-hit former Soviet Union have not recovered until today. There, the transformation in fact impoverished a sizable part of the population. The dramatic health outcomes caused by these socioeconomic dislocations, such as a decline in life expectancy, pervasive substance abuse, rising rates of depression and other mental illnesses and in domestic violence, may well be described as the "deaths of despair" of Eastern Europe—analogous to what scholars observe in the deindustrializing U.S. rust belt.[11]

From whatever angle we look at it, we must ultimately acknowledge that this is a story of economic crisis, the devaluation of labor, and the social stratification of society along unequal pathways for decades to come. This crucial insight does not contradict the notion that 1989 was a moment of democratic renewal, that the revolutions did bring economic prosperity, rising living standards, and modernization, exactly what many in the West had hoped for. But not everyone was able to reap the benefits of economic growth in the same way. Across the postsocialist world, elderly people, unskilled workers, and rural residents were much more likely to lose out than were younger, urban, highly educated individuals. People's position in the labor market at the time profoundly shaped their life course and what was in store for them after 1989. This is one elementary fact that needs to be recognized: today's outcomes are generated by yesterday's structures. Social inequalities bridge time, linking the present to the period after the revolutions. In this book, I take this perspective as a point of departure.

INTRODUCTION

Economics as a Matter of Justice: Nostalgia in the Making?

This view on the post-1989 period animates this book's core concern: *how do people make sense of disruptive economic change?* Social structure matters. The resources that people have at their disposal determine the degree to which they can exercise control over their economic lives. But culture also matters. Economics is not just numbers, not merely an objective force in the world. It is something that affects people in their lives. Economic facts are not read and perceived in a morally neutral way. They resonate, or fail to resonate, with existing ideas, values, commitments, and memories. We understand them affectively, with our minds and hearts.[12] In everyday life, the economy is experienced culturally, through existing narratives, scripts, and models of understanding. There is something about the way we relate to others through our sentiments about economics that makes us feel closer to others. Closer to some people, we may want to add—and perhaps less close to others. In this book, I put these considerations into practice. Key to this endeavor is to examine the meaning structure behind work, the sense of worth that individuals derive from regarding themselves and others around them as productive members of society. To this end, anthropological and ethnographic forays into postsocialist life and work worlds, like Elizabeth Dunn's study of workers coping with the privatization of a Polish baby food factory, Martha Lampland's as well as Chris Hann's accounts of the changing value of work in the Hungarian countryside, and Andreas Glaeser's ethnography of the merging of East and West German police in 1990s Berlin, provide intellectual landmarks.[13]

I propose a focused perspective on the experience of economic change by foregrounding the morphology of justice ideas. Why justice ideas? The post-1989 transformations entailed a central promise: that of individual achievement and social upward mobility in market society. This is an economic as much as a social promise, combined in the notion that one can be a worthy member of the new social order on the basis of one's contributions.[14] Conversely, if a person's sense of being valued as a contributor is undermined, if there are reasons to believe that his or her economic efforts remain unrecognized and undervalued, he or she will likely perceive this as a violation of a set of intrinsically held commitments and may also feel socially excluded as a consequence. Because people frequently

INTRODUCTION

seek to generate the sense of being a worthy member of society in the realm of work, we must pay particular attention to textures of meaning in this domain.

Some observers have identified sentiments of injustice as the main culprit for the distrust that prevails in postsocialist societies today. Survey researchers note that citizens are deeply disturbed by what they perceive to be endemic corruption around them. People are irritated by the fact that it was evidently not meritocracy but instead nepotism, thievery, and foul play that allowed some to rise to the top after 1989. What is more, they are found to dislike excessive inequalities because they value egalitarianism: in contrast to U.S. Americans but also to West Europeans, they favor more equal societies, societies in which the state assumes a more active role in taking care of its citizens, sheltering them from risks, and reducing the material differences between them.[15] Evidently, the ever-widening gap in incomes, wealth, and life chances after 1989 makes people angry because it contradicts their normative ideas about what a good and just social order looks like.

These are important insights, but there is a critical aspect of the dynamism in justice orientations after the fall of the Berlin Wall that we have yet to come to terms with fully. In this book, I explore justice ideas in greater qualitative depth, approaching their meaning against the horizon of the disruptive experience of the 1990s. This opens a vast trove of accounts of lived experience, and justice is a critical theme in many of them. People link their personal accounts to the level of society, not in the abstract but in the form of biographical knowledge. Their stories reveal *profoundly moralized ideas of economic change*. We must listen to them to truly understand the nature of the disappointment with the transformation period.

A perceptive reader will ask, Isn't this phenomenon driven by nostalgia for the socialist past? In fact, the power of nostalgia—a sense of loss and a longing for objects, people, or ways of living that are associated with the past—has been described in many ethnographies of postsocialist communities. If nostalgia, as a concept, is not defined as an irrational longing for a bygone past and instead conceived of as an immanent framework of meaning and reasoning that connects past, present, and future temporalities, then it is a useful analytical tool.[16] In this book, however, I am primarily concerned with unearthing memories of the 1990s, not with tracing recollections of life before the breakdown of state socialism. Positive or negative evaluations of the pre-1989 past may play an important role in them, but they are not necessarily dominant. By giving people space to articulate economic memories of the transformation period, I am interested in how they link different levels of temporality. Moving the site of memory closer to the present, I suggest, also allows us to understand the nature of loss better, namely, as something that arises out of the dynamic interrelation of expectations and experiences during the 1990s.

WHY DO INDIVIDUAL ATTRIBUTIONS OF DESERVINGNESS DOMINATE?

In interviews with sixty-seven respondents from a generation that has experienced the sea changes after 1989 firsthand, I reveal that, despite the structural nature of the post-1989 shifts, individuals employ a thoroughly moral vocabulary to make sense of them. The discourse of individual responsibility for economic success or failure is widespread. Even though they have experienced great economic and social shocks during the 1990s, they nevertheless believe that people got what they deserved. They conjure skills as a natural and pure source of economic success, and categorize those they deem incompetent as flawed in their character and *undeserving* of their material advantages after 1989. The sense of disappointment or demoralization arises from the feeling of not being recognized as a productive, contributing member of society—through work. Reasoning in this way, today, about thirty-five years after the initial moment of transitioning into market society, people respond to a prevailing moral discourse: the need to reject claims of being a victim of the economic circumstances and the imperative to write a legitimate biography for oneself and for those associated with the self.

This is a surprising finding. The sea changes of 1989 shaped people's life chances, often beyond their control. What is it, then, about the idea of individual responsibility that makes it so powerful? It is not that people naively buy into the transformation as a tale of success. Again, many are highly critical of skyrocketing inequalities and the way these changes played out, and they direct various grievances at the political system and at the Western *takeover* after the revolutions. The Western political model, after it had long been admired, is now, for many, a target of resentment, a "light that failed," as Ivan Krastev and Stephen Holmes succinctly put it.[17]

INTRODUCTION

To grasp why people see economic outcomes through a moralizing lens, we must look at the granular level of how they make sense of this period. I demonstrate that there is a space that nourishes these economic sentiments: the social experience of the transformation time. With the rise of market societies after 1989, individuals had to take a moral stance: whose career aspirations do they deem legitimate, who do they sympathize with and feel close to? Who do they seek to distance themselves from? Critical relations of equality, such as friendship ties, had to be renegotiated in the face of rising social inequality. Before 1989, there were no careers and life chances were leveled; after 1989, material trajectories suddenly diverged. There is a moral claim—a claim of having a legitimate economic biography after 1989—that individuals lay on their social environment. They expect others to share, and support, their assumptions about the ways in which economic worth comes to express personal worth. But the ideas about who deserves what and who was to blame for economic failure, I find, are only superficially about performance and effort—in fact, they are rooted in ideas of moral character. On these grounds, people recall how they would disassociate from others, how they would break formerly trusted ties of equality such as friendship ties.

I offer a theoretical prism that helps to grasp these genuinely sociological foundations of the post-1989 transformation experience. I call it the "moral framework." I demonstrate that this moral framework through which people understand change is a social framework. It is a web woven from concrete ties of social relations to friends, family members, and acquaintances. People apprehend key economic experiences as part of their social surroundings, in the midst of an ensemble of social attachments. The moral framework requires relational recognition. Ties to other people are critical sources of knowledge about the effects and implications of economic change in society and indispensable sources for a sense of continuity of the self. Despite the breakup of the formerly state-socialist world as a story about the rise of market society, we are missing the point if we understand it primarily as a tale of individualization. Instead, the transformation brought to the fore a genuinely cultural articulation of economic experiences and problems of loyalty and rupture in social ties. These are the themes of the moral framework. As I demonstrate, however, morality is not somehow naturally opposed to neoliberal reasoning. In fact, ideas of social worth based on meritocratic reasoning can be deeply moral.[18]

Comparing Czech and East German Transformations

If we wish to dissect the social ramifications of the crisis-ridden 1990s today, we need to do two things. First, we need to go further back in history. State socialism was a laboratory of authoritarian rule, but it was also a system of redistribution and recognition. Hence, the transformation is also a story about the dissolution of an old status order. Second, we should look at the period comparatively—after all, during this time, twenty-eight nations plus the unified German state emerged from what was formerly the Communist Party–ruled Eastern Bloc. Clearly, there is not just *one* experience of the 1990s. To understand this variety of experiences, a systematic framework of analysis that centers on critical processes of change is needed. I therefore embed the interview research on which in this book is based in a historical-comparative study. I focus on two societies from the Central European region: East Germany and the Czech Republic. Because these two societies have experienced a very different type of economic change in the 1990s, juxtaposing them sheds light on different objective parameters of change as well as on the ways in which people subjectively relate to them. There is also a deep analytical rationale for looking at these two cases. Any comparative approach runs the danger of getting lost in an abundance of differences. To avoid the pitfalls of this problem, I identify a shared historical trajectory out of which differences arise. East Germany and the Czech Republic offer such a shared historical trajectory. For four decades—between 1948 and 1989 for East Germany and between 1949 and 1989 for the Czech Republic—the two societies shared a similar political and economic profile that made them stand out from other state-socialist societies. Hence, the comparison is founded on the proposition that similarity before 1989 allows us to explore the role of differences after 1989 in a systematic way.

Among the similarities before the breakdown of state socialism, there is one that is particularly consequential for the argument of this book: each of the two state-socialist regimes promoted a social contract that was based, in the words of Claus Offe, on the principle of "economic integration."[19] They were highly industrialized, highly educated, labor-intense societies that sacralized economics as a source of collective belonging. Organized in a system that promoted and valued a deeply moralized idea of work—the notion of "productive labor"—in the late socialist period, people's identities were strongly enmeshed with their workplace. But after 1989, this model of economic belonging was broken by the massive downsizing of the labor force and the revaluation of skills according to capitalist markets. The old social contract was shredded from one day to the next. Yet the ways this happened, the specific mode by which those older identity resources were upended, varied in the two countries. East Germans were politically incorporated into West Germany and they were soon deemed "backward," "premodern," and "unproductive"—all while experiencing an economic crisis of historic proportions that left hundreds of thousands unemployed and most of the former industrial structure dissolved. Czechs, in contrast, experienced more continuity. Here, unemployment rates remained conspicuously low during the 1990s. Czechs' sense of economic belonging was reconfigured through an explicitly nationalist, gendered story of the transformation time that celebrated them as "manly" and "persevering" neoliberal subjects.

Those state-decreed narratives of economic change enter the moral framework, we will see, fueling a dire sense of social exclusion among East Germans but a relative sense of cohesion among Czechs. This difference underscores that the economic scripts and causal accounts promoted by those in power (answers to the question, Why are we going through this transition?) matter decisively.

East Germany, of course, is often deemed a special case of the transformation. Because of the incorporation of East German state and society into West Germany in the unification treaty of 1990, the assumption is that its story is very different from that of its Central Eastern European neighbors. For a long time, scholars have taken this narrative for granted and focused on comparing East and West German development after reunification. Although I also compare aspects of East and West German development, I do not treat them as the primary analytical tool. I set out with a different assumption, namely, that the comparison of societies with similar conditions at the beginning of the transition in 1989 is rewarding, a fact that has been relatively obliterated by the focus on liaisons among East and West Germans. West German developments after 1989 constitute an illuminating, although selectively important, "negative case" compared to those in East Germany.[20] This angle allows me to pose the question, Was a particular process really specific to East German postsocialist developments after 1989, or can it also be found in West Germany at the same time? In this way, it also indirectly benefits the analysis of Czech trajectories after 1989.

INTRODUCTION

A Focus on Work and Social Relations

In this book, I combine the historical-comparative analysis with biographical research on the transformation period. Comparative analysis is a branch of scholarship that has flourished in recent years. A landmark contribution was presented in 2011 by Polish sociologist Adam Mrozowicki, who surveyed Polish workers' experiences. Major oral history projects document Polish and Czech experiences from the perspective of different generations. These studies reveal that, in the ways people remember everyday changes of the 1990s, two issues are particularly salient: work and social relations.[21]

The interview research underlying this book was designed with this finding in mind. It enables a focus on people's work biography and their sense of change in social relations. To trace work experiences in depth, I compare accounts of people from two professional groups: engineers and health-care workers. This juxtaposition captures emerging labor market inequalities after 1989—care work evolved as a feminized, low-pay profession after the revolutions, while engineers were able, by and large, to generate sizable incomes soon after the system changed. The transformation of health care, to be sure, is a quintessential part of the overarching story of the departure from the old industrial social contract that constitutes the background thread of this analysis. The fate of health care is linked to trajectories of deindustrialization. Historian Gabriel Winant demonstrates this for rust belt America, noting that "the social formations left behind by manufacturing were—at the level of the population—disproportionately aged, sick, unemployed, impoverished, and yet relatively well insured . . . with the secular crisis of industrial employment, the working-class population demanded more care."[22] This is quite similar in fact to what we can observe in postsocialist societies, at least in Central Eastern Europe. The centrality of health care, both as a field of employment and as a service in demand, was a profoundly gendered and inevitable result of the epochal labor market shifts after the breakdown of state socialism. Considering the experience of health-care workers also means expanding our view beyond the iconic, dominant representations of the male industry factory worker in times of economic upheaval.

On the basis of this comparison, I demonstrate that the memory of disruptive economic change differs by social position in the present, and with it, by gender: engineers tend to portray economic success or failure as a matter of individual responsibility; health-care workers are more likely to remember economic change as a structural challenge. However, I also find that the fundamental dynamics of the moral framework are similar in both cases: the overarching problem of defining deserved economic outcomes after 1989, of crafting narratives of legitimate ways of coping with economic change as part of a larger memory of the period, is intertwined with the texture of social relations.

My aim is not to shift the narrative of 1989 around. In the past, a number of contributions have made such a claim, often in an attempt to explain the breathtaking rise of authoritarian right-wing parties and movements across the postsocialist world. The present analysis is more modest in its scope and simultaneously more ambitious in terms of theorizing perceptions of change. It highlights the significance of the cultural and relational dimensions of economic change and the ways they are linked to a historical consciousness of the 1989 revolutions. It offers a historical-comparative and cultural sociology of economic ruptures, showing that memories are intricately bound up with social relations, thereby contributing to the thriving fields of culture and networks as well as culture and inequality. It also attempts to deprovincialize the study of postsocialism by elaborating a sociological framework that is rooted in the analysis of inequalities and foregrounds the role of popular perceptions of justice within them. In all these ways, the book seeks to improve the tools that we have at our disposal to understand societal crises and their aftermath. Hence, while the historical context is specific (1989 was never just an economic crisis but the shift from one political system to another), there are many insights that are highly pertinent for contemporary issues—climate emergencies, health crises, inflation, and the automation of labor, to name just the most glaring ones—that we can derive from it.

Talking About an Uncharted Past

The people whose stories I tell in this book were mostly in their late teens or early twenties when the end of state socialism had arrived.[23] By that time, they had finished their education, and some had already worked a few years. A few respondents commented on my sampling choice. "I was so young back then!" Laura, a cartographer who was in her mid-twenties and had just had her second child in 1989, exclaimed, "It was folks in their

Importance of the age group informed

INTRODUCTION

forties and older who were struggling." To be sure, transitioning into a new system was an even greater challenge for those who had lived under state socialism for a significant part of their adult lives. It was much more than an economic shock for them: the world that they had come to inhabit was disintegrating. For most of the younger individuals I spoke to, market society arrived around the time when they were also settling into adulthood. Their memories of the period are variegated and vibrant. I approached my respondents with the intention of talking about their experiences of the 1990s. Some were initially surprised because they expected a researcher to care mostly about "big" events like 1989—the protests, the politics, and so forth—but not the "small" stories of their ordinary work lives after 1989. Yet it quickly became clear that people had a wealth of stories, memories, and lessons to share about this period of momentous change in their lives. It was also mostly uncharted territory. In 2016 and 2017, when I conducted the interviews for this book, the social and political significance of the transformation time was still relatively neglected in media and politics. This has only changed in the past few years, when observers became increasingly concerned about the success of right-wing populist parties in postsocialist Central Eastern Europe. In the remainder of the introduction, I define and discuss the moral framework in theoretical terms.

THE MORAL FRAMEWORK: A THEORETICAL OUTLINE

The moral framework provides a theoretical model of the ways people perceive and remember disruptive economic change. It is based on one elementary proposition: the memory of ruptures is guided by concerns about social inclusion. What makes a person feel that he or she is a worthy member of society? In our contemporary world, the answer to this question has a lot to do with economics.

Social inclusion is the classic problem in the branch of sociological thinking going back to Emile Durkheim. Durkheim was interested in how, given the modern arrangements of the division of labor society, the relation of individuals provided them with a sense of being part of the larger whole of society.[24] He argued that the degree of integration—and conversely, problems of disintegration—could explain people's political and economic orientations. Some may be in a better position than others to claim their membership symbolically, to perform their belonging in the image of

INTRODUCTION

society as a whole. We can also use the Hegelian tradition and frame the problem in terms of social recognition. German social philosopher Axel Honneth poses that social recognition is the force by which individuals gain and secure a sense of autonomy in society. A person's sense of accomplishment and confidence—in the professional, in the civic, as well as in the private realms—are all part of a social and normative ensemble in which the grounds for acclaim are social and never just individual.[25]

The twin issues of social integration and recognition are most often understood to concern the present: the assumption is that they are nourished by one's *current* status vis-à-vis the larger social ensemble. With the moral framework, I suggest that we also need to consider the role of memory to this end. It is not that the present is less relevant; rather, feelings of social inclusion or exclusion are charged with different *temporal horizons*, and *interpretations of the past* can be highly consequential for how people make sense of their location in a social arrangement. Memory can in fact be a force of social cohesion or a sense of disintegration in the moral framework.

To deepen this proposition, consider how Durkheim's ideas were developed further. One of his most eminent disciples, Maurice Halbwachs, drew on his ideas to elaborate the concept of social memory with an emphasis on social groups. Halbwachs, writing in the interwar period in France, maintained that the relations between individuals in the present are informed by shared images and narratives about the past, and those memories are nourished in groups. Hence, membership in a group—for instance, a type of profession, but even more so in what Halbwachs called the "mundane" world of family and friendship ties—ultimately determines one's view of the past. If a person's social attachments and loyalties change, then their relation to the past changes as well.[26] Today, social memory is commonly defined as a set of selective references to the past that affect the present, a force rooted not in individual consciousness but in collective dynamics.[27] It arises from the activities of conjuring, interrogating, or celebrating, as well as forgetting, deemphasizing, or dissociating from the past.

Halbwachs had already offered an explicitly relational understanding of memory. He also cautioned that memory is inherently unstable. This instability, in particular, has often been invoked in wholesale critiques of this concept by arguing that the past can be rewritten in any given moment, that everyone can invoke a highly selective version of it to whatever end they please. However, empirical research shows that (outside the realm of

INTRODUCTION

authoritarian politics, at least) the past is not all that malleable. In fact, the meaning structures of memory can be relatively persistent. Generational researchers, for instance, find support for what they call the "critical years hypothesis" across a number of national and global domains: events experienced by individuals who are in their adolescence and their twenties are most likely to be remembered by these individuals as "especially important" later in life. To cite an example from the United States, when the terrorist attacks happened on September 11, 2001, a younger generation of Americans was "available for a strong collective memory to take roots in ways that older Americans [were] not." Experiences are encoded and sedimented over time. While modified over time, they do not disappear or lose their import: "A collective memory can be thought of as being carried along, retaining its vitality as cohorts age and as new events take place."[28] This "vitality" of memory is the point here; it is at once dynamic and deeply engrained. Similar findings exist for other cultural contexts. Studying the memory of the so-called sent-down generation in China, sociologist Bin Xu demonstrates how people from the same generation but from varying class backgrounds encode biographical meaning and historical knowledge in different ways.[29]

Hence, there are empirical indications that the meaning dimension of memory matters for membership and social inclusion. What might be the role of this interrelation in the aftermath of economic crises and disruptive economic change? In fact, we don't know much about this problem.[30] There is a dearth of approaches to economic change in sociological thinking about memory. Scholars writing in this field are overwhelmingly concerned with political phenomena, with the legacies of mass violence, authoritarianism, and ethnic conflict for democracy in the present, but rarely do they address the significance of economic pasts in this way. Thus, we lack a clear conceptual basis for pursuing this question. In the following sections, I elaborate a theoretical approach—the moral framework—as a conceptual outline. The moral framework has two dimensions, which I subsequently discuss: first, the relation between disruptive economic change and justice ideas, and, second, the link between ruptures and social relations.

Economic Ruptures and Justice Ideas

In "unsettled times" of large-scale societal change, assumptions about the relation between state and society that are normally taken for granted are made explicit and are being contested.[31] In those moments, people are, more than ever, concerned with justice in society—with questions such as, What is a fair distribution? Who should get what, and why? The dominant ideologies that regulate questions of distribution manifest themselves, and their justifications are potentially called into question. Justice ideas also imbue the very crisis situation with meaning, turning it into a *crisis of inequality, of public trust,* or *of political legitimacy.* There are two interrelated levels at which this unfolds. The first level concerns the macro, society-wide meanings of disruptive change. The second level is smaller in scale: it concerns how justice ideas held by individuals are informed by temporal horizons. What links these two levels is that popular justice orientations are never merely about individuals; they are necessarily concerned with the legitimacy of the social order as a whole.

MORAL ECONOMY AT THE MACRO LEVEL: SIGNIFYING CRISES

To suggest that the society-wide dimension of disruptive change affects the moral framework is to acknowledge that it is not free-floating in time and space, that it responds to political, economic, and social processes as they unfold. This is the level of large-scale historical events and their signification.

From a macro-sociological perspective, 1989 constitutes a major societal turning point. Historical sociologists, in an approach that is sometimes referred to as eventful sociology, understand such large-scale caesuras as moments of radical contingency because they have the power to transform existing structures. In those moments, long-standing political and economic arrangements can shift and be steered onto new paths. Culture—ideas, narratives, and structures of signification—shapes and guides societal transformations: historical breaking points engender new vocabularies, new ways of seeing and explaining the world. Actors develop novel understandings of their goals and projects against the background of eventful experiences. As Robin Wagner-Pacifici suggests, events are more than a single moment in time. They are "restless" in that they do not have a determinate end point but drag on in time. "Events take shape" and "events live in and through . . . forms" such as language, visual representations, and modes of social association. Their power lies in making explicit the structures of agency, including the cultural imagination of agency. As Mabel Berezin puts it, events are at the same time cultural and political because

INTRODUCTION

they are "templates of possibility." Much like the sociology of memory, however, eventful sociology has concerned itself predominantly with the political nature of transformative events. Its favored topics are the shifting horizons of action in the aftermath of revolutions, mass violence, the rise and fall of democracy, and so on.[32]

So where do we begin if we are interested in the cultural signification of disruptive economic change? There is one school of thought that is, in fact, squarely concerned with this problem: writings on *moral economy* elaborated in social history, economic history, and anthropology. Two leading thinkers in this tradition, British social historian Edward Palmer Thompson and Austrian-Hungarian economic historian Karl Polanyi, understood historical crisis events as transformative for capitalist societies. They were inspired by Karl Marx, but they each crafted frameworks of analyses that aimed at dissecting the consequences of economic crises not only in their material but also in their cultural and social dimensions. They argued that it was necessary to trace the values and cultural systems of the communities who lived through periods of rupturing change—by reconstructing the immanent perspective of the subjects and the communities in question—because those frameworks of understanding guided the ways people made sense of it. What becomes evident from these writings is the extraordinary significance of justice ideas, of popular ideas about what constitutes a just social and economic order, in the context of transformative events.[33]

In his seminal *The Making of the English Working Class*, Thompson asked how the emergence of capitalism disrupted the social order of the early English republic of the late seventeenth and eighteenth centuries. He studied different communities and social groups—for instance, peasants, weavers, shoemakers—who lived through severe economic shocks such as land enclosure, the rise of precarious wage labor, and the devaluation of skills and status titles. Thompson found that communities would react to economic shocks in different ways and that how they did so was shaped by available value structures and cultural orientations as well as by specific work identities. Economic change was perceived as particularly disconcerting if people understood what was happening to violate an "older moral economy," a system of social customs, norms, and obligations upon which earlier economic arrangements were built. According to Thompson, for economic change to be perceived as

INTRODUCTION

gravely unsettling, the sense that it undermined the structure of *social relations*—the glue that held communities together in their social fabric—was needed. Polanyi came to a similar conclusion in his investigation of the crisis-ridden interwar period of the twentieth century in Europe: the problem that unfettered market forces undermined the economy's ultimately social end, a person's "social standing, his social claims, his social assets." Polanyi singled out the devaluation of labor as a key element in the mechanism behind this process.[34]

Why are social relations so central here? These writings underscore how, in the popular imagination of the economic order, there is a motif about the necessity of a social balance in it, an assumption that the social and the economic domain must stand in a harmonious relationship with each other. This sense of balance (also nurtured by, specifically, ideas of social order in Christianity) inspires ideas of legitimacy, and it is expressed in justice ideas: legitimate economic practices or arrangements must reflect principles that are rooted in the social domain. And so, in times of unsettling economic change, communities will draw from these older ideas of legitimacy; they will draw on the notion of a social contract that is *violated or broken*—"a consensus about what distinguishes legitimate from illegitimate practices . . . rooted in the past" to interpret the meaning of eventful change.[35] Preexisting cultural scripts are invoked to make sense of the novel situation. In particular, people's ideas about justice and a fair distribution of goods in society are consequential to the ways in which disruptive economic change is signified and then also acted upon. Thompson emphasized that justice ideas necessarily refer to the social, economic, and political order as a whole because they are concerned with the grounds of legitimacy.

Related to this point is that major events may recalibrate an existing system of redistribution and recognition.[36] The way the governing authorities communicate the need for change and the ways they respond or fail to respond to the claims made by social groups matter for how it all unfolds. The state offers narrative templates for the justification, the nature, and the direction of change—or, if the state fails to do so, then it also communicates by other means, such as negligence or repression. In times of societal rupture, relationships of power and of acclaim between the state and social groups are recalibrated on these grounds.[37]

INTRODUCTION

MORAL ECONOMY AT THE MICRO LEVEL: NOTIONS OF DESERVINGNESS

We may be inclined to dismiss the writings of Thompson and Polanyi as concerned with traditional and precapitalist economic formations, or otherwise outdated. Yet doing so would be a mistake. In our crisis-ridden contemporary world, we can hardly rely on the intellectual resources provided by modernization theory, with its exclusive emphasis on the future, alone. Instead, we must look for convergences between moral economy writings and contemporary research about justice, morality, and the perceived legitimacy of the social order. The moral framework can provide elements of such a synthesis. But how? I suggest we focus on people's ideas about *economic deservingness.* Notions of deservingness are moral-economic judgments that spell out the criteria by which people are seen as entitled to certain outcomes. On what grounds does a person deserve his or her wealth? Who is entitled to receive support after job loss? The answers to questions such as these also reflect normative understandings of the larger social order as rewarding some kinds of behaviors or properties and not others. The concept, then, promises to offer a link between the historical theories and contemporary welfare attitudes as well as a link between the micro and macro levels of analysis. Notions of deservingness are grounded in temporal reasoning; in fact, they are—as I will argue here—elements of a social memory of economic change.

A rich body of empirical work on social policy and welfare attitudes confirms that, in contemporary society, people care deeply about justice.[38] They hold strong views about fairness in the economic order, and those ideas have political impact. Using large-scale and cross-national surveys, researchers ask how individuals in different parts of the world reason about fairness in society and under what circumstances they regard economic and social inequalities as legitimate. This branch of research is sensitive to everyday reasoning about these matters, unearthing patterns of lay explanation and justification of unequal outcomes. There is a difference, for instance, between the ways people describe economic inequality and how they justify or explain it. Unlike philosophical approaches to these matters—like the debate between communitarianism versus libertarianism—scholars working in this area do not impose a normative standard of what is just but instead reconstruct patterns of beliefs and orientations empirically. One of

INTRODUCTION

the classic findings is that justice beliefs are generated through social comparison.[39] They are formed socially, as well as articulated relative to others. A major strand of social psychological scholarship in this field, so-called relative deprivation research, underscores that sentiments of injustice are often generated not on the basis of absolute levels of wealth, income, or status but by the sense that one is worse off in relation to others.[40]

Justice researchers find that people variously invoke one of three fundamental principles of distributive justice: merit, need, and equality. Each principle expresses a normative vision for the larger social order. Each has a different answer to the following question: under what circumstances are unequal economic outcomes in society seen as legitimate? The principle of merit deems legitimate the combination of individual effort and equality of opportunities; the principle of need proclaims that basic conditions (physical and psychological, social, cultural, or economic resources) have to be guaranteed so that an individual gains the capability to participate in the competition over resources; and the principle of equality holds that a just market order must work toward equality of outcomes and thus commonly calls for state redistribution to achieve this goal.[41]

These insights from empirical justice research add more nuance to theories of moral economy. Moral economy is often associated with precapitalist or anticapitalist values, and this reading is informed by a rich anthropological tradition and the seminal work of Polanyi. However, empirical findings by scholars who research justice ideas in welfare societies invite us to consider the possibility that meritocratic ways of reasoning may be articulated *as part of* a set of beliefs about justice and moral economic order.

Today, the meritocratic ideology is widespread across the Western world.[42] It deems material success to be a sign of superiority (based on effort, talent, and/or wit) and regards individual failure as legitimate if it is ultimately rooted in a lack of effort or adequate performance. Merit entails a promise of social recognition and inclusion because it allows individuals to claim respect not for who they are but for their choices and activities in the past—in the words of Daniel Miller, merit "looks backwards to what people have already done."[43] Hence, merit rests on the idea of individual *contributions* for which people can legitimately expect to be rewarded and esteemed. Merit refers to *earned* instead of *ascribed* rewards, to an act instead of an innate characteristic of an individual, as the source of legitimate returns.

INTRODUCTION

The critical issue then is that there is a moment of moral evaluation inherent to justice reasoning: on what grounds does an outcome (such as a certain amount of income or wealth, or a person's status in the labor market or a workplace hierarchy) count as *deserved*? Posing this question, what I am interested in is how the relationship between what someone did or did not do and what he or she receives in return is being specified. The very structure of notions of deservingness is based on a relationship between past and present. They rest on a moral evaluation of agency in the past from which the criteria for judging the legitimacy of present outcomes are derived. When we interrogate notions of deservingness, we trace people's reasoning about whether others are worthy of financial or emotional support or not.

In the literature, scholars frequently research the concept of deservingness in the context of attitudes about the welfare state. They interrogate public opinions about what groups in society should receive unemployment support and why. This strand of scholarship documents a dominant conviction that a person should not be rewarded for nothing (the idea that rewards must be based on reciprocity, or some form of contributing) and that the baseline for deserved economic outcomes must be a person's work effort. Public support should be strictly limited to those who are not able to work. For instance, in the European public, the elderly and the sick and the disabled are generally perceived as the most deserving of public assistance because their vulnerabilities are strongly understood to be beyond their own control; immigrants are perceived as least deserving.[44] Research on perceptions of the causes of poverty reveals that attributing responsibility is the single most important factor for how poverty is evaluated—if a person is perceived to be in control over his or her circumstances, if he or she is perceived to have caused the misfortune by his or her own doing, then he or she is seen as undeserving of public support. These evaluations in turn are often racialized, which suggests that ideas about agency are not independent from cultural assumptions.[45]

In the moral framework, notions of deservingness are not necessarily limited to questions of welfare support. To be sure, the insights from welfare research are concerned with instances of economic dislocation—so they are in fact highly useful for thinking about the cultural signification of disruptive economic change more generally. They also strengthen our proposition that justice ideas are anchored in a rich moral imagination about agency in the past. The criteria for what *personal responsibility* means in a situation of economic deprivation—for instance, what it would take to overcome a plight of hardship—are derived from socially shared images and definitions of the situation. Here, we are in fact in the realm of stories and narratives about agency. Cultural scripts are employed to arrive at moral judgments about what someone was able to do in the past and about what present outcomes can therefore be regarded as legitimate or illegitimate.

In the context of rupturing events and society-wide transformations, this allows us to hypothesize that notions of deservingness are embedded in larger narratives about economic change with cultural ideas about the causes, the nature, and the consequences of an eventful crisis. Seen from this angle, notions of deservingness may be regarded as part of social memory. After all, theories of social memory interrogate a closely related phenomenon: they seek to understand how people construe the space of agency in the past, how they assign responsibility in it, and how they derive implications for the moral location of individuals and groups in present society. In his theory of cultural trauma, Jeffrey Alexander explains how the cultural grammar of a binary between victim and perpetrator is fundamental to the remembrance of violent events. Who counts as a victim? "[W]hat group of persons were affected by this traumatizing pain? Where they particular individuals, or groups, or 'the people' in general?" And who counts as a perpetrator? "Who injured the victim? Who actually caused the trauma?"[46] Entire groups of people might be included in or excluded from agency through a moral logic applied to the past. They might be moved closer to the circle of those who are identified as responsible for crimes in the past, or they might be removed from these associations altogether. Delineating moral agency in this way determines how political and legal claims in the present are assessed.

To be sure, these observations refer to historical instances of political violence, mass atrocities, and genocide. It is doubtful, in particular, whether we can—or should—translate the category of perpetrator to the economic realm. But what if constructions of collective victimhood do in fact work in an analogous way in economic matters in one specific respect, namely, in terms of *abnegating the responsibility of victims*?

Memory narratives often seek to establish moral purity for the victims. Memory is concerned with acts of interpretation about what a person or a group of people was capable of doing in the course of the events in question and with retrospectively defining the space of moral agency. This is why, in acts of remembrance, people frequently express a pure version of moral agency for the self, one that is eager to keep polluting narratives—stories that move a subject or a group of people closer to the realm of responsibility and thus the realm of blame—at bay. The problem of having to define such a space of agency is, in fact, similar to that of the cultural construction of *legitimate victimhood* in the face of disruptive economic change. Seen from the perspective of memory, victimhood is not just an individual condition; it always concerns membership in a social group. We can take up this proposition in the moral framework, asking: how do notions of deservingness rely on or variously reject ideas of economic victimhood? What forms of economic victimhood are seen as legitimate given the prevailing narratives and cultural significations about the nature of the event?

Social Relations and Disruptive Change

We now turn to the second element of the moral framework: social relations and their meaning. If the way people perceive economic change is guided by concerns about social inclusion, the bonds that link them to others must have a critical role in it. After all, our sense of social recognition is nourished to a significant degree in existing networks of interpersonal connections, where we construe meaning through attachments to others. It is a social force that inhabits the very associations by which we navigate our lives and through which we develop and foster a sense of autonomous, moral personhood. George Herbert Mead famously argued that our sense of self is generated in relation to those who surround us; it is also nourished and constantly reshaped by those relations. Honneth notes that "we achieve our autonomy alongside intersubjective paths by learning to understand ourselves, via others' recognition, as beings whose needs, beliefs and abilities are worth being realized."[47]

Support networks—the ties that people maintain to care for each other materially and emotionally—matter in ordinary times. They do so even more in times of crisis, scarcity, and economic uncertainty. Network researchers find that the principle of reciprocity is an important mechanism that allows ties to persist during trying times. Reciprocity is transactional, as in the exchange of money or goods or, say, critical information

INTRODUCTION

about job opportunities. But it is also affective, as in the different ways that people care and provide for each other. Gender plays a crucial role in support networks: women are often expected to care for children and the elderly as well as to provide emotional support, a dynamic that is again aggravated in periods of economic downturn.

After 1989, across the postsocialist world, private support networks were critically important. This was in part a legacy of the state-socialist economy: during state-socialist rule, everyday goods and services were frequently distributed through informal means, in what came to be known as the pervasive *second economy*. Individuals and families organized their social relations around private "niches" of material, emotional, and informational exchange.[48] After the breakdown of state socialism, informality did not disappear. In fact, in regions that experienced a dramatic rise in poverty during the 1990s, like many in the post-Soviet world, support networks become more important than ever. Anthropologist have studied them carefully over extended periods. For Ukraine in the 1990s, for instance, one anthropologist finds that among those affected by economic deprivation, "the single most important factor for escaping poverty was the strength of an individual's social network. Regardless of the severity of individual circumstances, if a family had someone in their 'circle' with access to capital and money-making ventures, then the family escaped poverty with stunning regularity."[49]

Individuals don't go through trying times alone. Economic ruptures may affect entire webs of relationships such as families, trusted ties, and communities. In the late 1980s, Katherine Newman published *Falling from Grace*, a seminal exploration of this phenomenon. In it, she studied how, at the time, American middle- and working-class individuals and their families were affected by downward mobility. Newman found that economic grievances, stress, and feelings of insecurity all translated into the realm of close, trusted ties. There, they reinforced gendered role conflicts. After losing their jobs, husbands felt threatened in their ability to live up to the role of the breadwinning head of the family. Newman's analysis demonstrated how this sense of insecurity spreads socially, how "family cocoons" were weaved around feelings of shame, support, and mutual expectations about the right way to cope. Economic grievances functioned much like an elephant in the room—they were everywhere present but at the same time systematically silenced. Newman also found that health problems

INTRODUCTION

such as stress, depression, and alcoholism, which arise from economic deprivation, all had a relational dimension to them. Czech psychologists disclosed similar processes as part of the economic shocks of the 1990s. At the time, Czech marriages suffered from economic stress and uncertainty. Dramatically increasing divorce rates, as the authors of one study show, were caused by these problems. They also revealed that the perception of economic dislocation—and more specifically, the ways this problem was negotiated in social relationships—mattered above all. They conclude that "what generated irritability in the home was the way Czech spouses assessed their family's economic circumstances, not the family's more objective economic standing."[50]

These findings suggest that social relations are a source of knowledge about the world and that they have an inherent quality. As one contemporary strand of network theory emphasizes, people attach cognitive and affective meaning to interpersonal relations and act on these meanings, too.[51] The webs of associations that surround people are webs of meaning. In times of rupturing change, the stability of networks of meaning is potentially at stake. From the perspective of the moral framework, the relevant question is, Against the background of disruptive events, how do social relations themselves become an object of moral evaluation? Drawing on relational and cultural sociology, I suggest that there are two ways this can happen: through drawing symbolic boundaries and through the evaluating deservingness in strong ties.

DRAWING SYMBOLIC BOUNDARIES

People regularly draw symbolic boundaries, classifying others and locating themselves in a social space, articulating distance to (or from) others on the grounds of status-related or moral concerns. Pierre Bourdieu regarded the social world as a field in which individuals and groups compete for resources, status, and recognition. A cultural topography of social positions arises in this process. By giving an account of others, people reveal relevant criteria of affection or social proximity (who they want to associate with) and distance (who they want to avoid or dissociate from). By defining those who are outside their moral world, they also reaffirm bonds among those inside the *we* group. Those who are outside are often seen as representative of an entire group, with its own morality and way of

INTRODUCTION

life—something that also justifies the boundary from the perspective of the insiders. Frequently, these dividing lines are charged with racialized meaning, but social cues of status or the urban/rural divide can also be made legible and be culturally reinforced in this way. Tracing these acts allows sociologists to map the moral logic behind notions of *us* and *them*.[52]

In postsocialist societies, people make sense of social change in this way. One anthropological study of a small Polish village after the system change, for instance, documents how farmers, agricultural workers, village proletariats, and white-collar workers set themselves apart from each other. These four social groups had emerged in the process of social differentiation of the 1990s primarily on the grounds of varying access to landownership and property. In a similar vein, an ethnography of middle-class high school teachers in St. Petersburg documents a moral grammar that at once criticizes and embraces the logic of meritocracy. While they draw strong boundaries in relation to the "new Russians"—individuals who display their wealth aggressively and are deemed as arrogant, tasteless, and uneducated by teachers—they simultaneously affirm their deep-seated belief in the *civilizing* mission of the market, a source of moral worth for their own position in this new society.[53]

EVALUATING DESERVINGNESS IN STRONG TIES

Symbolic boundaries are concerned with how individuals position themselves vis-à-vis relatively distant others in society, but the moral framework is also concerned with proximate social ties and personal relationships that have a history, like friends and family relations. Sociologists call these relationships *strong ties*. The meaning dimension in such ties is not reducible to factors such as the size of one's network or the formal properties (such as physical distance or frequency of interaction). Here, meaning depends on the perceived quality of the ties. It emerges, as relational thinkers argue, as a property of the evolution and reciprocal dynamics of the relationship itself.[54]

In this realm, moral sentiments are variously attached to social ties because we tend to treat those relations not primarily as instrumental but as an end in themselves. Gabriel Abend suggests that some relations are linked to "thick" moral concepts, like dignity, cruelty, clemency, or friendship. Unlike "thin" moral concepts, these are not abstract prescriptions for how to act; rather, they are "constrained in their application by what the world is like." Here, morality is a binding force, a glue that makes people stick together. Webs of social obligations necessitate the application of thick moral concepts; at the same time, relations also depend on them. Moral sentiments, in other words, can be socially consequential: in relations guided by thick moral concepts, obligations can also be misrecognized and relational expectations can be disappointed.[55]

Justice and network researchers concur that people care about *balancing* their fundamental values in proximate relationships.[56] As a general rule, the principle of need is associated with social proximity, while the principle of merit is linked to more distant social relations. We tend to evaluate those who are close to the self by their circumstances, while we judge those who are socially more distant to the self according to criteria such as effort and performance. But how does this pattern play out in instances of changing attachments and, possibly, disappointed moral expectations? In periods of disruptive change, strong ties might undergo shocks. In eventful times, social geographies, social "alignments, . . . senses of belonging and solidarity" can shift.[57] The moral binding force of a relationship may be at stake when questions of loyalty and the sincerity of attachments move to the foreground. During rupturing periods, the question of who is deserving of my recognition moves to the fore. To find out what the consequences are is the task for empirical exploration. We must interrogate how notions of deservingness are construed in this "thick" space between social recognition and economic outcomes.

OUTLINE OF THE BOOK

The first chapter introduces the historical-comparative background. It reveals that East Germany and Czechoslovakia had many things in common before 1989 and that the transformation period restructured the economic and social foundations of these two societies in different ways. I trace the ways in which the rationale for shock therapy was communicated differently by policymakers, with lasting consequences.

In the second chapter, I portray biographical experiences with changing work environments after the 1989 revolutions by drawing on interviews. The issue of skills is essential in the interviews. Skills ensure a sense of continuity and provide a sense of legitimacy for one's economic efforts, allowing people to narrate a smooth personal transition from the pre-1989 to the post-1989 order. I demonstrate that skills are narrated as a moral

INTRODUCTION

foundation, and they are tied to the problem of social inclusion. East Germans feel that their economic expertise was not recognized after 1989, and on these grounds, they harbor a sense of not being recognized as contributing members of society. Czech memories of economic change are more ambiguous, but there is also a profound disappointment with the fact that the post-1989 political system fails to reward merit appropriately.

In chapter 3, I discuss what respondents regard as deserved or undeserved social mobility outcomes in the aftermath of 1989. People share stories about how others coped with disruptive economic change and thus offer rich insights into their imagination and memory of the period. I document the desire to maintain a moral distance from those who are understood to have *failed* in the transition to market society and those who allegedly have generated undeserved advantages, as in the (racialized) image of the "welfare cheat." Beyond personal stories, the episodes reveal elements of larger understandings of the post-1989 period, ways of making sense of key economic events and processes of the time.

In chapter 4, I ask how strong, trusted ties are linked to deservingness beliefs. Based on a review of survey evidence, I find that such ties have been ruptured more dramatically in the East German transformation compared to the Czech. An in-depth analysis of episodes of broken friendship ties reveals that it is the problem of justice—born out of recognition and misrecognition of one's efforts to cope with economic change after 1989—that haunts respondents to this day. Meritocratic ideas are entwined with the problem of social inclusion in this very personal and intimate realm. This underscores that the moral framework is a relational framework.

In the epilogue, I address deservingness in light of the rise of authoritarian right-wing populism in postsocialism. Around the globe today, right-wing populists thrive on sentiments of moral worth and exclusive, tribal solidarities. These actors promise to *restore* feelings of pride associated with the past and to *return* to a social order in which the market, not politics, rewards individuals. Right-wing populists' outsize success in the formerly state-socialist world—in Germany, they receive many more votes in the former East than in the former West; in the Czech Republic, they have received the largest share of the vote and entered government from 2017 to 2021—urges us to think more systematically about the role of economic memories of the post-1989 crisis and the role of the moral language of deservingness in this context.

Chapter One

HISTORICAL TRAJECTORIES

Without history, memory is open to abuse. But if history comes first, then memory has a template and guide against which it can work and be assessed.

—TONY JUDT, *THINKING THE TWENTIETH CENTURY*[1]

History as a template and fact-checker for memory

A SHARED LEGACY OF MORALIZING WORK

In the fall of 1989, when East German protesters flocked the streets to demonstrate against one-party rule, they displayed a banner that read "Stasi into productive sector!" People had enough of living in a police state; and they were fed up with a government that no longer, in their eyes, represented the true interests of working people.[2]

"There is no simple, coherent narrative of life under socialism, but rather multiple and, at times, contradictory ones," writes Jill Massino.[3] Under state-socialist rule, people's relation to the governing authorities and to the official ideology was fundamentally ambiguous. Political repression and the massive curtailment of fundamental rights existed side by side with a state-guaranteed system of social entitlements for large swaths of the population. The "welfare dictatorship," as one historian labeled this form of rule, systematically wrecked the life of some individuals and their families while simultaneously providing a materially stable and socially esteemed mode of living for others.[4] In the narrative that I offer in this chapter, the political dimensions of state-socialist rule are deemphasized, and its social and economic dimensions are foregrounded. I do not intend to downplay the pervasiveness and insidiousness of state terror. Instead, I trace the legacies of state socialism as a system of redistribution and recognition, a multilayered

Unbalanced government support

symbolic order that sustained a sense of belonging in economic terms. The key proposition is that popular experiences of the 1990s were shaped by the mode by which this system was upended. I demonstrate that East Germans and Czechs experienced radically dissimilar modes of economic change after 1989, and so the shared legacy of moralized ideas of work was differently reconfigured.

If the moral framework is animated by concerns of social inclusion, if the question of belonging is at the very heart of it, then we must delineate the key historical parameters and events that shaped notions and aspirations of social inclusion. This is the purpose of the present chapter. To achieve this goal, I take up elements of a social historical perspective. I also offer a historical and comparative overview over the post-1989 changes. I aim to paint a broad, context-rich picture of the forces that turned people's lives upside down during this period. I rely on two analytical building blocks. First, before discussing the 1990s, I consider elementary features of work life in state socialism. Second, I proceed comparatively, showing that rupturing change unfolded in different ways.

Different Political Pasts

Political scientists have often noted that country-specific pathways after 1989 were steered by elite actors. It mattered what institutions were built and how they were designed, what theories about the interrelation of markets and democracy were implemented and how this was done, and what networks of actors emerged successful in the course of the project of "rebuilding the ship at sea."[5] Yet we also need to ask how this large-scale experiment in societal reorganization was perceived by broader swaths of society. To this end, it makes sense to draw on a comparative methodology.

The fact that the German Democratic Republic (GDR) and the Czechoslovak Socialist Republic (CSR) came to resemble each other in their economic and social profile by the 1980s is by no means intuitive or readily apparent. In fact, they look back to very different, if not contrasting, political and national histories.[6] As modern nations, they emerged from different empires in the nineteenth and early twentieth centuries. The Czech lands (in proper historical terms, the Bohemian, Moravian, and Silesian lands) were part of the Austro-Hungarian Empire, while the eastern German territories were ruled by Prussia. In the political geography of the time, the

Czech lands were located at the periphery. German was the official language of the administration and the prized language of the arts; Czech was mainly relegated to the provinces, and bilingualism was widespread.[7] Czech nationalism was intricately linked to claims of independence from Austro-Hungarian rule. The East German territories, in contrast, were much closer—linguistically as well as geographically—to Berlin, the center of Prussian political life.

In 1918, when World War I came to an end, European empires collapsed. Now there existed, for the first time in history, a Czechoslovak nation and a German nation. It was an uneasy neighborhood relation from the beginning.[8] Distrust between Czechs and Germans, fraught by historical resentment, increasingly escalated into violence during the interwar period.[9] After Hitler came to power in 1933, it was soon evident that Germany did not recognize the legitimacy of the Czechoslovak state. Hitler first gained control of the German-speaking territories in the fall of 1938 after a diplomatic bluff with the Munich Agreement. By the spring of 1939, Prague was occupied by Nazi troops, and the systematic brutalizing of the civilian population began. After six years under Nazi rule, in the spring of 1945, Prague was liberated by the Soviet Red Army. Czechoslovakia was now in Stalin's sphere of influence. Berlin finally surrendered; however, the violence continued.[10] Meanwhile, Germany was divided by the Allied powers. The emerging Cold War border between West and East Germany was an outcome of geopolitical trade-offs and a cornerstone of the European postwar order. Germany's political role was to be constrained. To this day, national self-conceptions and public memories in both societies are shaped by the atrocities of the first half of the twentieth century.[11]

In light of this history, it is remarkable that Czechoslovak and East German societies developed a similar model of society after the war. This was, of course, a consequence of Soviet geopolitics and the redrawing of postwar borders. In February 1948, the Communist Party of Czechoslovakia (KSČ) came to power, marking the beginning of the regime that was, after the federation with Slovakia in 1960, officially known as the Socialist Republic of Czechoslovakia (CSR).[12] In October 1949, the German Democratic Republic (GDR) was officially proclaimed on the territories of the Soviet-occupied zone of Germany. The GDR was de facto a one-party state, ruled by the Socialist Unity Party of Germany, the East

German Communist Party (SEDt). From the beginning, the two societies assumed a special role in the Soviet power game. Given their immediate geographical proximity to the capitalist West, Moscow decreed them as *model* socialist states, a beacon for the achievements of the *socialist way of life*. Here, the superiority of Communist Party rule was to manifest itself to West Europeans. Moscow exercised tight control over the regimes and their respective national elites. As a result, they remained fairly hard-line ideologically for decades. In fact, the Czechoslovak and East German communist parties never conceded power to reform movements, in contrast to neighboring Poland, Hungary, and Yugoslavia.[13] In the crushing of the worker's rising of 1953 in East Germany and in the defeat of the Prague Spring of 1968 in Czechoslovakia, attempts at reform were violently thwarted. Berlin and Prague also deployed extensive resources to control and surveil the population. Although capital punishment was mostly avoided, political repression was ubiquitous. In the GDR, more than 50,000 people, or about one of every 200 adults, was, for some time at least, imprisoned or confined to internment camps, and the justice system was used as a tool of political persecution. Secret police surveillance was widespread and deployed a large number of *unofficial informants* (citizens pressured or lured into collaborating), particularly in East Germany. There, according to one estimate, about one in 180 citizens was an informant for the secret police. In Czechoslovakia, that number is estimated at around one in 867 citizens.[14]

Politically, the GDR and the CSR remained distinct. National integration was predicated on different political histories in each case. East Germans, who were essentially living in a divided country, shared a language with West Germans. Because of the Nazi past, ethnic or nationalist models of belonging were officially discredited in the GDR. Instead, the leadership claimed that this country and its people derived its identity exclusively from the fight against fascism and capitalism. From the perspective of Moscow, the very raison d'être of the East German state was to compete with the West, both economically and ideologically. Czechoslovakia, in contrast, was a united country, with two distinct, if mutually intelligible, languages. Here, the systemic challenge was to integrate the Slovaks into dominant Czech politics and culture. Prague maintained a highly fraught relationship to Moscow, which culminated in the dramatic events of the Soviet crushing of the Prague Spring in 1968.[15]

Industrial Politics, Industrial Lifestyles: Economic Integration

The GDR and CSSR developed a similar economic and social model, which, according to Claus Offe, was characterized by the principle of "economic integration." He notes:

> The GDR and the CSR, the "state socialist success stories," are integrated primarily economically and for all the notable differences between them, in the following ways they have more in common with each other than with any of the other countries . . . Their industrial potential was well established and constantly expanded owing to wide-scale pre-war industrialization, and per capita industrial output was correspondingly high. In addition, the fact that they are the only two of the six countries in which a strong labour movement existed before the Communists seized power also has to do with their pre-war history as industrialized societies.[16]

Social historians concur that these two regimes represented the apex of socialist industrial modernity.[17] Historically, the industrial sector had long played a dominant role in their economies. These were the heartlands of European manufacturing in the nineteenth century, as is illustrated, for instance, by the thriving border region of Saxony and Bohemia.[18] There, building on traditions of manufacturing and craft, industrial production in areas such as textile works, glass, machinery, and chemicals had flourished. At the end of the nineteenth century, workers from all over Europe flocked to the area, finding work in one of the many cotton mills, timber factories, or coal mines. Over the course of a few decades, cities in the region doubled and sometimes tripled in size because of labor migration. The region was interconnected by a dense railroad network. The accomplishments of the Industrial Age fostered an ethos of productivity and technological advancement, cultural values that were still cherished by later generations. The pride in technological progress and the self-designation as a community of problem solvers became a cornerstone of regional and later national identity in the Czech and the German lands.

In the postwar decades and under Soviet economic planning, Czechoslovakia and East Germany experienced a further expansion of their industrial base. The state took command of the economy, nationalizing firms.[19] Slovakia was designated the center for heavy industry and armaments;

in Bohemia and the southern East German lands, mechanics, metallurgy, mining, and the chemical industries were expanded. The share of the population employed in the industrial sector grew rapidly. In the Czech lands, it increased from more than 40 percent during the 1940s to more than 55 percent in the 1980s; in Slovakia, from about a third to more than half of the population during that time. Historical sociologist Anna Pollert notes that Czechoslovakia became the "workshop of the Soviet bloc, its mechanical engineering industry supplying hundreds of locomotives, trams, heavy trucks, and capital equipment every year."[20] In the GDR, about 800,000 new jobs in industry were added between 1949 and 1960. Employment in this sector continued to be the norm until the breakdown of state socialism.[21] Nowhere in the state-socialist world was industrial labor as advanced, and as ubiquitous—really, nothing short of a lifestyle *for* most of society—as in these two societies.

Soon, most politics was industrial politics. Scholars accordingly label the Czechoslovak and East German brand of state socialism the "bureaucratic" type.[22] It relied on a high degree of centralization as well as a technocratic profile of its ruling class. Private economic activity was strongly constrained—in contrast to Poland or Hungary, which permitted some business activity, especially in their larger agricultural sectors. Bureaucratic socialism administered a network of large, state-owned plants all over the country. Decision makers within those plants had only very limited autonomy because economic directives and production norms were generally decided top-down. Economic reform from below was not part of this model.[23] Industrial politics was symbolic politics, too. The regimes performed an image of their economies as firmly rooted in regional traditions. State propaganda was full of praise for dynamic virtues such as creativity and a technical mindset. For instance, in 1980s Czechoslovakia, a popular television series, *The Engineer's Odyssey*, linked the themes of productivity and creativity to the tradition of the industrial heartlands.[24]

Social Integration Through Work

The moral framework revolves around a desire for social inclusion. Approaching the pre-1989 histories of our two cases, we encounter a very specific historical constellation that crucially informed ideas about who does and who does not belong. The model of economic organization was embedded in a larger system of redistribution and recognition. Historian Martin Kohli succinctly characterized it as the principle of "social integration through work."[25] Its core elements were paternalistic and coercive labor policies that granted extensive social entitlements for both the male and the female working population; the existence of large, state-owned companies at the heart of economic and social life; low social mobility; and a dominant ideology of social conservatism that promised stability and rested on moralized ideas of work.

PATERNALISTIC LABOR POLICIES: COERCIVE INCLUSION

One goal of state-socialist labor policies was to commit as many people as possible to full-time work.[26] The SED and the KSČ were remarkably successful in this regard. By the 1980s, the share of adult citizens who were working was among the largest in the world. At the same time, in the GDR, around 90 percent of the adult population were employed.[27] The regimes also boosted the share of women in employment. In 1956, in Czechoslovakia, women made up 46 percent of the workforce; by the 1970s, almost all women in their mid-twenties were working, with at least one child at home.[28] Another goal was to raise productivity. The leadership wanted to increase economic output and, at the same time, appeal to people by granting them extensive social and economic rights. In practice, these two aims often contradicted on another. As elsewhere in the socialist bloc, labor was in constant undersupply, while worker-friendly policies were expansive. People were guaranteed access to employment, and it was nearly impossible for firms to lay them off.[29] Hence, economic planners had to find other ways to increase workers' productivity, like wage bonuses, symbolic praise (such as the titles of "shockworker" or "hero of work"), or peer pressure. Yet productivity levels remained below expectations. In the late socialist period, policymakers increasingly tried to find new ways to incentivize people individually. By the 1980s, the GDR leadership propped up the discourse of individual effort as the basis for economic rewards. One social policy directive from the time declared that "the principle of merit constitutes, and remains to constitute, the fundamental principle on which the distribution of work benefits in socialism is based."[30]

This is a crucial yet often misunderstood dimension of how power was wielded by the Communist Party. The leadership did in fact promote the idea of individual effort as the basis for legitimate rewards. The official doctrine of egalitarianism was narrowly conceived, always with the specter of economic free riding in mind. Individual gains were to be rooted in hard work, ambition, and personal commitment to the cause of national productivity. These ideas permeated the shop floor; the educational system; socialist consumer identities; and even people's intimate life, such as in their thoughts noted in poetry albums.[31]

Citizens were also punished for an allegedly flawed work ethic. State-socialist labor policies were profoundly paternalistic and often outright repressive. In the GDR, unemployment was officially abolished by 1955 (when a mere 25,000 were registered as jobless). This was the result of coercion.[32] The leadership wanted to employ as many people as possible and to reduce the number of individuals who received unemployment assistance.[33] In 1960, the Czechoslovak constitutional "right to work" was amended to "duty to work." The same change was adopted in the GDR just a year later, when the Berlin Wall was erected and the border to West Germany was militarized. These rules effectively turned unemployment and social welfare into a form of deviance. The norm was to be an active, fully participating member of the socialist workforce—people's work status was even recorded in their identification document.

In terms of gender, labor policies were ambiguous. On the one hand, leadership was committed to increasing female participation in the labor force. Women could receive training in male-dominated fields. Some could even pursue higher education degrees. On the other hand, women were generally employed in less well-paying and less prestigious sectors, such as the consumer-oriented light industries. Manual labor in the most esteemed branches of the economy—such as the raw material and heavy industries—was male labor. Despite the rhetoric of emancipation, women often had to perform a double role: they were often working full-time and providing domestic care simultaneously. They were also less likely to be rewarded for political engagement than men. In Czechoslovak plants, for instance, Communist Party functionary positions were nearly exclusively occupied by men. In practice, the mechanism by which political personnel was recruited on the factory floor resembled an "old boys' club."[34]

Employment in health care is another instructive example. Health care was a near-exclusively female profession, though, of course, a great number of leading doctors and other medical specialists were men. In the postwar period, female employment in this field was still linked to a larger project of modernizing society, it was framed as a "political commitment to [female] emancipation".[35] Yet, in the late-socialist period, this vision had all but disappeared. In post-1968 Czechoslovakia, the notion that care work was to be "naturally" performed by women came to predominate, very similar to how the issue was generally seen in the Western, non-socialist world.

THE STATE-OWNED COMPANY: A SPACE OF SOCIAL ENTITLEMENTS, NETWORKS, AND IDENTITY

The symbolically charged idea of work found its manifestation in social spaces such as the large, state-owned company. These companies existed in most branches of the economy and were at the heart of the Czechoslovak and the East German industrial and social model. These institutions were simultaneously spaces of work, welfare, community organizing, and private sociability. Not unlike the social wage model of the postwar decades in the United States and Western Europe, they granted both material benefits and social esteem—a degree of respectability—to workers. Those who worked at a plant received a living wage, but they also had access to a range of social entitlements including housing, child care, health care, educational opportunities, pensions, and sometimes car ownership. In a sense, state-owned companies acted like communal structures. The firms also functioned as the primary hubs for the informal exchange of goods and services, the networks that provided access to everything that money could not buy in state socialism.[36]

They were also spaces of sociability. Citizens spent a lot of time at work engaged in all kinds of social activities together, and they sustained professional and amicable ties with their colleagues. In Czechoslovak industrial plants, so-called workplace clubs provided a cultural and recreational space in the spirit of "socialist education." Sports, theater, dancing, lectures, music, and photography were among the regular social activities of workers. These clubs were devoted to advancing the cause of "living labor," to blurring the distinction between private and public spaces, and bringing workers closer to the "practice" of socialism.[37] It was assumed this would also increase workers' morale and result in higher levels of economic productivity. In East German plants, small units of workers formed "collectives." As part of a collective, workers were supposed to "work, learn, and live as a socialist." This was a widespread form of social organization. According to one estimate, in 1988, around 84 percent of East German industrial workers were members of a collective.[38] In the collectives, a strong work ethic prevailed—"an almost religious faith in 'productive work'"—that effectively functioned as an institutionalized system of social, relational control.

LOW SOCIAL MOBILITY

As we will see later in this chapter, the dynamic interplay of expectations and experiences that crucially shaped people's experiences of the 1990s was partly also informed by normative ideas about a "typical" biography from the time before 1989. The communist parties' proclaimed goal was to augment the life chances of working-class people and to promote working-class ethics as a model for society as a whole. Disadvantaged families and their children were to be treated preferentially. And really, in postwar East Germany and Czechoslovakia, wide-ranging changes in the social structure were enacted that granted children from disadvantaged backgrounds access to education and secured stable jobs for manual workers.[39] In the long run, however, the two regimes failed to create a sustainable model of mobility for working-class people. In the late socialist period, their social structure had become petrified, and upward mobility had become a privilege of the politically loyal class. According to one estimate, in 1980s GDR, the chance to leave one's working-class background behind and rise to an upper service-class position were lower than in West Germany at the time.[40] In late socialist Czechoslovakia, for an individual to move up the social ladder, it was necessary that he or she come from a politically loyal family. Over time, political recruitment and political networks—proximity to the party and to those in power—had become the single most consequential determinant of economic success.[41] Access to higher education was a political privilege. By the 1980s, East German and Czechoslovak universities had become exclusive training grounds for the children of the upper functionary class and the intelligentsia. The lucky few who were able to enter higher education were designated to join the ranks of the managerial class. The subjects available to study where overwhelmingly technical, such as the natural sciences and engineering, while nontechnical curricula were irrelevant at universities. Technical knowledge was considered superior to humanistic knowledge (philosophy and social science was seen as scientific only if they were rooted in the "natural" laws of historical materialism). Socialist modernity was a technical modernity, and mobility aspirations were oriented toward these principles, too. The technocratic profile of the governing elite also shaped political reactions to the attempts to reform society during the Prague Spring in 1968. There was a pervasive anti-intellectualism in the KSČ, which the leadership could mobilize in their fight against dissidents and nonconformists in this critical moment. They stigmatized reformers as individuals who preferred talking to working, who were effectively *useless* to society.[42]

This begs the question: was there really ever a *promise* of social upward mobility in the sense of a vision that people would orient their lives to? Competition in the Cold War system certainly shaped people's expectations. The communist parties promoted an image of the GDR and the CSSR as egalitarian *worker societies*, superior to what they deemed as the socially fractious, capitalist rat race in the West. But there was also a mundane quality to the absence of social mobility, a sense of what was *normal*. Decisions such as where and how to enter the workforce did not seem like a career choice for most citizens, at least not in the Western sense. People were generally expected to take up available jobs. Most people would not have considered moving (and were not permitted to move) somewhere else to find a better job. Czech oral histories of the 1980s reveal a subtle idea of social equality. Despite the worsening plight of the economy, people's impression that their work was needed granted them a sense of social inclusion. The lack of Western life choices was also tangible in living spaces. As German sociologist Steffen Mau, who grew up in a typical socialist high-rise in the city of Rostock, notes, it was nothing exceptional if your neighbor next door happened to be a decorated Communist Party functionary. This person might wear the same clothes, go to the same shops, and maintain neighborly relations in the same manner as everybody else. This quotidian character of equality underscores why social mobility might not—or not always, at minimum—have seemed like a desirable goal for many.[43]

A PLACE OF "TRANQUILITY AND WORK": SOCIAL CONSERVATISM AND THE MORALIZATION OF WORK

Given the lack of an overarching political vision and the impossibility of reform, the SED and the KSČ sought to legitimize their power by other means. Social historians determined that they did so by promoting an ideology of social conservatism, which rested on fear mongering based on profoundly moralized notions of work. In a departure from the postwar understanding of work as a social and collective right, it came to be increasingly defined as a private, moral duty. After the crushing of the Prague Spring in August 1968, the idea that socialism could be reformed from within was essentially dead. The leadership wanted social order above all. Czechoslovakia after 1968 was to be, in the words of the Moscow-loyal president Gustav Husák, a place of "tranquility and work," "where every worker, every farmer, every member of the intelligentsia can concentrate on their work so that we can think about all issues in a quiet atmosphere."[44] In reality, however, the KSČ adopted a new governing style that was based on sowing distrust, animosity, and paranoia. After 1968, the so-called era of *normalization* began with widespread political and economic purges among former reformers and their confidants.[45] The leadership concentrated on defining enemies from within: reformers, intellectuals, and nonconforming individuals from all walks of life were branded as capitalist agents who were charged with undermining job security, price stability, and wages. The goal was to appeal to citizens' conservative sensibilities. By exploiting the fear of change and conjuring an image of moral crisis, those in power fashioned themselves as the force of stability in society.[46]

After Erich Honecker's rise to power in 1969 in the GDR, the SED adopted a similar strategy, although with a greater emphasis on appeasing citizens materially. Promising a "constant improvement of working and living conditions" under the banner of the newly proclaimed "unity of social and economic policy" after the Eight Party Congress of 1971, the SED's policy priorities were formulated around wage stability; housing; and the support of families, particularly of working women.[47] It also promoted a conservative crisis discourse. The leadership was struggling with the fact that the country was losing population. Scores of East Germans were leaving or attempting to escape. This clearly demonstrated to the world that many citizens did not in fact think of the GDR as the better part of Germany. The SED reacted by intensifying the strategy of scapegoating political opponents, ethnic minorities, and even the poor for their alleged lack of commitment to the socialist project.

Moralized notions of work, such as an individualized meaning of "productive labor," were employed to discipline citizens. The courts increasingly relied on moralized, milieu-based definitions of deviant behavior. Through civic as well as penal law, the state persecuted individuals with charges like "socially deviant behavior," "asocial behavior," and of being a "goldbricker" or a "parasite."[48] After 1968, a legal, encompassing definition of the charge of "asocial behavior" was implemented. It was now officially defined as a "violation of public order," to be determined in cases of "defiance of norms out of an unwillingness to work." It was to be punished by "education through forced labor" or prison. Shortly before the GDR ceased to exist, about a fourth of the prison population was convicted based on the "asocial behavior" charge. As social historians note, these developments reveal how earlier, class-based explanations of deviance were abandoned and replaced by milieu-based explanations. As a disciplining mechanism, these laws were used to target citizens' attitudes and opinions, never just behaviors.[49]

Similarly, in late socialist Czechoslovakia, state violence was directed against individuals who were deemed a threat to the *healthy* socialist community. A law targeting "parasites" and "goldbrickers" had already been passed in 1956, but the full-fledged fight against so-called asocial behavior only began in the 1970s.[50] The Czechoslovak law defined parasites as individuals who "systematically avoided 'honest work' and let them be supported by someone else or obtained the means of subsistence in some other 'dishonest' manner." This behavior was punished by multiple years in prison (this charge was decriminalized only in the mid-1990s). Like in East Germany, the charge included a range of suspicious behaviors and intentions, among them prostitution, which was understood as a willful decision not to take up "regular" work.[51] The root causes for "socially deviant behavior" were identified in family morals and upbringing, as well as in a lack of "socialist attitude." Young people who did not look and dress according to the norms of the time (like boys wearing long hair) could also be charged. Promoting such milieu-based explanations of *unruly* and socially *detrimental* behavior only created the cause for the authorities to act. Ultimately, the goal was to increase support for the socially conservative ruling ideology.[52]

"At no time did the state-socialist leadership wish to miss its moral appeal to the 'we' of an 'orderly working' subject, at the expense of those who remained 'below,'" notes one historian.[53] Whoever was regarded as "unwilling to work" was seen as damaging the community from the inside. Paranoia and constant fearmongering put a strain on the social texture.

Those who suffered most were dissidents and the individuals stigmatized and persecuted by these policies. But they also had a harmful, socially divisive effect on the broader society. This was the language of state propaganda, but it effectively also undermined the foundations of community life. People grew suspicious of each other as the state forced them to demonstrate their commitment to *healthy, work-oriented* communities. The moralization of work hardened the relations between state and society and sowed distrust among citizens.[54]

From the 1970s onward, a deepening recession was underway. A constant supply of cheap, heavily subsidized Soviet energy was no longer something that Eastern European policymakers could count on after the oil crisis of 1973. The leadership in Prague and East Berlin was hard-pressed to sustain the resource-intensive model of the "welfare dictatorship." The GDR accumulated foreign debt because it was increasingly dependent on importing goods and technologies from the West, while its own exports stagnated. No one in the West wanted to buy socialist cars. These trends fostered the regime's dependency on West Germany, its main creditor. The Communist Party leadership, of course, preferred to look the other way.[55]

East Germans and Czechoslovaks experienced economic stagnation. At the same time, they also went through a deeper crisis: a fracturing of the model of social integration through work. As social divisions deepened, one question was moving to the foreground: who has a right to full membership in society? Nativism and racialized dividing lines deepened. In East Germany at the time, there was talk of "idle" Poles who allegedly took advantage of "hard-working" citizens.[56] In Czechoslovakia, violence against Roma and the Vietnamese minority was on the rise. The 1980s spike in hate crimes against migrant workers and ethnic minorities was fueled by a new combination of racism and economic resentment. The cultural logic behind definitions of "productive labor" had become significantly less universal and decidedly more privatized in meaning. It had increasingly morphed into a logic of symbolic boundaries between those who are, by virtue of their identity, *deserving* or *undeserving* of belonging to the community. This was the situation in the fall of 1989, when it all swiftly—and unexpectedly—came to an end.

The breakdown of state socialism represents not just the end of a political regime—it signifies the dissolution of an older social contract. Gábor Scheiring, referencing Barrington Moore, calls it a departure "from moral codes about the hierarchies of authority, the division of labor, and the distribution of goods and services."[57] The historically patterned forms of sociability that were intertwined with a logic of economic redistribution, and the ideas of entitlement and fairness that inhabit it, constitute the background against which the moral framework of the 1990s emerged.

DIVERGING PATHS AFTER 1989

The Revolutionary Moment

When the Iron Curtain collapsed, millions were liberated from terror, propaganda, and the rule of the self-serving and corrupt leadership. What many had been long hoping for—a moment of accountability, justice, and democratic renewal—had finally arrived. It was a shift from one temporal regime to another: from the backward orientation and nostalgia of the late socialist period to the contingency and hope of the democratic future.

In the fall of 1989, the opposition movement gained momentum. In Prague, in November, students and workers organized mass protests; went on strike; and "churned out tens of thousands of declarations, flysheets, bulletins, posters, and open letters."[58] By December 1989, power was lying in the streets. Shortly before New Year's Eve, president Gustáv Husák resigned, and Václav Havel, leader of the opposition movement Civic Forum, was elected the first democratic president of the country since 1948. In Germany, demonstrations were preceded by the opening of the Hungarian-Austrian border in September 1989. Even though the passage to Austria was officially restricted to Hungarians, many East Germans took advantage of the opportunity to escape. Soon, protests in major cities such as Leipzig and Berlin intensified.[59] Moscow's reluctance to intervene weakened the SED leadership. Erich Honecker was forced to resign on October 18; his successor resigned just a month and a half later. When the Berlin Wall fell on November 9, the door to German reunification was thrown open. These events triggered the manifold changes in the political, economic, and cultural foundations of these societies that are known as the postsocialist transformations. In 1990, in Berlin and Prague, as well as in Warsaw and Moscow, policymakers and their international advisers were convinced that things had to move fast and that deep-seated change was necessary. From this moment on, the German and the Czech pathways diverged.[60]

HISTORICAL TRAJECTORIES

A German Marriage, a Czech Divorce

On October 3, 1990, the two Germanies were unified, while the Czech and the Slovak republics parted peacefully on January 1, 1993. East Germans were "getting married," while Czechoslovaks were "getting a divorce." As with any substantial shift in relations, each had lasting and unintended consequences. The German marriage was a radical political and economic experiment. The GDR was dissolved and incorporated into the Federal German Republic in 1990. Practically overnight, East Germans experienced an elite takeover by West Germans. Between 1990 and 1994, about 35,000 civil servants, judges and political experts entered East German administration offices. This in turn significantly lowered East Germans' chances to rise into elite positions for years to come—many positions remained occupied by West Germans for decades to come.[61] The proposition offered to former citizens of the GDR was that they would be part of a single nation and be able to think of themselves as Germans again. There was a tacit assumption baked into this, namely, that they lacked a stable identity, that decades of state-socialist propaganda had left them without a sense of belonging. In many ways, this turned out to be a shortsighted proposition. While the West German political class promoted a kind of soft nationalism couched in metaphors of family reunification, emboldened nativists and neo-Nazi groups soon launched a campaign of violence against migrants, ethnic minorities, and leftists in the eastern provinces—all in the name of the German nation. During the 1990s, many provinces and towns in the territories of the former GDR experienced an outburst of nativist violence. The period came to be remembered as the baseball bat years. This did not fit into the official narrative of reunification.

The Czech story, in contrast, was a tale of becoming a nation of its own. The federation of Czechoslovakia ceased to exist on New Year's Eve 1993, when the Velvet Divorce from Slovakia was accomplished. The fact that this process was entirely peaceful stunned many observers at the time because brutal nationalistic wars were being waged not far away, in the Balkans, after the dissolution of Yugoslavia. But the Czechoslovak "short goodbye" was really an elite deal.[62] An iconic photo taken in 1992 shows Václav Klaus and Vladimír Mečiar, the Czech and Slovak leaders, as they casually converse in the garden of Brno's modernist Villa Tugendhat to determine their nations' fates—an image that conveys a sense of nonchalant patrimonial, aristocratic rule more than of democratic deliberation. One issue that fueled the divorce was that policymakers disagreed about the desired model of economic transformation. Czech and Slovak elites envisioned different routes of reform, with the Czechs pressing for a more radical approach and the Slovaks for a more gradual one. The split paved the way for the revival of nationalism. Slovaks, who had typically harbored a sense that they were underrepresented in the federal institutions, could now think of themselves as the masters of their own fate. Czechs in turn could find comfort in the fact that economic growth in their country would no longer be slowed down—as the thinking went—by Slovak underperformance.

Next, I trace elementary features of structural change that shaped the ways in which social identities were differently reconfigured after 1989. While East Germans experienced economic dissolution in the form of disappearing industry, skyrocketing rates of unemployment, and increasing wages, Czechs experienced a relatively high degree of industrial preservation, with low levels of unemployment and low wages. It mattered how German and Czech elites variously communicated *shock therapy* to the population. East Germans were subject to a patronizing discourse that blamed them for economic failure; Czechs were offered a cultural script of resilience and masculine economic nationalism by their respective leaders.

THE GERMAN PATH: DISSOLUTION

After German unification was realized on October 3, 1990, East Germany ceased to exist as a political and legal entity.[63] West German leaders, convinced that the GDR industry suffered from a perennial backwardness, wanted economic integration as quickly as possible. Consequently, monetary union was introduced already in July 1990, prior to political reunification. The East German currency was now exchanged at a 1:1 (1:2 for larger sums) rate, which gave East Germans extensive purchasing power overnight. Wages rose steeply. In contrast to neighboring transforming societies, this resulted initially in an upward valuation of East German industry. It was excellent news for customers, but it was a serious problem for domestic firms because their products were too expensive from one day to the next for their main trading partners in Russia and elsewhere in the former bloc. Privatization was next on the agenda. Policymakers looked for ways to transform state-owned property (everything from flats, trains, and roads to the state-owned companies was formally possessed by GDR citizens) into property that can would be valued and traded at market prices. In Germany, a single institution was responsible for this mammoth task, the federal agency *Treuhandanstalt*. The agency sold off the large, formerly state-owned enterprises fast in an auction-style process in the hope of attracting competitive prices. In this model, unlike in the Czech *voucher privatization*, East German citizens did not receive a share of the former state-owned property. The principal idea behind the *Treuhand* privatization model was the faster, the better. Such was the spirit of the time—and it was also profoundly shortsighted. The agency found itself in a weak bargaining position with investors and was forced to sell off many firms far below their value. The consequence was the near-total demise of East German industry. In its four years of existence, *Treuhand* managed over 13,000 economic units, from which only a fraction survived.[64] "When *Treuhand* proudly announced in 1994 that it had completed its task, it had incurred a loss of more than 250 billion marks rather than making the expected six hundred billion profits on privatization," writes historian Philip Ther.[65] A heated controversy about the causes of this disaster is still ongoing for Germans. All things considered, it was really a combination of factors that produced this outcome: foreign debt and the structural weakness of GDR firms; the dramatic loss of competitiveness generated by monetary union in 1990s; and mistakes made during privatization, especially the focus on speed rather than infrastructure and sustainability.

The social consequences were dramatic. Unemployment levels skyrocketed. The East German workforce shrank from 9.8 million people in the fall of 1989 to 5.8 million in 1992.[66] In the first year after the fall of the Berlin Wall, the number of people without a job rose from practically zero to around 1 million in a population of merely 15 million people. Unemployment soon turned into the defining experience of the period, reaching levels that were, at the time, "probably unprecedented in the entire history of industrial society."[67] In search for a job, more than 1.5 million people left East Germany for West Germany or left the country between 1990 and 2006. Joblessness and the threat of job loss reached far into the emerging middle class. At the same time, wages rose steeply. East Germans could now think of themselves as full members of a consumer society. Wages also rose in the public sector, which often constituted a "safe haven" of employment because it was relatively shielded from the dangers of job

HISTORICAL TRAJECTORIES

insecurity, and the state was—unlike in other transforming societies—paying relatively well.[68] However, this initial increase in wages did not bring social upward mobility. In fact, most East Germans struggled with social downward mobility at the time.[69] It was a deep labor market crisis. Sociologists find that how a person was able to cope was primarily determined by his or her skills and educational credentials—in fact, credentials acquired *before* 1989 were a critical factor in whether one would be able to remain at a job or find a new job at the time. In other words, the qualifications that people had acquired before the fall of the Berlin Wall turned out to be crucial for weathering the crisis. How a person fared in the early 1990s also often determined their long-term trajectories. About one-third of the East German labor force became "extremely vulnerable to unemployment," about one-third remained in employment but was confronted with "sharp changes in the occupation ladder in terms of status and occupation," and about one-third could "master the restructuring process without severe losses in terms of status or occupational capital in the long run."[70]

In the early 1990s, a great number of East German institutions of political, economic, and cultural life quite simply disappeared; they were replaced by West German institutions. The health-care system, for example, was comprehensively restructured. Large health facilities known as policlinics, which typically combined teams of doctors and nurses in surgery, dentistry, physiotherapy, and other services in one building, were rapidly dismantled. The speed at which this happened was remarkable: in 1990, around 87.4 percent of doctors working outside hospitals were practicing in policlinics, but at the end of 1994, this number was down to a mere 3.3 percent.[71]

For East Germans, business opportunities were notably scarce. During the 1990s, becoming an entrepreneur did not pay off. In many cases, being self-employed was primarily a means to avoid unemployment.[72] There was not much to gain for East German entrepreneurs because, "in stark contrast to other transformation countries, very few windfall profits were made and thus nouveaux riches are not visible."[73] It was a far cry from the promise of meritocracy. As sociologist Martin Diewald points out, economic success, at the time, had nothing to do with a person's belief in merit and hard work.[74] The radical flattening of the former industrial structure and the shrinking of firms were part of this problem. During the course of privatization, valuable pieces of the former GDR economy were quickly sold off to resourceful West German or international investors. Small and medium-sized East German businessowners were left with little resources to develop. In the long run, this compounded their disadvantage. Businesses had little opportunities to grow and often did not withstand West German competition. Around three decades after 1989, this pattern is still visible. There are few large, viable economic structures that allow for vocational training and within-firm upward mobility in eastern regions.[75] East Germans also still earn less than West Germans. The gap in wages again widened during the 1990s, and it still persists in many sectors of the economy today. The promised economic convergence materialized only selectively, and some disparities grew wider over the past thirty years. Wide-ranging welfare cuts and labor market reforms that were passed in the mid-2000s hit East Germans hard, suppressing incomes and accelerating the rise of a low-wage sector.[76]

Extensive state action, in the form of subsidies and welfare measures by the federal German state, helped cushion the catastrophic social consequences in the early 1990s. As it was dismantling the GDR's economic infrastructure, the government launched a large-scale effort to reintegrate East Germans into the labor market. Between 1989 and 1994, more than half of working-age East Germans participated in some form of labor market measure, some several times.[77] These programs could not tackle the deeper problems, however, in particular the devaluation of firms and labor and the lack of social upward mobility.[78] Instead of becoming autonomous subjects in a market society, East Germans found that their economic fates mostly depended on the (West German) state.

THE CZECH PATH: PRESERVATION

For Czechs, the transformation time was a very different experience. Here, policymakers' priority was to avoid mass unemployment and to preserve key industries (initially, the goal was also to keep them in domestic hands). It was a less radical approach, if still a form of shock therapy. Like in Germany, economic planners believed that there was only a small window of opportunity for reforms, so things had to move fast. A key priority was to reduce the size of the labor force, especially the share of women in it. Employment declined by around 8 percent between 1990 and 1992 across all sectors of the economy, and by a whopping 31 percent in agriculture.[79] Price liberalization was to happen fast, too. Thus, in Czechoslovakia, the

HISTORICAL TRAJECTORIES

average price level increased by more than half in the first year after the revolution. This came as a shock to many, in particular the elderly.[80]

The Czech reform model was authored by Václav Klaus.[81] Trained as an economist and well connected in technocratic circles in 1980s Prague, he was drawn to neoliberal thinking long before the revolution. After the split from Slovakia in 1993, and as the first prime minister of the Czech Republic, Klaus was able to implement his reform package, which included measures such as slashing firm subsidies, deregulating the economy, weakening unions and workers' associations by curtailing their bargaining rights, introducing means testing in social assistance, and reforming the pension system.[82] However, some social standards were maintained. Rent control, housing subsidies, a minimum wage, and the maintenance of corporatist labor market institutions were guaranteed.[83] The social cushioning measures avoided widespread impoverishment. In 1992, around 3 percent of Czech families lived below the poverty line. In Poland, where welfare provisions were dismantled more comprehensively, poverty affected around 15 percent of the country's families during the same year.[84] The bedrock of Klaus's reform model was the preservation of jobs, to "[keep] the employed in work and the unemployed employable."[85]

Privatization was implemented in two steps. In the first phase, right after the revolution, small businesses were returned to former owners or sold to private investors. In the second, after the split from Slovakia in 1993, so-called voucher privatization, which targeted the large, state-owned companies and totaled a third of assets of all firms in the country, was implemented. Every adult Czech citizen would receive a share of the former people's property and be able trade it on the market. The idea behind this model of privatization was to allow "ordinary citizens to get access to property quickly and without [existing] capital" and thus create a society of domestic shareholders.[86] Two-thirds of the adult population participated in these programs, so there was a popular, democratic element to them. However, voucher privatization was prone to corruption. Given the weak regulation of the financial sector—the government was in fact promoting the deregulation of finance as a key driver of economic growth—insider information about the value of firms or the timing of their selling was exchanged in informal networks. In this situation, some well-connected individuals—emerging oligarchs—managed to buy cheaply, sell expensively, reap profits, and thereby reduce the value of the wider population's piece of the asset pie. One particularly consequential form of corruption was the practice of handing out loans to unprofitable and unviable firms so that they could be sold off at high prices. The accumulation of bad loans resulted in a national banking crisis in 1996 and 1997. To counter the recession, banks were sold off cheaply to international owners. Firms began to compete for foreign direct investments, and the goal to keep businesses in domestic hands was abandoned. Major branches of the economy became dependent on foreign capital and foreign ownership. For instance, the German car giant Volkswagen produces the popular Škoda brand in Czechia today.[87]

The Czech path of reform nevertheless left key economic infrastructures—above all, industries such as cars, machinery, steel, and chemicals—intact, which in turn kept unemployment comparatively low. The difference compared to East Germany was like night and day. In the Czech Republic, a mere 3 to 4 percent of the population were without a job in the early 1990s, and unemployment remained low until about 1998, when the recession forced firms to restructure.[88] Unemployment rates were "not just conspicuously below those in other post-communist democracies, they were actually lower than anywhere in Europe, and second-lowest among all OECD [Organization for Economic Co-operation and Development] countries."[89] There was a stark gender disparity, however, because joblessness affected many more women than men. The situation was particularly dire for members of the ethnic Roma minority, who frequently lost their jobs and faced massive labor market discrimination beginning in the 1990s.[90] Wages remained exceedingly low. Sociologist Jiří Večerník wryly commented that, after the revolution, "for the majority, jobs continue to be 'socialist': easily available and poorly rewarded." However, a new logic of worth did emerge around work. Now, private sector work, particularly in financial services, was highly rewarded, while public sector activities were poorly remunerated. Incomes rose in niche sectors such as banking, management, technology, and other specialized fields, but they stagnated or fell in education, social services, and health care. The main continuity from state-socialist times was in fact the gendered pattern of worth. Female work was devalued, as it was before 1989, when education and health care were regarded as "non-productive" activities.[91]

The health-care sector is a paradigmatic example in this respect. Policymakers, inspired by the Washington Consensus, agreed that labor costs in the public sector were too high. The shift in the mode of financing health care from a model in which the state centrally administered health-care coverage under state socialism to one involving competing health insurance providers and semipublic and corporate forms of administration in hospitals and health-care facilities effectively cut costs. It also meant that health care was operating on an increasingly tight budget. The Czech state has been particularly frugal when it comes to health-care spending. In 1990, about 3.6 percent of Czech GDP was spent on health care (in Germany, the figure for that year was 6.06 percent), but that figure had grown to a mere 6.46 percent by 2019 (compared to 9.83 percent in Germany).[92]

How did individuals with business ambitions fare? Was this now a society governed by the principle of meritocracy? Becoming an entrepreneur was a more viable option for Czechs than it was for East Germans. In fact, they were enthusiastic founders. So many people decided to set up their own businesses during the 1990s that this country soon had the highest share of self-employed people in the postsocialist word.[93] However, social mobility patterns were meritocratic only on the surface. Once we dig deeper, we can see that powerful structural forces guided life courses after 1989. As sociologist Akos Rona-Tas notes, the vast majority of newly founded Czech small businesses were rather unviable; typically, they were characterized by "low investment, lax record keeping, using the home as an office, and lack of geographical expansion."[94] As in Germany, skills and educational credentials acquired *before* 1989 played a crucial role during the early phase of the transformation.[95] After an initial uptick, overall levels of social mobility declined. Between 1989 and 2009, family origin, together with the dynamics of capital accumulation, crystallized as the principal determinants of life chances.[96] As we saw, gender disparities widened. Economists sometimes explain the gap between male and female earnings by underlying differences in education and skills. However, Czech developments of the 1990s tell a very different story. When state socialism broke down, the level of education was similarly high among both men and women. The widening gulf in incomes after 1989 was therefore driven by gender discrimination in labor markets as well as by conservative family policies, but not by a lack of expertise or work ethic among women.[97] After the turn of the century, when the Czech government adopted another set of neoliberal reforms that targeted child care, pensions, and taxes, those inequalities were further entrenched.

Old elites managed to benefit, too. Individuals who were able to draw on insider knowledge of firms and informal networks from the time before the revolution found themselves with excellent chances of becoming successful entrepreneurs and businessowners after 1989. But it was not the former political leaders, the heads of the Communist Party, who profited the most. Sociologists Jiří Večerník and Petr Matějů call the Czech type of elite change a "revolution of the deputies" in which "individuals in the highest positions (directors, general directors) have been replaced by less politically compromised professionals who were, from the standpoint of power, members of a kind of 'second league' (mostly their deputies)." Taking advantage of privatization, technocrats would rise to power after 1989.[98] These individuals had often received technical, economic, or administrative university training before the breakdown of the old regime. Czechs, of course, took note of the fact that economic success after 1989 was often based on insider knowledge. As inequality and wealth concentration exacerbated, citizens were increasingly disillusioned about privatization.

We saw that, in both cases, the logic and the direction of change after 1989 was deeply shaped by structural forces. It was not primarily a question of individual agency. How do people make sense of these forces in the moral framework? Before beginning to unpack this question in the following chapter, I turn to an analysis of the dominant narratives about economic change that were publicly available at the time.

Framing Economic Transformations: German Patronizing and Czech Masculinizing Narratives

Who gets to define the meaning of the transformations? Who gets to say what the telos of painful economic change might be? In the moral framework, economic change is not just a numbers game—people perceive, interpret, and evaluate it against horizons of cultural orientations and normative expectations. For the remainder of this chapter, I stick to the macro level of analysis, focusing on dominant narratives about the economic transformations that circulated in the public sphere. Political and economic elites, as well as academics, journalists, and other producers of culture, crafted a set of stories that communicated the rationale of economic change to the broader public. Like any narrative, they contain elements of causal explanations for success and failure.[99] From the perspective of the moral framework, I assume that, while people do not necessarily agree with them, they will, in one way or another, respond to such public stories. They may also inform people's personal experience—and perhaps later, their memories—of the period.

The prevailing narrative of the 1990s was a neoliberal discourse, a story about how people are individually responsible for economic success and failure. We can identify two versions of this general theme in the German and Czech public spheres. East Germans were confronted with a patronizing narrative, which blamed them for economic weakness after 1989. The implication was that East Germans must become someone else during the transformation. For Czechs, in contrast, the problem was framed as one of overcoming weakness, of resilience in the face of economic difficulties. The implication was that Czechs must mobilize their hidden powers and return to their more authentic self in this process.

In Germany, the power imbalance between East and West persisted long after 1989. Equality remained elusive. As we saw, East Germans were able to occupy only a small fraction of leadership positions in politics, economics, culture, and the media. Thus, the public conversation about the GDR past, the fall of the Berlin Wall, and the transformation period was generally dominated by West Germans. As we saw earlier, one theme was that East Germans were now addressed as *consumers* on an equal footing. Apart from this, they were frequently depicted in a patronizing way. A range of cultural clichés circulated about them in the public sphere. One study that compares the representations of former GDR citizens in four leading newspapers (all of them West German because East German papers had ceased to exist) in the early 1990s finds that the image conveyed was overwhelmingly pejorative: East Germans were regularly depicted as "backward," "lazy," and "unfamiliar" with the challenges of democracy and market society. For their part, East Germans felt treated as "second class citizens" already soon after 1989, and this sentiment only deepened during the 1990s.[100]

How was East German *economic agency* portrayed after 1989? We may consider the publications of economic think tanks to approach this question because their narratives were generally widely distributed in the media. Here, we can see that economic specialists were concerned with one macroeconomic problem, above all: the productivity gap between East and West. The East German economy was less productive, and the questions were, What caused this deficiency? and How can the process of catching up be accelerated? Writing in the newsletter of Institute for Economic Research (IFO) in Munich, one of the leading German economic think tanks, economist and IFO president Hans-Werner Sinn outlined the following explanation in 2000: "The financial means at the disposal of East Germans . . . exceed their own performance by far. . . . A large share of resource consumption in the East is financed by the West." Ten years into the transformation, Sinn suggested, East Germans still had not managed to "stand on their own feet," and West Germans had to sustain their advanced lifestyle. This he called—referencing a similar diagnosis about Southern Europe—the "mezzogiorno problem" of East Germany. What was the root cause of this predicament? According to Sinn, the problem was that East German wages were too high and that they did not reflect the actual level of qualifications, or "human capital." Citizens of the former GDR, in other words, were underqualified or not working hard enough. Around ten years later, on the twentieth anniversary of German reunification, the narrative had evolved. An IFO report from 2009 noted that the productivity gap was ultimately caused by a structural weakness of East German firms, a legacy from state-socialist times. Now, the problem was found to rest not primarily with workers but with firms. This interpretation—although it contained important observations about the deficiencies of the late socialist economy—deemphasized the fact that political choices after 1989, in particular policy decisions around monetary union and the model of privatization, had shaped the structure and the economic opportunities of the firms in question. Economic weakness was still, in part, presented as an *intrinsic* feature of the East Germany economy. The only solution therefore was the most radical one: the legacies of the past must be left behind. More balanced accounts that also discuss the role of privatization as a causal factor for lower levels of productivity can be found only in recent publications by think tanks.[101]

The Czech story could not be more different. Here, the population was addressed with a domestic voice that sought, above all, to justify the need for market reform.[102] It was coupled with a strong anticommunism, the prevailing mood in the public sphere at the time, in which "any voices which attempted to evaluate aspects of the previous regime in a more complex way" were "immediately attacked for advocating a return to the old order."[103] Prime Minister Klaus, in particular, had mastered the discourse of *shock therapy* as a form of a painful but ultimately gratifying experience.

He was able to do so because he stayed in power for eight years, the longest of any postsocialist head of government in the 1990s. Klaus regularly communicated his ideas to the public. His favorite theme, in fact, was the meaning of economic change, which he linked to a specific interpretation of the Velvet Revolution and thus also to a vision of Czech democracy. In 1990, he proclaimed,

> There still persists a distrust of the market, an unwillingness to leave our fates in the hand of impersonal mechanisms . . . and by contrast a belief in the effectiveness of politics . . . and the possibility of a political solution to economic problems. To overcome this, we need a much deeper revolution than that which occurred after 17 November [the beginning of the Velvet Revolution], a revolution that won't be visible on squares and in mass demonstrations, but which will take place inside all of us, which will last much longer, the results of which will long be binding.[104]

For Klaus, the real meaning of the revolution was the shift away from politics and toward the market. In his understanding, politics was always and everywhere the source of problems, and only the market could offer solutions. Consequently, 1989 was to be nothing less than an epistemic shift in the life of Czechs. The need for reform was a moral mission: a purification from politics and a journey toward inner strength. In such a situation, sacrifice—individual economic sacrifice, in particular—was tied to a higher goal.[105] Klaus regularly spoke of the need to "tighten our belts," never failing to strike a sacralizing tone.

This was a masculinizing discourse. Klaus consistently linked his transformation narrative to male fantasies of empowerment and nationalist revival, effectively branding a form of economic nationalism. For instance, he justified his reform package—his attack on the welfare state—by a discourse of male strength, the dignity of work, and the idea of domestic ownership. Bringing all these themes together, in 1994, he cited a Czech member of the early twentieth century Habsburg Parliament in Vienna, František Ladislav Rieger (a fighter for greater national autonomy under imperial rule), with the following words: "What we need above all is work—real, sustained work both spiritual and industrial. That will help us most rapidly to adulthood, to manly force, to power and to honor."[106] At the same time, Klaus also invoked the pragmatic, harsh language of transactional politics—the language of the *deal*—promising that unemployment would be contained but that people would have to accept moderate wages for some time in return. Voucher privatization was also part of the economic nationalism theme. This mode of privatization suggested to citizens that they had an active role in the emerging property regime. Vouchers were "a kind of election ballot for the chosen transformation strategy and a symbol of its economic returns in the future."[107] Accordingly, privatization was framed as an investment opportunity; and Czechs were called on as financially prudent, independent, and smart subjects. In their advertisements, investment funds suggested to potential customers that this was the opportunity and the moment to become the "master" of their "future" and that of their children. Notably, the funds directed this language of investment as a matter of responsibility and maturity exclusively at men.[108] The neoliberal "return" to "normalcy" was, in effect, everywhere imagined as a social order that was naturally dominated by men. Although people lost trust in these schemes after a range of corruption scandals came to light later in the 1990s, the idea of voucher privatization as a form of however vaguely defined "people's capitalism" did foster popular support for the government's reform agenda.

The masculinizing economic nationalism provided a rationale for coping with change. The interpretations promoted by a major Czech economic think tank, the Center for Economics and Politics (with Václav Klaus at the helm) after the turn of the century reveal striking differences to what we saw in the German context. Here, the diagnosis of a lack of productivity or low productivity—which, as we saw, was the principal concern of German economic commentators—is largely absent. The Center for Economics and Politics also defines the 1990s as a time of crisis. Yet here, macroeconomic deficiencies and labor market problems are not seen as rooted in the productive sector but in a different set of phenomena, such as the swift change from an "artificial" to a "natural" price regime.[109] The overall sphere of production is coded as the realm where value is being created and hence as a source of economic pride—similar to before 1989. After the Czech Republic joined the European Union in 2004, an additional theme emerges as part of the economic nationalist discourse: that of blaming domestic deficiencies on Brussels's regulatory drive—the infamous "Brussels bureaucracy."

From the perspective of those in power, this nationalist framing of the transformation challenges seems to have worked remarkably well. During the 1990s and beyond, pro-market orientations persisted in wide swaths of the Czech population, even in groups that were objectively disadvantaged by the changes. An ethnography of female factory workers conducted at the turn of the century, for instance, finds that they drew on these narratives to make sense of their own experience of change. In 2004, the Czech Republic was the only country in the region where the number of people who believed that their family was among the "winners" of the transformation was greater than those who thought it to be among the "losers." Despite widespread anger about stagnating wages and corruption, many Czechs could draw on an optimistic narrative that provided a positive telos for change. In sum, we can distinguish two variations of the neoliberal theme that are also different stories about modernization. The masculinizing narrative, suggesting that Czechs must only overcome their weaker selves in order to thrive in market society, was presented as a reform agenda *from within*. East Germans, who were addressed as consumers but otherwise frequently reminded of their economic deficiencies, were to be modernized *from without*.[110]

Chapter Two

REMEMBERING ECONOMIC CHANGE AFTER 1989

traditional values at stake

> That working people felt these grievances at all—and felt them passionately—is itself a sufficient fact to merit our attention... The issues which provoked the most intensity of feeling were very often the ones in which values such as traditional customs, "justice," "independence," security, or family-economy were at stake, rather than straightforward "bread-and-butter" issues.
>
> —E. P. THOMPSON, *THE MAKING OF THE ENGLISH WORKING CLASS*[1]

VARIETIES OF CRISIS EXPERIENCES

In her oral history study of a Czech-Austrian border town before and after 1989, historian Muriel Blaive reports the story of a woman who, when interviewed and asked if the term "Velvet Revolution" meant anything to her, tried to make up her memory and replied: "Ah yes! But that was in Prague!"[2] This is not a contested vision of 1989. Rather, it seems that the specific political-iconic reading—that of mass demonstrations, and a claim for political change—is not part of her experience. Hers is likely a more *vernacular* understanding: smaller, less official, and focused on her local environment. When we are interested in people's biographical accounts of the period, we should refrain from taking the public narratives about 1989 as our point of departure. Listening to how people make sense of change in subtle and idiomatic ways is the goal of this chapter. With the broad societal pathways discussed in the previous chapter in mind, I zoom in to trace the ways in which people remember concrete economic shifts and construe a sense of rupture in them.

This brings us back to our main theoretical proposition: that the way disruptive economic change is remembered is guided by the problem of social inclusion. In the moral framework, people link past and present in a way that sustains ideas of economic worth. They draw on preexisting

REMEMBERING ECONOMIC CHANGE AFTER 1989

cultural orientations and social identities—what Thompson called the "older moral economy"—to signify and evaluate ruptures. In this chapter, I identify a relevant pattern in biographical narratives of economic change. People conjure these older understandings by invoking skills, by narrating core competences of their professional identity. Skills are a structure of meaning; they link the time before 1989 and after 1989 in a way that is consistent from a subjective point of view. But these meanings, I demonstrate, are also shaped by varying cultural parameters. We encounter a difference between East German and Czech accounts. Among East Germans, there is a pervasive sense of exclusion, nourished by memories of economic humiliation and by how the value of their skills was never properly recognized in unified German society. Czechs, in contrast, offer a more ambiguous story of the transformation, characterized by a combination of pride in skills and a profound disillusionment with how the post-1989 political order fails to value work. In both cases, the legacy of moralized ideas of work underpins popular perceptions and memories of economic change.

Engineers and Health-Care Workers

Large-scale crises affect different groups in society in different ways—existing inequalities of health, economic resources, welfare support, and community support create disparate crisis experiences on the ground. The COVID-19 pandemic has brought this elementary sociological insight into sharp relief. We can discern similar patterns already after the breakdown of state socialism. At the time, a person's age, ethnicity, gender, skills, education, and location were among the primary factors that mediated the economic impact. As we saw in chapter 1, a person's status in the labor market in the early 1990s often shaped his or her life long after the initial changes. This also serves as a reminder that we cannot describe the intricacies of crisis experiences at the level of the population as a whole. Instead, we must be systematic about *whose perspective* we are foregrounding and what this choice implies for how we come to think about the crisis event more generally. This is why, in this chapter, I trace biographical accounts of individuals from two professional fields, engineering and health care, comparatively,

Why engineers and health-care workers? Engineers plan, design, build, and screen things. Health-care workers make sure that people are well. The former is a predominantly male profession; the latter is predominantly female. Engineers typically see the world from the standpoint of technical rationality, from the standpoint of producing objects and designing processes that are useful to society. Health-care work, in contrast, has a social end. It is often characterized as a process-oriented activity (such as alleviating suffering or caring for someone who is terminally ill) that does not have a single product or outcome. We need to be careful, however, about how we assess this proposition. A common prejudice holds that health-care work is a form of unskilled labor, something that anyone can do, which is not how those who practice the profession see it. Health-care workers, in the words of one anthropologist, "judge themselves and each other as professionals based on how well they are able to care for the patients in their charge," which requires them to fulfill a range of complex tasks, including physical, administrative, medical, and emotional labor, simultaneously. It is possible to distinguish at least four meanings of health-care work: "face-to-face working with patients, dealing with patients as a whole person, the comparatively open-ended nature of the nurse's duties, and the personal commitment of the nurse to [the] work."[3]

The main rationale behind comparing accounts from individuals in these two professions is that the departure from the old social contract looks quite different for them because 1989 variously shaped their economic opportunities and hence their life chances. The value of engineers' skills in the labor market increased after 1989 while that of health-care workers stagnated. Hence, their relative positions in the system of social stratification were differently preconfigured. These are still, broadly speaking, two professions of the middle class; we will not gain systematic insights into experiences of marginalization and impoverishment nor will we gain insights into windfall profits after 1989 by foregrounding these perspectives. In them, however, the conditions for experiencing change were differently aligned.[4]

Seen from a historical perspective, engineers occupied a central position in the state-socialist project. Technical expertise and technological progress were at the very heart of the socialist modernity, with engineering at the forefront. In her book *Red Prometheus*, historian Dolores Augustine, for instance, finds that a special, reciprocal relationship existed between German Democratic Republic (GDR) engineers and the party. Engineers also fared comparatively well after the 1989 revolutions, primarily because their skills and competences were transferable, in demand, and increasingly well paid.[5]

REMEMBERING ECONOMIC CHANGE AFTER 1989

ENGINEERS

This transition was much smoother in the Czech Republic than in East Germany. In East Germany, as hundreds of thousands of jobs in the industrial sector disappeared in the early 1990s, engineers were confronted with the prospect of unemployment, especially in regions where many plants were closed for good and large technical departments were radically downsized.[6] For Czech engineers, unemployment was rarely a concern. Industries were restructured, but many skilled jobs were retained. For many, the benefits of the market economy soon became manifest because higher education credentials allowed them to earn comparably high wages and to climb the social ladder soon after 1989.[7]

HEALTH-CARE

In contrast, the fate of health-care work is, in many ways, a story about the continuity of the inferior value granted to this type of work by society. In late socialist Czechoslovakia and the GDR, health care was valued very little. Nurses were not considered part of the working class; their skills were not regarded as "productive." Already, health care was an almost exclusively female profession.[8] Czechoslovak and East German nurses generated low incomes and worked under relatively harsh conditions.[9]

After 1989, work life improved, but new problems arose. The commodification of health care—driven by reformers' concern, as we saw in the previous chapter, to increase efficiency and to reduce labor costs—was arguably the most momentous change. In the Czech Republic, the introduction of market-based financing mechanisms in health care resulted in the dysfunctionality of medical services and depressed wages. It also contributed to the field's further feminization. "As Czech men moved into the private sector beginning in 1990," notes Jacqui True, "the public or civil sector became even more feminized than during the socialist regime." Wages for Czech health-care workers remained well below the national average wage throughout the first decade after 1989. Labor costs in the Czech public sector were among the lowest in all of Central Eastern Europe.[10]

East German health-care workers fared better in this respect, primarily because their employment by the unified German state meant that they received relatively high wages and offered them a degree of job stability during the turbulent 1990s. In this case, the realignment of the health-care sector was marked by two parallel dynamics. On the one hand, thanks to the resourcefulness of the (West) German state, East German health-care workers' wages grew initially amid job stability because the health-care field expanded after 1989. This was exceptional at a time when many branches of the economy were affected by job insecurity, downsizing, and reductions in the labor force. On the other hand, in a longer-term perspective, health-care workers found themselves in an occupation that was marked by underinvestment and mounting downward pressures on labor costs. Wages in the East, while rising initially, would continue to hover at around 70 to 80 percent of West German levels for decades to come. Here, too, policymakers sought to introduce pricing mechanisms (effectively transferring West German institutions to the East) in the hope of increasing economic and medical efficiency.[11]

Small Ruptures: Breaking Points at Work After 1989

How do people remember the economic change of the 1990s in their everyday lives? The memories are variegated. One commonality stands out from the beginning: in all of them, we can find episodes of how the shift to market society played out in people's quotidian experience—how broader change materialized, for the first time, in their work life. I label these stories "small ruptures."

We often encounter small ruptures in stories about how firms were shrinking after 1989, something that left a lasting impression on workers and employees. In the early 1990s, market reformers uniformly believed that the large, state-owned companies would have to be downsized, reorganized in smaller economic units, or dissolved altogether. From the perspective of workers and employees, this brought job insecurity and often the loss of colleagues. Rudolf, fifty-seven, an East German foundry engineer, has worked for the same firm for his entire life. Before the revolution, the city-owned foundry was casting parts for the East German car industry. In the early 1990s, managed by the privatization agency *Treuhand*, it was bought by a West German firm, downsized, and later sold to an international investor. Rudolf was able to keep his job:

[Before 1989], we were more than a thousand people, only in this part of the firm. There were many more parts; all of the buildings in this area were part of it; a lot has been closed down after the transition. This foundry survived, together with a small aluminum foundry, and a laboratory; the latter is an independent business. [The number of workers] was reduced to around 200 because nearly all the contracts were lost . . . It was clear relatively early on that my position wouldn't be cut as long as this business is operational. But there was this uncertainty—what is going to happen to this firm once there is a new owner? You didn't know what changes were coming.

Rudolf's memory of the firm's downsizing is shaped by the fact that he was able to stay. As luck would have it, and as he sees it, he was able to remain. This allowed him to record the process of reorganization from the inside. It dragged on for years. Rudolf remarks that it was not until 1994 that people were newly employed in the foundry; management's priority during this entire period was to downsize. During this period, the owners also frequently changed—something that was typical at the time, when ownership in firms administered by *Treuhand* could sometimes change every few months. As Rudolf remembers it, the disruptive episode of firm restructuring is not limited to a single moment but constitutes an ongoing process, a resurfacing tension and recurring possibility of loss. Notably, quantitative changes, such as the decline from 1,000 employees to 200, play a key role in Rudolf's account. Like others who witnessed firms shrink, he has a crystal-clear memory of the statistics of employees and colleagues in his department at the time. Here, the numbers are more than raw data; they convey social meaning. People often draw on such statistics to illustrate changes in work environments. A sense of loss also permeated Czech industrial enterprises at the time because many large combinates were reducing their labor force, although skilled employees, such as engineers, enjoyed a relatively high degree of job security.[12]

Health-care workers also remember downsizing. Yet in this field, unlike in industry and manufacturing, there was a growing demand for labor after 1989. The health-care sector expanded. Still, hospitals and clinics were restructured in elementary ways. Prior to the revolution, health-care facilities were generally large and centrally administered. Large policlinics were transformed, and single units and wards became smaller and more autonomously organized. The process of decentralization informs health-care workers' memories of shifts in the organizational and social composition of their workplace during the 1990s.[13]

Job loss was a defining experience of the period. For those who could not stay at their jobs—as was true in East Germany for most of the workforce—job loss constituted a small if potentially highly consequential rupture. Because unemployment was nearly nonexistent in the late socialist

GDR and Czechoslovakia, it was a novel and profoundly unsettling experience. Before the fall of the Berlin Wall, Björn, sixty-seven, used to work at a large GDR combinate as a test engineer. His former department was dissolved as a result of privatization, a process that dragged on for years. By 1994, when he finally received a notification of dismissal, he had gone through a prolonged period of uncertainty and fear over his employment status at the firm:

> I was employed at the technology department . . . After 1993 came the time of a wave of dismissals. Entire departments were leveled to the ground . . . At the end of 1994, it was "finite" for me, the end. In 1995, I was finally unemployed. In 1996, I started a retraining measure, the labor office offered this training for engineering personnel. It was geared towards quality control; we were "back to school," and we were taught—next to other things we already knew—we were taught English and some technology in quality control.

Björn, a diploma engineer, had received a prestigious education in the 1970s. He had no reason to assume that someone would, one day, question his qualification. Yet after his dismissal, he found himself stuck in state-subsidized retraining measures. He was far from the only one—according to one estimate, more than half of adult East Germans participated in some type of labor market measure between 1989 and 1994.[14] Given that jobs were in short supply, these programs were often unsuccessful. Like many others, Björn remembers them as bureaucratic, tedious, and humiliating. His dismissal in 1995 was also not the last time he experienced joblessness. The episode was the first in several phases of unemployment and job insecurity; the last time he was out of work was shortly before his retirement in 2017. This is not an exceptional biographical trajectory for East Germans of Björn's generation.

Anxiety about the *possibility* of losing one's job is widely remembered as a small rupture, too. "People were murmuring, 'we're going to have to lose a few pounds.'" one person recalls as a defining sentiment of the early 1990s. Czechs also perceived this threat. While East Germans faced a more grim labor market situation, unemployment rates were skyrocketing in some Czech regions such as Northern Bohemia, too.[15] Before 1989, one's employment situation was generally stable, and the sense that one has to compete with others over available jobs practically did not exist; this stability exacerbated the fear of unemployment. The breakdown of state socialism came unexpectedly, so people had to adjust swiftly to the new reality. Now, economic insecurity was a reality, and many experienced it as something that did not just affect themselves but also their coworkers, their firms, and their communities. Those who were forced to go often asked themselves: why me, why not someone else? Looking back today, people often harbor bitter memories of shattered social solidarity when recalling the ways in which fear of job loss drove a wedge between former coworkers.[16]

Finally, some remember the start of entrepreneurial activities as an economic turning point after 1989. They would set up their own business or manage a spinoff. For these individuals, a firm's dissolution was not so much an ending as the beginning of something entirely new. Instead of dissolution, their memories evoke images of economic inception, creation, and growth. Václav, fifty-eight, is a Czech structural engineer. He was employed at the combinate *Sportprojekt*, a state-owned company that planned and implemented sports buildings, such as pools or stadiums, around the county. After the Velvet Revolution, Václav teamed with a group of former coworkers, one of whom had just founded a business:

We were a bunch of guys, relatively young, without a big plan, who started from zero . . . In 1992 and 1993, when society was changing, that's when you started to see certain patterns. The competent ones started to look and see what options there are, like a colleague of mine who went to work in Austria. I also left *Sportprojekt*. With two other colleagues, we decided to create something. We'd be self-employed, really starting our own business . . . Well, I, of course, remember, or better, I know, that at the time of this founding of businesses a person has a certain level of fear—"what if I don't make it, what if I don't get contracts?" I also know that's normal, this uncertainty, everyone who starts something is worrying, "should I really do this?" Nothing happened to us. though, we were lucky/ I think that the field just worked, it just grew!

He soon became a shareholder in the new enterprise. For Václav, the early 1990s were a time of plentiful economic opportunities. To him, the initial rupture—his departure from the formerly state-socialist firm—was the beginning of linear, progressive time, a story of modernization of self and society. In his account, the revolutions of 1989 allowed people to put their entrepreneurial skills to practice, to implement what they had long been dreaming of. Here, economic and political (in the sense of publicly available) meanings of 1989 are closely aligned. According to closely related research by Veronika Pehe, this is in fact a very powerful strand within the public memory of the 1990s in the Czech Republic today—despite the fact that its main carrier group at the time, students and businesspeople, was a rather small elite group of people. Pehe calls it the "transformation nostalgia" for the "wild 1990s."[17]

Downsizing, job loss, fear of job loss, and entrepreneurship are different if sometimes interrelated memories of ordinary experiences of the aftermath of the system change. They are all critical temporal markers in a person's work biography. They indicate moments in which the broader societal changes materialized in personal work lives and career trajectories; hence, they are remembered as critical junctures that structured work lives into a *before* and *after*. These ruptures could sometimes occur years after the initial system change. Because they often follow their own temporal logic, we may regard them as "vernacular" memories of 1989. Overall, such memories do not necessarily align with official narratives of the revolutions but instead are informed by everyday concerns and people's immediate local environment.[18]

Imbuing Economic Ruptures with Meaning

People may imbue biographical ruptures with temporal meaning, and they then become part of larger, overarching narratives. When constructing their life story, individuals link the past to the present in different ways. They create narrative threads, some of which are later resolved, while others are not. How a person narrates his or her agency in the past—how he or she portrays consequential decisions at the time—informs the memory of economic change. Here, I distinguish two ways in which small ruptures may enter more overarching narratives: stories of success and stories of enduring. In the former, the subject emerged stronger because he or she had successfully mastered the challenging past; in the latter, ruptures are portrayed as something beyond a single person's control.[19]

Consider the example of unemployment. People can remember this experience in different ways. To be sure, joblessness is never an insignificant experience. Sociologists know that long-term unemployment in

REMEMBERING ECONOMIC CHANGE AFTER 1989

particular is associated with manifold negative outcomes such as material deprivation, stress, psychic harm, abuse, and social isolation.[20] The fact that hundreds of thousands of East Germans lost their job during the 1990s— that there clearly was a collective dimension to this crisis—does not make the personal experience any less troubling. As sociologist Gábor Scheiring has shown, economic dislocation after 1989 caused and aggravated a variety of troubling health conditions, such as alcoholism and depression.[21] Still, from a present-day perspective, some people recall job loss at the time as a challenge that they had to accept as a test of their commitment. This leads them to interpret the fact that they managed to overcome this plight as a proof of their perseverance and work ethic. Gustav, a sixty-eight-year-old East German cybernetics engineer, is an expert in the field of ultrasonic technologies. Before the fall of the Berlin Wall, he used to work at a large state-owned company. The firm was disbanded after 1989. The ultrasonic unit initially survived, but when a foreign investor took over the plant in 1994, it was downsized. Gustav was in charge of overseeing the shrinking process and letting people go, only to be laid off himself soon after. A sequence of unemployment episodes followed from there:

In the mid-1990s, I was unemployed for the first time. This, of course, was a particularly terrible time to be unemployed, the labor market looked really bad everywhere! So I received a qualification in a retraining measure that went on for more than a year . . . In August 2006, I was unemployed again; the labor market still didn't look terrific . . . I took up a job at a firm that produced heat exchangers, but they resettled their production [in] Poland, so in December 2008, I was unemployed again . . . Every visit to the labor office is a catastrophe! It was like that for me—it was unbelievable. If you're not on good terms with your adviser there, it's a catastrophe. The process never worked for me, not in the least! . . . This is about motivating yourself, especially when you're a little older. The last time I was unemployed, I was fifty-eight. This is why I cannot understand when people are complaining: "I'm fifty-five and I can't find a job!" It amazes me how people can just give themselves up like that!

Despite these demoralizing experiences, Gustav narrates his story as one of personal development and success. He emphasizes that he managed to triumph over economic hardship because he was able to mobilize inner strength and an extraordinary work ethic. Gustav stayed mobile: he moved to different parts of the country to avoid remaining unemployed. His technical qualifications allowed him to adapt to new circumstances. Focusing on moments of success in his own biography, Gustav is convinced that this was a time of great possibilities, a time when everyone could go, as he notes, "from rags to riches." To him, a key lesson from the time is that hard work will get you everywhere.

Contrast this with Ursula's account, a story of enduring. Ursula, sixty-three, works at a utility company in an administration unit. She was originally trained as an engineer and employed at a state-owned combinate before the system change. Thousands of people from all over the city used to worked there before it was radically downsized beginning in 1990. She remembers that she was "among the first" to be laid off; within just two months after the fall of the Berlin Wall. Since then, her work biography has been marked by a recurring sequence of unemployment, precarious employment, and retraining measures. She could never stay at a job for more than two years:

> [T]hen [in 1990] I was unemployed. I then started my retraining career. In 1994, I participated in another retraining as assistant of the management, and then my traineeship at the municipal utility company started . . . That was May to December 1995. After that, I was unemployed again. Then the municipal utility company fetched me again, first as an assistant worker, then as a regular employee, but then I was unemployed again . . . In 2000, I took an English course. At that time, I was practically unemployed all the time, always in retraining . . . I have so many certificates that no one has any use for! . . . Without luck and connections, you couldn't get in anywhere.

Ursula brings a printed CV to the conversation, as in a job interview, claiming that she would otherwise lose track of the many interruptions of what she ironically refers to her "retraining career." The way Ursula recounts these experiences is circular: "then, I was unemployed again;" "then, I started at that job; then, again unemployed." Even though she is currently working, she knows that she will have to look for a new job one last time before retiring. Hers is not a linear story, not a narrative of growth. There are no uplifting lessons to be drawn from her memories. Ursula acknowledges that the labor market situation in the 1990s was driven by larger forces beyond her control. To be sure, her account is reflexive and rich in references to her own agency; she remembers her own creativity and also her pride in coping with these problems. Yet she firmly rejects the idea that her personal choices, let alone her motivation to work, did make a difference in this situation. She adds that, "I must say, when you have work yourself, it is so easy to forget what it is like to be jobless. Talk is cheap! You tell yourself, well I got work, why doesn't she? . . . And you forget that it is precisely not the case that anyone gets work if they just want to. In fact, I have to remind myself again and again. You have to be careful not to jump on the bandwagon." Her experiences afford her a detached realism.

Gustav, who tells a triumphant story despite experiencing numerous instances of joblessness, was also relatively advantaged. Thanks to his specialized training in cybernetics, he enjoyed better chances in the labor market than Ursula, who was forced to work in low-skilled jobs after 1989. They did not enjoy the same economic opportunities when the system changed. Nevertheless, their stories reveal that episodes of economic rupture in the past can be differently imbued with meaning in the present, thereby forming economic memories.

Coping with Change

Work life shifted profoundly after 1989. The rapid decline of the industrial and agricultural sectors and the rise of services reconfigured the very foundations of economic life across the postsocialist world. Commodification and consumerism advanced. The introduction of the market principle played out differently in various branches of the economy. While scholars have meticulously described the institutional and political dimensions of this process (and often portrayed elite decisions and life worlds), little is still known about how people perceive significant changes in their work environments. How did those larger shifts manifest at work? In this section, I focus on discerning patterns in the way engineers and health-care workers remember crucial instances of change. These accounts are articulated from the point of view of particular professions. At the same time, they are biographical. These are not objective descriptions of change, as in an economic history of the period. They are recollections by individuals who *coped* with disruptive change and so their memories are shaped by this agentic quality.

TECHNOLOGICAL ADVANCES

The 1990s are remembered as a time of great technological advances. Engineers recall that they were often at the foreground of innovative developments. Computerization and digitization hardly left an area of this profession untouched. It revolutionized basic activities such as drawing, projecting, and calculating. Work processes became more efficient but also more complex. Computerization changed the division of labor within firms, usually resulting in smaller departments and more flexible forms of collaboration. Some subfields of the profession—like those tied to the former East German car industry, the former Czechoslovak heavy military industry, as well as many purely manual activities—were made redundant during the 1990s. While some areas, such as construction engineering, could master the transition smoothly, retraining and further specialization was necessary everywhere.

Things moved very fast after the system change. Western accounting, financing, and legal frameworks had to be implemented from one day to the next. Computers became widespread in engineering offices, and English (instead of Russian) was now the lingua franca in the field, which was challenging, especially for senior employees. While engineers generally embrace the technological advances of this period, some also reject the notion that innovation was based solely on imported knowledge from the West. They cast doubt on the idea that Easterners were *catching up* to a higher standard of expertise. Walter, seventy-two, an East German construction engineer, remarks that, in the early 1990s, "there were lots of materials that we were not familiar with . . . the level of development was higher in the West, a lot higher! But as far as the activities are concerned, there are no differences at all." He asserts that the technology gap between East and West was a difference in degree, not in kind. In his view, technological change did not affect the substance but merely the surface of work. For Walter, domestic expertise—East German engineering skills—in fact constituted the critical resource for implementing new technologies and workflows. He emphasizes that he was able to adjust thanks to his GDR-style education, which had schooled him in the core values of the profession such as technical competency, creativity, a readiness to improvise, and attention to detail.

In health care, there were wide-ranging advances, too. Before 1989, health-care work was a relatively static field. Czechoslovak and East

German hospitals (even if among the most advanced institutions of their kind in the state-socialist world), were often underequipped. Hygiene standards were low. The range of tasks a nurse had to perform was generally much wider than it is today. In addition to attending to patients, they were expected to clean beds, rooms, and hospital kitchens, and wash the dishes. Petra is a Czech health-care worker in her late fifties who works for a church-affiliated elder-care organization. She recalls how, as a nurse at a Czechoslovak hospital in the 1980s, she had to perform all kinds of tasks that were only loosely related to health-care work: "We worked as nurses, but at the same time, we also worked as paramedics, and, most of the time, also as cleaners . . . It happened often, especially over the weekend, that the cleaning lady didn't show up. So what could we do? We grabbed the mob and cleaned the rooms. We were practically in charge of everything in those hospitals."[22]

After 1989, improvements in working conditions in hospitals and health-care facilities came as a great relief to Petra. As new equipment became available, basic tasks could be performed more easily. A theme that many remember vividly is the introduction of one-way usable syringes and cannulas after 1989. One person remarks that she felt like she was in "paradise" when she did not have to do disinfections by hand anymore. Earlier, nurses had to sterilize syringes, gloves, diapers, and dressing material, which took a lot of time. Nurses visited clients by bike or public transport, and they often had to return to the hospital to sterilize the material after each visit multiple times a day. People spent hours on these tasks. The introduction of electronic beds and lifting tools made interacting with patients physically less straining. Hygiene also improved significantly. New medication and better supplies made work much more efficient and orientated toward the needs of patients.[23] As a whole, health-care work became more formalized and specialized. Some also view these changes ambiguously because specialization upended an older division of labor. This sometimes meant that certain tasks could not be performed by individuals who were not officially licensed to do so anymore.

Still, health-care workers are proud of their education. Some refer to the training that they had received before 1989 as more "encompassing," "generalist," or "socially oriented" than today. In their view, it provided them with a certain degree of flexibility that young colleagues lack. Some also deem their education as more substantively orientated toward what the job is really about—the needs of patients—than what people are trained to do in the highly differentiated, specialized system that prevails today. One nurse asserts that she is "glad to have received my education during socialist times," claiming that she did not have to acquire *any* new skills after the system change. Another person, while praising the fact that, as a nurse, she was able to take advantage of many opportunities for specialization after 1989, finds that these trainings were good additions to what she considers the gist of her work, claiming, "[W]hen I'm at the bedside [interacting with the patient], I am still the same person I always was."

ACCELERATION

After 1989, work life became dramatically faster. The shift to a capitalist market economy signaled the departure from an older, different rhythm of work. Anthropologist Katherine Verdery notes that state-socialist production regimes followed the distinct rhythm of the planned economy, in which periods of intensive labor and stress were followed by periods of underemployment and waiting.[24] During the state-socialist period, time could be scarce in some moments and abundant in others. Now, in a market economy, time is always and everywhere a scarce resource. Václav, the construction engineer and successful entrepreneur, reflects on how what was considered a normal time budget for activities such as planning, designing, and projecting before the 1989 revolution had radically evolved: "I remember one of my first major contracts; it was a sport hall here in the city . . . I was designing it as a young designer, and I did it for two or maybe two and a half years, only designing, and then I built it for eight years, right? Today they would draft such a hall in a year, and they would set it up in another year and half."

In the capitalist time regime, an engineer's products are subject to change during the design process. As clients' needs and preferences evolve, engineers have to adjust constantly. Time has also become a priced resource in the competition over clients and contracts. To be competitive today means to outpace others. This change can be a potential challenge to a core professional value of engineers: the commitment to designing high-quality products.

Health-care workers also remember acceleration as a defining experience of the 1990s. The specialization of tasks tightened work regimes. Now patient interaction was measured in time units. In elder-care, small tasks like washing or lifting became standardized by the minute, Such interactions now had to be documented meticulously, which took up an increasingly large amount of health-care workers' time. Barbora, a Czech nurse in her late fifties who works in the neurological ward of a midsize hospital, remembers how time was already in short supply before 1989: "when we rinsed the metal needles, cleaned the tubes, prepared the sterilization. Today, all of this is gone . . . But the time you save thanks to one-way bandages is the time you lose on administrative tasks." Like Barbora, many vividly remember how the new, demanding pace of work created a profound contradiction between what health-care workers think constitutes good and efficient work, and what they are able to do in practice. Health-care workers regard lack of time as a serious systemic problem in health care today. While this criticism goes beyond the assessment of changes after 1989, East Germans and Czechs think of acceleration as a *direct* consequence of the marketization and commodification of hospitals and health-care facilities during the 1990s. Acceleration brought increasing stress. Fulfilling the various professional demands afforded by this work is challenging, especially for an older generation of employees. As one person puts it, before 1989, "physical stress was intense; today it does your head in."

Time is a critical resource in health-care work. Time must be committed to single patients for medical tasks, advice, and documentation, but also for listening, interacting, and creating a sense of human connection. This is particularly important in elder-care, which is committed to principles like compassion, dealing with a patient as a whole person, and caring about a patient's practical needs. These are vital dimensions of professional and patient-oriented ethics. Sara is an East German in her late forties who used to work as a nurse and today manages an elder-care facility. She summarizes this problem as follows:

Make no mistake: An elder-care worker has to do an incredible job. She has to be socially competent; she has to go from one human being to the next. If there's dementia involved, she has to immediately switch, in her mind, "so now I'm talking with Mr. Maier, next to him is Ms. Mueller, I have to choose my words." So that's a top performance already there. In addition to that, she has to sit calmly at the computer, write everything down, plan and calculate . . . it's social work which is demanding mentally; in addition to that it's physical work, which is taxing in elder-care, and then there's technical work. And you can't delegate anything!

To many, stories of acceleration summarize what they think is fundamentally wrong with care work today. Acceleration threatens to undermine the complexity of professional responsibilities by necessarily constraining health-care workers' role, often to a single task. Lack of time is a serious problem, not only because it is exhausting and decreases the quality of services but also because it demoralizes workers. It makes it very hard if not impossible for health-care workers to maintain professional standards at work. The way respondents expose these difficulties are reminiscent of so-called moral injuries in the medical professions, an issue that has gained significant attention during the COVID-19 pandemic, when health-care systems around the world were pushed to the brink of collapse. "Moral injury," which is increasingly recognized as a condition with strong adverse psychological implications, "is generally assumed to result from exposure to events that involve either perpetrating or witnessing actions that violate one's core beliefs."[25] In some cases, economic memories of the 1990s contain a sense that fundamental professional principles were violated.

MONETIZATION AND PRIVATIZATION

After 1989, in line with the neoclassical idea that the market, not the state, is the only legitimate source for determining the value of goods and services, prices were liberalized. Engineers remember monetization vividly. From one day to the next, they had to make offers and secure contracts. As Walter, the construction engineer, recalls, "Calculation was new to us, entirely new. We used to have prices that were set by the state, according to price order PR206. That was the name, you could look it up in the books and get the prices. On January 1, 1990, we had to start—I remember very well—we had to start calculating . . . Suddenly we were in competition."

Engineering offices opened sales departments and began to pursue profitable projects, either independently or in cooperation with government agencies. Wages increased. Those who managed to avoid job insecurity and establish themselves in a profitable field could capture sizable incomes already a few years after the revolution.[26] Today, many find that this had been long overdue. They think of this change as a shift away from the *artificial* wage regime of state socialism toward a *natural*, merit-based system of remuneration after 1989. In the Czech Republic, as we saw, there also exists a powerful cultural script about the early 1990s as a moment of sheer unlimited entrepreneurial opportunities, a time conducive to all types of economic adventurism.[27]

Perhaps surprisingly, however, many East German and Czech engineers have decidedly negative memories of privatization, or the process of transferring public property into private hands. In fact, many recall it as a disaster. Among Czechs, the process is associated primarily with domestic corruption; among East Germans, it is often coded as the pinnacle of the hostile *takeover* of their economy by West Germans. Václav, the Czech construction engineer and entrepreneur, associates privatization with nepotism and illegitimate political interference. He takes great care to emphasize that his own economic activities after 1989 had nothing to do with it, stating that "we started from zero; we did not privatize anything." Václav asserts that he never used state resources in his own business activities. In his view, this is really a moral issue. He regards economic success as deserved only if it is independent of politics. The very term "privatization," in Václav's account as in that of many others, serves as a symbol for illegitimate sources of affluence after the revolution.

Health-care work was profoundly shaken by monetization and commodification. The shift from a centralized system toward more autonomous, semiprivate forms of health care generally occurred in two forms: first, through the rise of corporate models in hospital financing, management, and ownership, and second, through the emergence of a private sector for outpatient care. In East Germany, some small hospitals were privatized in the early 1990s; the privatization of large facilities followed after the turn of the century (in 2009, about 30 percent of German hospitals were privately administered). As in the Czech Republic, the overarching goal was to increase cost efficiency. During the 1990s, Czech hospitals were increasingly privately operated; although a small number of private facilities were founded, most were still owned by regional governments. They continued to operate on a shoestring budget. Marketization only deepened after the turn of the century. In 2003, several Czech hospitals were converted into joint-stock companies, and today the majority of them are joint-stock companies. However, marketization failed to tap new sources of funding. Instead, the lack of public investment in infrastructure and staff resulted in problems such as a decline in available hospital beds, understaffing, unpaid overtime, and a continuous pressure to cut labor costs.[28]

Workers recall how, suddenly, a stay at the hospital became a commodity; how, because of technological improvements and the rise of market logics, hospital bed occupancy became increasingly expensive; how there were now strong monetary incentives to limit a single patient's time at the hospital.[29] The limited availability of hospital beds based solely on cost factors was deeply disturbing to people who had known a system in which this was never a priority. Sara, the head of an elder-care facility, remarks, "[B]ack then [in GDR times] we used to treat people in the hospital who did not necessarily have a diagnosis . . . Our beds were full also with people who would otherwise have remained out on the street. The system provided a cushion for them. That disappeared from one day to the next!" Some feel that their relationship to patients and to patients' families was negatively affected by the new emphasis on money, and financial interests had a profound effect on health care after 1989. They are disheartened by some clients' attitude toward them as mere "service providers." A Czech nurse complains that patients started to think of nurses as "maids." Now, the thinking went, "I'm paying, so you have to take care of me!"

BUREAUCRATIZATION

Social scientists concur that the breakdown of state socialism fundamentally weakened state capacities and state resources across Central Eastern Europe. However, many people who went through these changes do not see it like that. They do not remember the state to have ceded power to the market. Instead, they are convinced that the state interfered in the transition process, especially in the realm of work. In popular memories of the 1990s, state action appears in the mode of "bureaucratization." This very notion keeps resurfacing in accounts of economic change. "Bureaucratization" refers to the numerous novel legal arrangements that entered and reshaped work environments after 1989. The introduction of a private property regime and advances in technological, financial, and ethical standards all required new forms of government oversight and control. People remember this shift as a new quality and dimension of state regulation. For instance, Elisabeth, a sixty-two-year-old East German engineer who, together with her colleague, heads a female-owned, small architecture firm today, expresses mixed feelings about the fact that measurement norms were "Westernized" after 1989. "There was all the restructuring in terms of regulations! For us, it was hard to fathom. We grew up with the old standards, back then we called it TGL [Technische Normen, Gütevorschriften und Lieferbedingungen]; now suddenly the DIN [Deutsches Institut für Normung] was authoritative. The construction law was also entirely new to us." Frequently, engineers criticize what they regard as too many and sometimes irrational and self-contradictory regulations. One person laments the "short-livedness" of regulations, arguing that, before 1989, things were more stable and transparent. In this view, before the system change, failing to abide by the (economic) rules did not have as many negative consequences, at least from the business perspective.

Shifts in legal frameworks also reconfigured the relation between health-care providers and their patients. Health-care workers remember how, after 1989, they were required to document patient interactions and receive patient consent for medical procedures. So-called expert standards were introduced, suggesting fixed protocols and procedures and requiring the documentation of patient food intake, movement, accidents, and/ or injuries. Filing was increasingly done electronically. As a consequence, nurses now had to spend a lot of time in front of computers. Barbora, the Czech nurse who criticized the rise of acceleration earlier, remarks:

> And with that came the enormous rise of administration. You have to get the patient's signature for everything. He has to agree to hospitalization; otherwise you have to send the papers to court. He has to agree to surgery; otherwise you have to find a legal guardian . . . This in turn means stress because [the nurse] has to care not only about caring for the patient well but also about doing the documentation well. We didn't have that. If you compare the [socialist] case record of a patient with the same diagnosis, it was tiny; today it is such [an enormous] file!

Many recall how documentation has made work more time consuming. One person remarks that bureaucracy "destroys you as a person." Another person bemoans that "our work here in elder-care is obstructed by hundreds of thousands of regulations and laws." Health-care workers are also troubled by the gradual implementation and extension of an external system of control after 1989. Today, Czech and German health-care markets are private or semiprivate, but government agencies are responsible for supervising and enforcing standards in the public and the private sector to ensure, for instance, proper classification of insurance levels. These agencies regularly visit facilities and evaluate their work. Thanks to technological advances such as digital patient files, the system of supervision operates very efficiently. Insurance levels and medical procedures are standardized. The risk of miscalculating—a consideration that played a minor role in state-socialist allocation economies—drives management decisions in health care today. Thus, health-care workers' activities are controlled and evaluated by a sophisticated, multilayered system of public, medical, and corporate interest. The degree of medical and administrative control exercised by institutional actors before 1989 pales in comparison. Some workers see this as a sign of lack of trust in their skills and abilities. Luisa, an elder-care worker in her fifties remarks, "[B]ack then [before 1989], people had trust in our work. That we would do it the way we had learned to do it. Now, people are questioning that." While she supports the legal changes in principle, she takes issue with the fact that people have come to rely on legal solutions to problems that she regards as ordinary challenges of this job. What she perceives as a lack of trust in her skills undermines her sense of autonomy at work.

THE RISE OF MEDICAL ETHICS

The rise of medical ethics is an important thread in health-care workers' recollections. Before the system change, patient rights were often willfully ignored or undermined. Coercive methods and informal, arbitrary power dynamics were widespread in late socialist Czechoslovak and East German hospitals and medical institutions. After 1989, a comprehensive legal and moral framework that safeguarded patient rights was finally implemented. To Nora, a forty-nine-year-old Czech specialist who works in a hospice, the introduction of ethical standards in patient interactions and patient rights after 1989 came as an enormous relief. It ensured, finally, "that the patient was treated with dignity . . . that the dignity of this person came first, so that he could live his life in this facility with all dignity and respect, under the conditions that were acceptable to him."

Health-care workers still remember the inhumane practices of state-socialist medical institutions, when arbitrariness in decision making, hierarchical style, and disregard for patient needs were all considered normal. Patients and their families depended on the goodwill of their caregivers and whoever was in charge at the ward. Health-care work was also sometimes practiced as a form of political repression. Individuals were assigned to psychiatric wards as a form of political punishment. Tanja, an East German nurse in her fifties who supervises a child psychiatric ward in a large hospital today, remembers how, before 1989, patients were kept in rooms with bars, sometimes tied to their beds against their will, and regularly sedated using medication. It was only after the fall of the Berlin Wall that she could finally perform her work according to an ethics that was oriented toward patients' needs. When Tanja first learned about therapy as a medical practice, it changed the way she looked at the field of psychiatry as whole: "To regard the patient as an independent individual, not to patronize him . . . Slowly, respect [by health-care workers], and the consciousness that these people are merely psychiatrically disabled, emerged. They were treated like aliens before! . . . After the transition, the bars were removed from the windows. More and more, problems were resolved not by using medication, but by music therapy, sport therapy, or painting."

The rise of medical ethics was not always an easy transition. Before 1989, coercive and disciplinary measures allowed health-care workers to exercise a certain degree of control, providing them, for instance, with the means to deescalate conflicts and calm down patients. Somewhat similar to what sociologist Joanna Wawrzyniak documents in interviews with Polish workers in industrial milieus, there exists a form of nostalgia for informal workplace hierarchies in the late socialist period, often called "family"-like relations at work. Now, after the revolutions, a different set of social skills was required to deal with conflict. Still, in the eyes of most, it is only thanks to the rise of medical ethics that health-care work can be performed today in a way that is true to its fundamental principles.[30]

SKILLS AS A MORAL ANCHOR

We saw that individuals remember sensitive themes and topics in the ways their work lives changed after 1989. Small changes were rooted in larger shifts in the economic order—in privatization, commodification, specialization— that manifested themselves at work, where they posed practical challenges that individuals confronted and reflected on. In their stories, we could see that the meanings people create concern everyday challenges at work but also something more fundamental, namely, claims about the intrinsic value of work activities.

Let us consider this point in more detail. In the preceding discussion, a recurring motif was that individuals were able to navigate disruptive change by mobilizing their skills. Their training, and the specific expertise it had afforded them, proved to be an important resource for coping with shifting standards of valuation and new work rhythms. As life-course and biography researchers note, skills have a double function: they are exchanged for money on the labor market and, at the same time, constitute a valued object in themselves. For a person reflecting on his or her work biography, skills are "negotiated agency," providing a sense of what one was granted to do in terms of institutional credentials (a tacit and instrumental dimension), as well as in terms of what one could do in the sense of one's innate capabilities (a reflexive and personal dimension).[31]

The meaningful dimension of skills is particularly consequential for how people make sense of economic change in the 1990s. We saw that engineers and health-care workers, when remembering the changes in question, engage in *delineating* and *narrating* what they consider to be core skills of their profession or notions of what their job is substantively about. They distinguish between the surface and the depth of their work. The latter in particular provides them with a sense of biographical agency. Engineers refer to *technical competency* as a core value of their education before 1989 and as the genuine basis of economic success after. Health-care workers point to a *generalist* education before 1989 that provided them with the means to think outside the box instead of being narrowly focused on single tasks. This flexibility and their deeper knowledge about the meaning of patient orientation in health-care work allowed them to cope with the difficulties of the 1990s.

In this way, skills provide a sense of continuity as well as consistency, a temporal anchor for the self in changing environments. To be sure, they are *imagined* as stable and robust. As work environments changed, the competences that were in demand also shifted. However, the idea that skills constitute an invariable substance, really a foundation of knowledge, has an elementary biographical function. It provides cohesion in a structure of meaning over time. Skills represent what a person was trained to do in the past, feels empowered to do in the present, and will be capable of doing in the future.[32] Thus, they also function as a vehicle for communicating a subjective sense of the order of time around the system change. They create a smooth transition between the two systems from an immanent perspective, a sense of a stable self as it moved forward through time, by linking one's education before 1989 to the mastering of economic difficulties in the 1990s and finally to the present day.

Because they link past and present, skills are a core element of the moral framework. They grant individuals a sense of self—really, with a sense of having stayed *true to oneself*—after 1989. In memories of economic change, ideas about the substance of one's work are inseparable from ideas of a morally grounded, temporally consistent self.[33]

Doesn't this concern with skills, on a deeper level, really express sentiments of nostalgia for the socialist past? By rushing to this conclusion, I would argue that we risk losing analytical purchase. Nostalgia, often understood as the wish to return to an embellished past, has frequently been diagnosed as an irrational force, a social malaise in postsocialist societies. However, the memories documented here are not irrational ways of longing. The stories provided by engineers and health-care workers are primarily statements about work—about what constitutes *good, effective, productive* work—and so we should take them seriously as such. After all, as we saw, these are the meanings that people give to skills, skills that allowed them to cope with disruptive change during the 1990s.

The accounts of economic change that we have considered here are very often statements about a moral and also a rational basis of work performance, often coupled with a critique of contemporary society. In this respect, they are frequently linked to ideas of how workplaces were organized differently before 1989, how they would function differently—and in a more personally fulfilling way—as social spaces. One Czech engineer, for instance, laments the loss of a "culture of work" after the breakdown of state socialism. People often point out that, in state-socialist workplaces, they were able to maintain collaborative relationships with their coworkers (the "collectives" or "brigades"), relationships that many imagine retrospectively as *healthier* because they were undisturbed by market-induced status competition. Ethnographers who study postindustrial settings, like Kinga Pozniak in her study of the former Polish steel town Nowa Huta, often encounter such sentiments.[34] Such sentiments rarely express a wish to return to life under communist rule as such—at least in the Central

European context—because they are typically coupled with a strong rejection of the larger pre-1989 political order, which is seen as a failing, deeply unfair system.[35] Instead, people's sense of loss relates to specific domains of life, and very often, as historical sociologies of deindustrialization confirm, the sphere of social relations in the workplace.[36]

To approach accounts of the 1990s as *economic memories* instead of preconceptualizing them as nostalgia leaves open the possibility that some of them positively or negatively relate back to the period before 1989 but not all of them necessarily do. As we saw in this chapter, some may be concerned primarily with making sense of turbulent change during the 1990s.

SKILLS AS A PROBLEM OF SOCIAL INCLUSION

Skills do not only play a crucial role in economic memories of the 1990s; they are also intricately linked to a sense of social belonging. People draw on existing cultural orientations and work identities to make sense of rupturing shifts. As we saw in chapter 1, the GDR and Czechoslovak regimes had prized full-time work and (near) full employment as the main pillars of social cohesion. In their everyday lives, citizens were confronted with a deeply moralized universe of meaning around "productive labor." Yet East Germans and Czechs went through the 1990s on very different terms: the former in the mode of dissolution of industrial structures, accompanied by a patronizing narrative about the transformation, and the latter in the mode of relative preservation of industries, couched in a narrative of manly economic nationalism. For East German engineers, job loss was an imminent threat, which was not true for Czech engineers. How does this disparity affect economic memories, and with them, a sense of social inclusion?

The Rupture in East German Economic Memories

As discussed in chapter 1, despite the promises of reunification, relations between West and East Germans remain charged to this day. In politics and the media, citizens of the former GDR have been depicted for a long time as backward and too immature for democracy. As we saw, in economic narratives about the post-1989 period, the productivity gap between East and West was the dominating theme. And memories of *economic humiliation* are pervasive in biographical accounts today. In this section, I suggest that these episodes point to a larger political predicament, namely, the perceived lack of economic integration of East Germans into German society. This problem does not concern only the persisting wage gap between East and West. It concerns the claim to be recognized, on the basis of skills, as a worthy, productive member of society.

Looking back to the early 1990s, East Germans engineers often remark that, at the time, it became evident that their work ethic was much more profound than that of West Germans, that they possessed a superior, if unassuming, kind of economic expertise. They depict West German knowledge as superficial or, at best, complementary. Björn, the test engineer who went through many episodes of joblessness despite his strong qualifications, remembers how West Germans really only excelled at one thing, namely, acting *as if* they were competent: "In the technical field, people are no different from anybody else . . . I always used to say, around the time of the Wende [period of transition after 1989], we lacked a year of training in drama school. Meaning, they were better at performing, better at selling their stuff. When they arrived with their enormous printouts, they got you excited, but once you read them [more closely], there wasn't much to it. This kind of performance, we never learned how to do it, and we certainly never will."

In contrast, according to another respondent, East German engineering is based on "detailed knowledge" and the ability to "construct details logically . . . We received a very good training back then." Many invoke the value of technical competence as an East German trait. An engineer's technical orientation is a seemingly neutral category, one that can be measured objectively, independent from political judgment. The focus on technical expertise allows East Germans to narrate their work biography as untainted by the politics of GDR society. It also allows them to reject West German claims to superiority and to turn the tables on them. Many regard the *selling attitude* as a typical quality of West German engineers. To Walter, the construction engineer, the field of engineering in the East was forever altered the moment West German "salesmen" entered it: "Today, those who are usually in charge in these firms are salesmen, or lawyers, but not engineers anymore. The salespeople are obviously at the top end of the hierarchy." Walter adds that East Germans were still the ones who actually *created* value in the firms: "They [West Germans] did earn quite a bit thanks to our work. Those who actually did the job all were people from here."

The selling attitude may well be advantageous, but it has nothing to do with the fundamental ethos of engineering. Engineering is about attention to detail, goal orientation, thoroughness, creativity, and love of detail, all of which East German engineers associate with their education. Markus, a sixty-one-year-old structural engineer who set up a family business the moment the Berlin Wall came down, recalls how, in the early 1990s, his abilities were tested by a West German business partner for whom he had drafted a construction static. At the time, West German engineers already exclusively relied on computers, producing drawings that Markus found "hard to comprehend." But Markus, like he was used to doing, drew the static by hand. His outline explained the technical processes from the ground up, as in a mathematical demonstration. He recalls how the contractor came to realize his own ignorance. He was skeptical, even dumbfounded at first, but after a while he conceded that he had not "held anything as proper, as beautiful in his hands for a very long time." Markus's proficiency was confirmed.[37]

The readiness to improvise is another consecrated value. People often link it to a kind of savviness that was necessary to navigate the state-socialist economy of shortage. As Björn notes, "As a GDR engineer, you had to make something out of nothing. Your creativity was in demand, you had to create something useful out of whatever little was at hand." Another person argues that West German businesses "readily" employed East German engineers after the fall of the Berlin Wall because there was "one thing we were particularly good at, and that was improvising." The creativity theme is also connected to innovation, another foundational value in engineering. East German engineers, as we saw, embrace technological change but reject the idea that innovation is exclusively a feature of market society. Instead, many think of it as an innate quality, rooted in a person's mindset and education.

Health-care workers echo this theme. Some recall bitterly how their professional autonomy was undermined after 1989. In some cases, qualified East German personnel were no longer permitted to perform certain medical tasks such as drawing blood, providing certain types of medication, or giving medical advice to patients.[38] This was agonizing to individuals who had received the appropriate training and regularly performed these activities in the past. Verena, an elder-care worker who is in her late forties today, calls out this problem:

You're trained as a nurse, but then you're not allowed to perform the work! . . . A lot of the [discontent] was about responsibility; this played a major role. The fact that we can do less today because, during GDR times, we were allowed to do more. The skilled worker was differently valued than today. I have to say it outright; a lot has been taken away . . . I took an exam, I laid a nasogastric tube, removed surgical clamps, performed an infusion, drew blood. I can't do that anymore today! I'm not allowed to draw blood anymore; they took it away from us because of the Wende . . . It was humiliating for many skilled workers.

West Germans are remembered to have exercised economic power in arbitrary ways.[39] Another person recalls how, in her role as the head of an elder-care facility, she had to administer these changes: "We had to say, 'from today on, you're not allowed to use the syringe anymore, from today on, you're not allowed to distribute that medication!' And that was bad, obviously, a lot of tears were involved." Just like engineers, health-care workers also cite these stories to assert the value of the work. They react to having their competences called into question, turning the tables on West Germans and emphasizing the superior quality of their own education. Sabine, forty-nine, a nurse who went to live and work in West Germany in the early 1990s, returned to her hometown after a decade. Being able to compare workplaces and work environments in this way only affirmed the sense that her East German training was in fact superior: "It was better! The education I had received here was much more encompassing, it was deeper . . . It was a mode of learning for adults, more independent, a freer type of learning . . . I think I carried these leaning tools along from the GDR."

People firmly reject the notion that German unification brought a more modern, more sophisticated economic knowledge to the East.[40] Specifically, as we saw in this chapter, their stories are informed by memories of *economic humiliation*. This sense of misrecognition, to be sure, was never exclusively nourished in the domain of work after 1989; we can also encounter it in the political and private realms (we saw in chapter 1 that East Germans were regularly caricatured in the news media even after German unity). Yet, as we saw in this chapter, East Germans express a sense of exclusion from the greater social texture of German society precisely at the seemingly neutral level of economic expertise and knowledge.

Their accounts problematize a rupture in the recognition of skills, which is also a break in the meaning structure of normative ideas about work after 1989. Evidently, people's memories of economic expertise—their ideas of what they have always been good at—are not politically neutral. These stories bring into sharp relief that economic memories are in fact an integral part of a sense of social and political belonging.

The Ambiguity of Czech Economic Memories

Czech engineers' and health-care workers' recollections of the value of skills during the 1990s, in contrast, are marked by ambiguity. As we saw, Czech elites likened the path of economic reform after 1989 to an inner journey, calling on citizens to mobilize secret powers and confront hardship in order to flourish in market society. The return to a market order was couched as a "natural" development. They also promised that the country would *return to the West*, which implied that wages would soon approximate Austrian or German levels. Yet this never happened, not even after the Czech Republic became a member of the European Union in 2004. Recognizing this is particularly disturbing for health-care workers, who earn only a fraction of their colleagues in Western Europe. Anna, forty-eight, who is a mobile elder-care worker for a nonprofit organization, recalls: "[The wage gap] surprises me a lot, such a long time after the revolution. Say I want to travel to Austria. My wage, in Czech crowns, doesn't allow me to buy anything there. The difference is simply enormous. And this is a neighboring state! Aren't we working just in the same way, isn't our industry working in the same way? Yet we still get paid worse. I'm surprised. It's a bit of a disappointment."

Freedom of travel was a central promise of the 1989 revolution. The fact that, so many years later, a person cannot *afford* to take a vacation is a bitter realization. It casts doubt on the political promise that the Czech Republic would become a full member of the Western community and also on the economic promise that the period of belt tightening and austerity would come to an end after a while. After all, Václav Klaus's brand of transformation nationalism was justified by its collective goal, namely, that Czechoslovakia would emerge as a stronger, wealthier, and more esteemed nation at some point. Yet wage levels remained far below those in the West for decades. Consequently, in their memories of the 1990s, engineers and health-care workers are careful to detach their pay from qualifications and work performance. Skills are a genuine if unseen source of recognition in their accounts because the political system has failed to deliver on its promise to reward merit. The fact that wages never came to reflect effort is taken as evidence that people were up against larger, arbitrary forces after the revolution. Many are convinced that these distorting forces originated in the realm of politics, not in the sphere of markets and work performance. The resulting sense of powerlessness is often coupled with the cynical insight that, deep down, it would have been naïve to expect to be rewarded appropriately.[41] But this remains an ambiguous position. Overall, Czech accounts of changing work lives after 1989 are characterized by a combination of great pride in skills and a marked emphasis on a positive, *healthy* attitude to work as a biographical commitment, and a profound disillusion with the political system's valuation of these things.

A Legacy of "Productive Labor"

Notwithstanding the vast differences in the mode of change they went through after 1989, East Germans and Czechs both remember the 1990s as a time that profoundly challenged their economic worth. In biographical accounts of changing work lives, they draw a distinction between the *surface* and the *depth* of work, with intrinsic knowledge of certain skills as the representation of the latter. In references to skills, selective aspects of life before 1989—in particular, domains of life that are seen as independent of politics, like workplace relations—can be salvaged without embellishing the state-socialist regime. In memories of the period after 1989, skills provide biographical continuity. Their neutral, persisting quality makes them appear as the source of legitimate claims to be rewarded in market society. In this way, skills are not just technical or instrumental but moral. As a claim of social worth and social inclusion, they constitute a meaning structure that is informed by the legacy of "productive labor."

Chapter Three

DESERVING AND UNDESERVING OTHERS

By the imagination we place ourselves in his situation, we conceive ourselves enduring all the same torments, we enter as it were into his body, and become in some
measure the same person with him, and thence form some idea of his sensations, and
even feel something which, though weaker in degree, is not altogether unlike them.

—ADAM SMITH, *THEORY OF MORAL SENTIMENTS*

Inequalities are more likely to be turned into questions of character if people start
out equally.

—RICHARD SENNETT AND JONATHAN COBB, *THE HIDDEN INJURIES OF CLASS*

THE SOCIAL TEXTURE OF JUSTICE

How do people perceive and remember disruptive economic change? So
far, we have shed light on biographical narrations and the role of skills in
them. How people think about justice after the 1989 revolutions remains
yet to be explored. When discussing the theoretical underpinnings of the
moral framework, we saw that a large body of social science research suggests that people make sense of justice by looking to their social environment and comparing their own situation to that of others. They read and
interpret the social cues around them. Hence, we now turn to the following
question: how much control, do people believe, did a person have over his
or her economic fate with the advent of market society after 1989?

Structural, external forces exerted enormous power over a person's
life course after the system change. The skills that he or she had already
acquired before the breakup of state socialism, age, gender, ethnicity, and
location—possibly even the size of the firm that he or she was employed
in when privatization began—all these factors could shape decisively how
much control over the circumstances a person enjoyed. Yet these objective
conditions tell us nothing about how people subjectively *imagine* agency,
how they understand the degree to which a person was able to make decisions autonomously at the time.

In this chapter, I show that this question is central to the way economic change is remembered. Pursuing it offers a window into notions of deservingness after 1989. These are narrative accounts and judgments about what someone did or failed to do and can therefore legitimately expect to receive in return. Notions of deservingness are embedded in temporal horizons: they are based on an image of agency in the past. Yet, crucially, deservingness also extends beyond the individual person. Social comparisons, as a form of reasoning about justice, are not limited to local contexts because whenever people advance a claim to the injustice of a particular outcome, they necessarily invoke a larger principle of social legitimacy. Claims about who deserves what, about what a fair distribution looks like, are tied to views about society at large.[1] *Temporal, local, and wholly social*

I reveal in this chapter that, surprisingly, many people tend to embrace the idea that a person is individually responsible for economic success or failure after 1989. These judgments are not independent of people's social position in the present. Generally speaking, engineers are more likely to provide individualized accounts than are health-care workers. Czechs also embrace such interpretations more readily than East Germans, who, as we saw in the preceding chapters, have experienced deeper labor market ruptures. At the same time, the language of individual deservingness is the dominant proposition; it is much more widespread than we may think. I identify two tropes that sustain it: the idea of 1989 as an economic beginning, and the inclination to reject economic victimhood as a collective fate. Both illuminate the ways in which deservingness is embedded in something broader than accounts of individual trajectories, namely, in economic memories of the 1990s. *COLLECTIVE FATE*

HOW THE 1990s AFFECTED POPULAR JUSTICE IDEAS

Before we address notions of deservingness, we must first revisit what we know about how the transformation period has affected people's sense of justice more broadly. There are some surprises here. Researchers have documented a highly unusual trend in postsocialist Central Europe, and the Czech Republic and Germany were at the forefront of it. After 1989, deeply ingrained, long-standing justice ideologies seemed to be shifting. So-called order-related justice ideologies are culturally robust ideas held by citizens about what the role of the state in the economy should be. These ideas are historically formed, they become entrenched in the institutions of a given welfare regime, and they are typically passed down from one generation to the next. In Central Eastern Europe, the dominant justice ideology is egalitarianism.[2]

During the turbulent 1990s, however, egalitarian beliefs were challenged. One team of researchers observed a shift in public opinion away from egalitarianism and toward market justice. They found that this trend was most pronounced in East Germany and the Czech Republic. In these countries, in 1991, they detected a "revolutionary zeal" when the "average endorsement of the capitalist principles" was "higher than that found in Britain, West Germany, and the USA for the same year."[3] In the early 1990s, people enthusiastically embraced market society. At the time, East Germans expressed very little concern with unfairness in society and reported a degree of confidence in meritocratic ideals that exceeded that of West Germans.[4] These sentiments were not just a corollary of enthusiasm for democracy—they were, in fact, rooted in a genuine commitment to economic performance and work-related ambition: "sixty-two per cent of easterners agreed with the statement that 'life is a challenge, in the face of which one has to use all one's efforts to achieve something,' 17 per cent more than in the west . . . Twenty-seven per cent rated work as 'the most important human activity,' whilst 57 per cent regarded 'work as important for personal well-being' as against 9 per cent and 36 per cent respectively in the west . . ."[5] The enthusiasm did not last long, however; support for market justice was challenged and in part even reversed by the mid-1990s. Feelings of disillusionment and cynicism took hold across transforming societies because citizens sensed that unfairness and corruption was increasingly pervasive. People grew skeptical of the idea that above-average incomes and wealth could in fact be attained through hard work. Instead, they began to associate it with nepotism and dishonesty. On these grounds, researchers posit that the principle of egalitarianism *returned* as the dominant justice belief after the bout of enthusiasm for market society.[6] The comparison to West Germany is instructive in this regard. The pattern of support for justice ideologies remained stable over the same period in West Germany, which underscores that the changes were in fact driven by transformation experiences in the East. The Czech Republic saw a similar trend, where, in the early 1990s, commitment to reform was high, and the conviction that the state must retreat from society found widespread popular support. The idea that everyone would benefit from these processes was widely accepted at first.[7] Czechs—much more than citizens in neighboring societies—associated the early phase of the transformation with a sense of collective upward mobility. For instance, until about 1995, about 25 percent of workers declared themselves to be moving upward, only 8 percent as downward. The share of people who reported economic hardship during the transformation was also relatively small.[8] Overall, here, the phase of enthusiasm lasted for a comparatively long time. The partial disillusionment with market justice set in, however, in the second half of the 1900s, when major corruption scandals around the privatization program came to light. The sense of betrayal was pervasive. In the Czech public, the word "privatization" was now generally used synonymously with illegitimate wealth accumulation and corruption.[9] Still, the notion that the market constitutes a *natural* force that should not be interfered with—observed early as an important cultural theme of the Czech transformation by anthropologist Ladislav Holy—and that it was therefore the solution to problems generated by the institutional mode of change did not lose appeal among the wider population. While they did diminish trust in the political system, it seems that the corruption scandals of the 1990s did not substantively undermine people's belief in market justice in this country.[10] On the whole, in Central Europe, this process of disillusionment was never as profound as in post-Soviet societies. In Russia, for instance, sentiments of disappointment with markets and democracy grew so deep that, even before the 2022 war in Ukraine, surveys found that a significant share of the population would return to Communist Party rule if they had a choice to do so. "Red nostalgia," as some call this phenomenon, is not a major issue in public opinion in the Czech Republic or in Germany today.[11]

Egalitarianism may have returned, but it has never been the same. Across postsocialist societies today, there is a strong inclination in the public to think of poverty as a personal failure. This way of reasoning individualizes social problems. In a comparison across Western, Eastern, Southern, and Northern Europe, a 2014 study highlights that "support for the individualistic explanation [of poverty] is strongest in the East-central European countries." Eastern Europeans tend to blame poverty on the poor themselves. This complicates the assumption that postsocialist citizens (still) support the idea of equality of outcomes through welfare redistribution, as in egalitarianism. In that study, around a third of Czech respondents advance individualistic poverty attributions, making it one of the countries with the highest levels of moralizing explanations in the European comparison.[12] Somewhat more in line with what could be expected, a study comparing poverty attributions between East and West Germans reports that, because of widespread experiences of unemployment and social downward mobility after 1989, "East Germans tend to believe in external factors [for poverty] more strongly than West Germans." Yet in East Germany, the picture is not that straightforward either. The authors remark that in East Germany, "the distinction between dominant and challenging beliefs is less clear" than in the West. East Germans' preference for egalitarianism is not a stable legacy from state-socialist times. These orientations were shaped by manifold social and political dynamics after 1989. For instance, the authors of this study suggest that it is conceivable that (some) East Germans express support for egalitarianism not because they genuinely believe in it but out of an attitude of defiance toward the (discursively) meritocratic West German order.[13]

Finally, to what extent can justice beliefs be explained by individual status attainment after 1989? At the aggregate level, there is evidence that social mobility after 1989 shaped these orientations. Those who fared better are more likely to support the principle of merit; those who fared worse are more likely to reject it. However, there are also cultural factors at play. For instance, some researchers detect an "extraordinary mentality" among high-status East Germans who discursively reject certain manifestations of market society, likely as a sign of disapproval of the West German order. The way people assess the transformation period as a whole—not just their individual experience but also in terms of society at large—matters decidedly. There is evidence that, during the 1990s, a person's evaluation of the collective economic plight of East Germans shaped his or her thinking about economic justice more decidedly than individual status. Similarly, for the Czech Republic, researchers find that the rise of support for meritocratic ideals after 1989 was driven by the perception of economic opportunities more than by their objective distribution.[14]

TELLING STORIES ABOUT OTHER PEOPLE'S FATES

Four Accounts of Deservingness

People's ideas about justice were affected by their experience of labor market change and the rise of inequality after 1989. In this chapter,

DESERVING AND UNDESERVING OTHERS

I draw on the moral framework described in the introduction to illuminate these issues from a qualitatively deep perspective. I aim to reconstruct people's subjective sense of temporality as well as their reasoning about justice when telling stories about others. As the theoretical frameworks discussed in introduction suggest, notions of deservingness refer to concrete, everyday life experience. People consider particular economic outcomes, such as a situation of economic hardship, or a particular labor market position or income level, and then ask whether this outcome is justified given the conditions by which it was generated.[15]

I explore *deservingness accounts* as they are articulated by respondents. A deservingness account is a type of narrative reasoning. Individuals communicate moral beliefs by referencing other people in their environment and by telling stories about their fate.[16] Deservingness is based on relational references, that is, people who a respondent has come to know and/or is still in touch with. Through these stories, individuals articulate symbolic boundaries—they locate themselves in a social space, narrating the moral self as either proximate or distant from others.[17]

Table 3.1 provides a systematization of deservingness accounts. The primary challenge for the analysis is to distinguish causality as attributed by respondents. The difference between internal and external attributions, as elaborated in social justice theories, is gauged here. Notions of an internal force (character) can be distinguished from notions of an external force (structure). The latter references conditions that constrain such as age or health, or enable moral agency externally, such as learning, support networks, or social capital, locating the force primarily outside the individual.[18] Respondents meaningfully link outcomes back to agency, thereby assigning (or deflecting) individual responsibility and creating moral tension in a narrative arc. Accounts of character are associated with the principle of merit; accounts of structure are associated with the principles of need (if targeting individual capabilities) or equality (if arguing for an outcome independent of individual capabilities).[19] I distinguish four accounts of deservingness in this way (see table 3.1): accounts of deserved economic success, accounts of deserved economic failure, accounts of undeserved economic failure, and accounts of undeserved economic success.

DESERVING AND UNDESERVING OTHERS

TABLE 3.1
The Moral Structure of Deservingness Accounts

Positive Outcome		Negative Outcome		
Overcoming Hardship		Failing to Overcome Hardship		Enriching Oneself on the Back of Others
Character (willpower, attitude)	Structure (luck, social ties, age, health, etc.)	Character (willpower, attitude)	Structure (bad luck, lack of social ties, age, health, etc.)	
Deserved success	Neutral account (used to relativize deserved success)	Deserved failure	Undeserved failure	Undeserved success

ACCOUNTS OF DESERVED ECONOMIC SUCCESS

Accounts of deserved economic success after 1989 are commonly accounts of another person overcoming various kinds of hardships typical for the transformation time, like periods of unemployment, job insecurity, or involuntary retraining.[20] Stories of deserved economic success foreground the level of individual responsibility for economic outcomes. It is held that hard work and a certain level of individual sacrifice are required to achieve success and that success is legitimate to the extent that it is based on a moral conviction. People foreground character attributes and individual dispositions when identifying agency, in attributes such as a "forward-looking" or "hard-working" attitude and "savviness." The lessons they derive from these accounts include adages such as "You can do it if you really want to," "Whoever wants to work will find work," "Every man is the architect of his own fortune," "Without work, there's no treat,"[21] and "You can't wait for someone to take care of you..

Blanka, a Czech health-care worker in her late fifties, recounts how her husband, trained as a car mechanic, lost his job in the early 1990s. She uses his example to make a more general point, namely, that avoiding failure is a matter of individual ambition:

> When my second husband returned from the army, the owner of the garage told him: "I can't have you work here; we are already three [people working here] and we don't have work." [After a while] finally, he found something. It was an unpleasant experience. But I have to say, since I know it, whoever wants to work will find work. We have some of those types in our

street—they will not work; they will not work. In our family, we don't have that. We are not like that. We were always used to working . . . Everyone has to take care of himself. You can't wait for someone to take care of you!

In a similar vein, Robert, sixty-one, an East German entrepreneur who founded his own engineering business after the system change, refers to the time after 1989 as one of "great opportunities." He tells the story of a relative who was "muddling through" for years, not doing anything "proper" but at some point finally understood that "you have to take matters into your own hands":

> There were these closed-minded people who, out of principle used to say, "You took so much from me, now please take care of me." . . . I have a brother-in-law, he was around thirty at the time of the transition, and he tried to always muddle himself through. Capitalism grants you to do that for some time. Now this guy had—I have to say, for some time I employed him—he had cancer, had to undergo surgery, couldn't work. Now he works at a security firm, so he can sit there and finally do something. And now, he told his buddy who still idles time away doing nothing, "Get lost, you keep on complaining!" Never would I have thought he'd dare tell him his opinion!

In the change of mind about his relative, Robert identifies a moment of moral agency, which he welcomes as a type of purging of an immoral past. Today, it creates a justified outcome because it makes the other person think more like him. He regards it as deserved to the extent that character and economic outcomes align in this story. Like Robert, people assign individual responsibility by telling stories of deserved success, but they often also relativize it in parts by introducing structural, circumstantial elements that point to exceptions.

ACCOUNTS OF DESERVED ECONOMIC FAILURE

Many report stories that advance individualized explanations for economic failure after 1989. People in the stories are regarded as "stuck" in their plight. Their agency is narrated as lacking in willpower or principled convictions, similar to what researchers have found in the field of poverty evaluations. Immoral motives, such as envy, closed-mindedness, or a vainglorious pursuit of money, are frequently associated with this. People often summarize the gist of such accounts in proverbs such as "It all comes back to you," "You can't save everyone," or some variation of the notion of a "survival of the fittest." Ralf, fifty-five, is an East German engineer who personally found the changes of the 1990s difficult to cope with. Ralf shares the story of his former friend from the same village who, even though he enjoyed the same education as the respondent himself, was phlegmatic and chose not to pursue a technical career after the transition. He therefore never got his feet on the ground:

This former friend of mine, he is simply too stubborn, I'd say. He's a trained electrician; he would not have had any problems to find work as an electrician. He starting working at some business that did carpeting or something, so he abandoned his proper life as an electrician and when, at some point, the shop was closed down, well he couldn't find anything! . . . It's his fault, he's too stubborn. He's not flexible enough . . . At some point you don't want to listen to him complaining. So the relationship weakens because you are not interested in it anymore.

In stories like Ralf's, a person's willpower is implicated in their economic success. Based on the assumption that the capability was there, lack of will is identified as the main cause of failure, making their trajectory a logical and necessary consequence of a set of decisions at a certain point in time in the past. The critical decision identified by Ralf was abandoning the realm of technical skills. Accounts like his consistently reflect an image of the post-1989 labor market and economic environment as principally favorable to those who are willing to work and are ambitious. Some who tell stories like this also negotiate political issues through this logic. For instance, one person reports knowing someone who worked for the secret police before 1989 and then failed economically in the new system after 1989. This generated a sense of justice and personal satisfaction—here, market justice serves to "purge" the political past.

Martin, sixty-seven, was trained as an electronics engineer in the German Democratic Republic (GDR). The system change has profoundly unsettled his own work biography, but with much delay. In the 1990s, he oversaw computerization in the planning department at a spinoff of a formerly state-owned firm. Economic restructuring brought "mounting stress." Thus, in

DESERVING AND UNDESERVING OTHERS

2003, he became sick and was forced to leave his job. He recounts the story of his former bosses, both party secretaries, who were initially successful after the system change because of their political connections in the previous regime. This had put them in a position to reap the rewards of entrepreneurship after 1989, even though they were poorly qualified:

> They were not planners; they had never done any planning back in the GDR. One of them was from Berlin, which was advantaged in GDR times . . . Therefore, shortly before 1989, they were put into these high-level positions and given the opportunity to take over the business—on the basis of their political position alone. So they "devoured" [the firm], took over, but really they had no idea how to run an engineer's office. Thanks to the good overall economic situation, money came in easily for them after 1989 . . . In 2004, the business finally crashed . . . because of mismanagement.

According to Martin, it was only a matter of time before the business would fail because the managers lacked both technical and business expertise. In 2004, finally, when going bankrupt, they received a deserved punishment for incompetency. In Martin's story, it was the force of the market that balanced things out. It literally put an end—if with some delay—to the political arrangements from GDR times, when underqualified but politically loyal individuals were rewarded with leadership positions. To some extent, it also redeemed Martin's own suffering.

ACCOUNTS OF UNDESERVED ECONOMIC FAILURE

In accounts of undeserved economic failure, people criticize the merit principle and advocate a position that points to the limits of character-based explanations. They use these stories to underscore the importance of the principle of need. These convictions are expressed in sayings such as "You can't blame it on the person," or "Help people to help themselves.." Björn, who experienced unemployment multiple times after 1989, tells the story of a brother-in-law who founded a business but made bad choices because of limited knowledge:

> Around the time of the transition, there were lots of people who started their own business, who were naïve and got cheated by some random strangers

who told them, "Well, you need this and that now." And so they indebted themselves, went bankrupt . . . These people were lacking information. You can't just do these things with your own hands. I have someone like that in my own family. A brother-in-law set up his own construction firm after 1989; well, the end of the story was now ten years ago, [when] he became insolvent. They've been living at the poverty margin ever since.

Björn's account highlights how East Germans were expected to play by the rules of the free-market economy, although they lacked the chance to learn them. Many people who tell such stories, Czechs and Germans alike, also bring up the issue of age, with a large group of people regarded as having been "too old" to be able to learn the tools of the trade. Others point to more existential problems, like depression or alcoholism. Stories of undeserved failure are not principally detached from individual attributions of responsibility. Instead, they introduce another level that explains the kinds of character traits that allow individuals to achieve or fail. Equality of opportunity is questioned by pointing to skewed structural conditions, such as the lack of available jobs, age disadvantages, the requirement of new skill sets, or the lack of social support. Most people advancing notions like this have a profound sense of individual agency in economic matters, but they differentiate by introducing the principle of need when it comes to the question of what it takes to get there. This is a model of explanation that regards individual autonomy as born of dependency. Health-care workers, both East German and Czech, more frequently recount stories of "undeserved failure," introducing the principle of need more often than do engineers. They do so by pointing to a greater number of factors, such as age, mental or physical impairments, or the need for a stable social environment and support from others.

ACCOUNTS OF UNDESERVED ECONOMIC SUCCESS

These accounts are exceptional because, unlike the others, they do not entail an evaluation of an experience of economic hardship. There is thus a different logic for evaluating someone's agency attached to it, expressed in lessons such as "people get by cheating." Accounts of undeserved success are stories of people taking advantage of others by engaging in nontransparent or otherwise morally questionable financial activities that contradict the merit principle, but they are also stories of luck (referencing a system that allows for such "luck" and "connections" to prevail over market justice) and stories of individuals who take advantage of "undeserved" welfare money, as in moral discourses on welfare eligibility.[22]

These accounts often involve former Communist Party members or secret police informers whose economic success after 1989 serves as an illustration that something is wrong with the market order. Czechs are particularly concerned about illegitimate means of attaining wealth after 1989. Corruption and illegitimate privatization practices come up as an important theme in many conversations. Some tell stories about "turncoats," former "reds" (Communist Party functionaries) who quickly became "capitalists." Jan, an engineer and architect in his late sixties, was employed for more than twenty years before the revolution at a Czech cooperative specializing in socialist housing construction. In 1989, when the former boss was dismissed for political reasons, Jan became the director of the firm. He reports the story of one of his former coworkers as an example of someone who was failing in his profession but became successful because he knew how to take advantage of the new rules of the game: "This person has been working with us in the cooperative . . . Today he's the major's representative. We had laid him off back then because he was incompetent. It's hard when you know his profile. Everyone knew about each other; we knew about his working morals, about his personal qualities . . . So the people we kicked out for total incompetence back then are the ones who make politics today."

In a similar way, another Czech engineer creates a dichotomy between decent, economically productive people and those who "eat off politics" after 1989, suggesting there exists an entire class of people whose political connections are the reason for their economic advantage. Through these stories, people cast doubt on the notion that 1989 brought equality of opportunities. This is most often articulated as a political instead of as an economic problem. When telling stories like this, people often point to political privileges or networks that enabled some to game the system.

Stories about alleged "welfare cheats" can also be found in this genre. Barbora, a Czech nurse, has a negative perception of an acquaintance who she regards as reaping an "undeserved success" of receiving payments from the labor office. In her view, for the first decade or so after the revolution, the conditions allowed individuals to take advantage of the system in this way:

> At the time, when my son was in ninth grade, he had a classmate whose mother was a learned retailer . . . She was laid off . . . And so she went to the labor office, and lived off social support. And then my son comes to me and says, "Mami, they are so poor, her [friend's] mother is on benefits alone." And then he told me the sum. And I said, "Just compare what she has, because she's at home with the kids, and she still has two thirds of my pay!" I work the entire month, I go to work every day, I have . . . responsibility, and still I only get a third more than this woman who is at home? . . . She can do the housework, she can cook, she often has free time on her hands . . . This is what people could get away with in the first ten years after the revolution or so, such were the times.

Barbora is deeply disturbed by the fact that, at the time, she earned just a little more than someone who, in her eyes, was unwilling to work. In her view, this would not have been possible in state-socialist times. Another Czech health-care worker, who expresses her frustration about the fact that people purportedly take advantage of welfare benefits after 1989, argues that she misses the time when there was a *duty* to work—late socialist Czechoslovakia, when these things were allegedly still in order. Some Czechs draw similar boundaries to the Roma minority in racialized references to presumed "welfare cheats." A growing number of studies are exploring the significance of such racialized boundary-drawing—acts of stigmatizing migrants, refugees, or members of particular ethnic minorities as undeserving—in the postsocialist context.[23]

East Germans have strong views about West Germans, who are remembered as patronizing owners, investors, and bosses after unification, adding—as we saw in chapter 2—insult to injury of the dissolution of East German industrial structures by devaluing their work ethic. Some respondents draw a parallel between former "reds," the old communists, and West Germans. In their view, both have achieved undeserved success. Stories of undeserved success and excessive wealth accumulation generally tend to focus on rather distant individuals: they are somewhat more abstract than other accounts.[24]

SOCIAL POSITION AND NOTIONS OF DESERVINGNESS

As we saw earlier in this chapter, sociologists concur that social position shapes justice beliefs. Research shows, for instance, that East Germans who had experienced long-term or frequent phases of joblessness after 1989 believed less and less in internal factors for economic success. Similarly, whether Czechs held egalitarian or inegalitarian views after the system change was soon "linked to [their] position in the social stratification system."[25] Generally speaking, this pattern also emerges from the interviews. The kind of social position that people attain grants them a particular perspective, a specific experiential horizon by which they reflect on and judge material trajectories. It undergirds the way engineers and health-care workers articulate deservingness accounts. On the whole, engineers, whose chances of experiencing upward social mobility after 1989 were greater, are more likely to advance a meritocratic reasoning than are health-care workers, who are more inclined to introduce criteria that point to circumstances beyond a person's control. East Germans are also more critical of individual attributions of responsibility than Czechs. Their respective professional identity and ethos—which is intertwined with gender—arguably also plays a role here. It is part of health-care workers' everyday jobs to consider other people's needs; they know about the many ways in which a person's physical and mental abilities can be constrained by his or her circumstances. For them, unlike for many engineers, careers after 1989 were seldom oriented around the logic of *winning* or *losing* in a market environment. Competition, in turn, was a distinct reality for engineers after 1989. Social status mattered and continues to matter more in this field than in the health-care professions. On the basis of such varying experiential horizons that are shaped by labor market chances after the system change, some are more inclined to advance individualistic narratives about the sources of social inequality than others.

Yet there are stories that do not fit neatly into this pattern. Some engineers went through periods of unemployment but nevertheless insist that individual effort matters before all. Some health-care workers whose incomes and social mobility chances continued to stagnate are still convinced that after 1989, a person had to take matters into her own hands.[26] Overall, meritocratic reasoning is much more widespread than we would expect.[27] Most of the stories are guided by the idea that there is, in principle, an *orderly,*

DESERVING AND UNDESERVING OTHERS

symmetrical relation between what someone voluntarily did and what the person gets in return. On the whole, then, our analysis of deservingness suggests that the idea of individual responsibility for economic outcomes after 1989 is the dominant proposition. We may say that it functions like a working hypothesis: it is generally regarded as valid until contradicted.[28]

DESERVINGNESS AS EMBEDDED IN ECONOMIC MEMORIES

Ideas of individual deservingness dominate. We can identify two recurring tropes that sustain them. The first is that 1989 constituted an *economic beginning* for society as a whole, which carries a consequential assumption, namely, that there was equality of opportunity after the system change. The second is that people can legitimately claim to be *victims of economic circumstances* only under exceptional, narrowly defined circumstances.

1989 as an Economic Beginning

The predominating theme that, after the revolutions, *you finally had to take matters into your own hands* is grounded in a temporal logic: 1989 is imagined as an economic beginning. It is widely accepted that, in political terms, the revolutions signify a shift from an old to a new order in which the old regime is associated with stasis and petrification, and the new order with change and modernization. Freedom, autonomy, opportunity, and agency are all associated with the new order. This juxtaposition has been reiterated in countless public representations and commemorations of 1989. But it is also more than an official memory. The idea that the period after 1989 represents a new temporal order also shapes people's biographical sense of the progression of time. It refers to a common, socially shared space of eventful experience.

In idiomatic designations (see table 3.2), the post-1989 period is charged not just with political but also with economic meaning. It is a space of economic agency.[29] This goes hand in hand with the assumption that it also represents a moment of equality of opportunity. Equality refers to the fact that each and every person was confronted with the new reality in a similar way: people had to make choices—on the labor market, in their business, in their families—that would be met with consequences. Decisions suddenly mattered in this *window of opportunity*. To be sure,

DESERVING AND UNDESERVING OTHERS

TABLE 3.2
Idiomatic Designations of Temporal Orders

	East German Designations	Czech Designations
Pre-1989 *stasis*	GDR times (*DDR-Zeiten*)	Under totalitarianism (*za totality*)
	Period before 1989 (*Vorwendezeit*)	Under communism (*za komunismu*)
	Before the transition (*vor der Wende*)	Before the revolution (*před revolucí*)
Post-1989 *change*	Period after 1989 (*Nachwendezeit*)	Postrevolution time (*porevoluční doba*)
	New time (*neue Zeit*)	After 1989 (*po převratu*)
	West time (*Westzeit*)	After November time (*polistopadová doba*)

this assumption is grounded in a notion of human dignity and autonomy. But as a temporal logic, the proposition of equality of opportunity after 1989 legitimizes unequal outcomes in the present. From research on justice beliefs, we know that meritocratic ideas necessarily rest on the idea of equality of opportunity. If everyone has similar starting conditions, individual achievement truly makes the difference. This is a powerful consequential proposition. Inequality scholar Leslie McCall demonstrates, for instance, U.S. Americans' views of meritocracy are not stable but instead depend crucially on how they situate and evaluate equality of opportunity historically. In other words, the stories that people tell about the structure of opportunities in the past truly matter for the way that they evaluate inequalities in the present.

This is also true in postsocialist societies today, more than three decades after 1989, where it is not required that people normatively judge that there was equality during state socialism. Rather, what matters is that the event of 1989 is perceived as the *beginning* of a process of rising inequality. Hence, when people compare themselves to others in the present, they reference the year 1989 as the point of departure for processes of social differentiation. This is precisely what sociologist Martin Kreidl documents among Czechs during the 1990s. He notes that "the more the people believe in equal opportunities, the more they support the individual explanation of inequalities. The feeling of having equal opportunities thus appears crucial, both for adopting and refusing the dominant ideology [of meritocracy]." This suggests that we should think of deservingness ideas *in the present* as embedded in eventful imaginations of what rules applied *back then*.

Deservingness is an element of larger cultural apprehensions, of economic memories of the past.[30]

Rejecting Economic Victimhood

Another trope that reinforces ideas about individual responsibility is the inclination to reject other people's (purported) claims to be *victims of the economic circumstances* after 1989. This comes as a surprise. After all, in their recollections of the post-1989 period, people often cite events and processes, among them privatization, corruption, wealth concentration, and unemployment, that underscore just how limited people's control over their economic fates really was. None of these, as Karl Marx would have it, are the conditions of people's own choosing. And the memory of these events is deeply antagonistic, infused with a profound sense of injustice. In light of their evocative power, we may even think of them as negative, economic *lieux de mémoire*: in the sense of French historian and memory scholar Pierre Nora, they are situated in time and space, they crystallize shared meanings, they are highly affective, and they inform collective identities in the present.[31] Privatization is frequently narrated as a plunder of the former socialist *people's property*—by Czechs and East Germans alike. People were cheated, and their ability to participate in a free competition over resources was undermined. Corruption squarely contradicts the assumption that there was equality of opportunity. It is a widely shared perception that, after 1989, a small group of individuals— usually, former party elites and *turncoats*, or in the case of Germany, West Germans—took advantage of the chaos at the time and tried to monopolize resources early on. So how could an ordinary person hope to accumulate wealth based on individual effort and an honest commitment to work in this situation? Unemployment is another case in point. Because mass joblessness in the 1990s was caused by the West German institutional *takeover* of the GDR economy, it would be absurd to blame job loss on East Germans individually.

Even if many invoke these themes in their criticism of the injustices of the transformation period, it does not follow that they permit others to blame their situation on external circumstances. Many are in fact adamant about this point. Some resort to a form of reasoning that suggests a peculiar order of time to make this case. They maintain that, in

DESERVING AND UNDESERVING OTHERS

the period immediately after the fall of the Berlin Wall, some groups in society were collectively disempowered. But into the 1990s, as things evolved, they had to face up to the new reality of market society just like everyone else, the argument goes. An East German engineer and entrepreneur, for instance, refers to the federal German privatization agency, the *Treuhand*, as one of the "biggest criminal organizations in history." It had "squashed" the East German economy. Yet he also insists that the time after 1989 was one of "great opportunities" and blames those who did not take advantage of them individually. While he accepts that unemployment was a collective problem in the beginning, he holds that after this initial phase, "you cannot blame it on the system." In a similar vein, a Czech construction engineer paints a bleak picture of economic developments after the Velvet Revolution, linking the success of *turncoats*, who could draw on their political networks from the old regime, to widespread corruption during privatization. He nevertheless suggests that the ability to "take advantage of opportunities" was decisive for economic success after 1989. In his view, today, "those who lament the new material differences do not deal with the fact that it is their own fault." These ways of reasoning, as we saw, squarely contradict the sociological finding that people's life chances were decidedly determined by their labor market situation in the early 1990s.

Scholars have often interpreted the widespread anger about corruption, social inequality, and foreign dominance found in postsocialist societies today as the result of people's egalitarian sensibilities being violated by what happened in the 1990s. But this—at least for the East German and Czech examples—is only part of the story. As we saw, there is a pervasive sense of injustice, but people also tend to think of economic outcomes after 1989 as individually deserved. They engage in memory work, construing narrow and rather idiosyncratic criteria for what constitutes *legitimate economic victimhood*. The assumption is that some individuals were needy or dependent for a time, but the proposition that entire groups of people, collectively, suffered lasting economic damage after 1989 is not easily embraced. It contradicts the trope of individual agency and responsibility.

From this, we can see that the way economic agency after 1989 is construed, and whether someone's circumstances are regarded as within this person's control or not, is a matter of meaning making. Morality, a "fellow-feeling" guided by the imagination in Adam Smith's sense,[32] relates to an imagined plight of others against the background of this shared experience of disruptive economic change, and it takes on shape by virtue of being narrated and fostered in stories. The relevant interpretations do not happen outside a consciousness of historical time.

So far, however, the picture we have gained of the moral framework is still incomplete. In order to see what is missing, we must now turn to the realm of close social relations after 1989, which is the subject of chapter 4.

Chapter Four

THE SOCIAL EXPERIENCE OF THE TRANSFORMATION PERIOD

The first thing to go was friendship . . . Suddenly, everyone was too busy, they had to go out and make money.

—SVETLANA ALEXIEVICH, *SECOND-HAND TIME: THE LAST OF THE SOVIETS*

Friendship cannot escape the laws of historical gravity: Two friends are still two incorporated social histories that attempt to coexist.

—DIDIER ERIBON, *RETURNING TO REIMS*

A WEB OF MEANINGFUL RELATIONS

In the analysis in the preceding chapters, we saw how people draw on frameworks of meaning that foreground individual agency in the way they narrate change after 1989 to the present day. First, this was visible in their emphasis on the importance of skills, understood as individual competencies; and second, we observed that many adhere to an overarching story about how the breakdown of state socialism hailed the advent of a new era of opportunity and choice. When it comes to understanding popular justice orientations, however, a substantial element is still unaccounted for: what was the mode by which economic change after 1989 was experienced and apprehended? People do not go through episodes of vast societal change by themselves; these shifts do not take place in a social vacuum. Instead, people experience them as part of a social arrangement—a web of meaningful relations in which they are embedded.

Trusted social ties with family and friends are critical sources of support during times of uncertainty. They are also a social space of meaning making in which shared ideas and narratives about unfolding events are generated and nourished. There is a link between events and the social ties that a person can rely on to orientate the self in a changing world: people make sense of external shifts *together*.[1]

THE SOCIAL EXPERIENCE OF THE TRANSFORMATION PERIOD

But what if these very bonds of trust are themselves subject to change? When relations change unexpectedly, problems of solidarity and justice arise. This leads us to ask, What does the experience of shifting social ties reveal about a person's moral apprehension of the larger story of societal change? This question is explored in this chapter. To be sure, this is an ambitious task. It is impossible, of course, to reconstruct comprehensively social change in the post-1989 era. We are confronted with a condition of overdetermined change, as social scientists call it: there are a variety of forces at play that shape how people, relations, and constellations of experiences might interact. To dissect the problem, we need a specific structuring angle, a viewpoint that enables us to zoom into and magnify the cultural dimension of social change. We can gain such a perspective, as this chapter suggests, by studying the meaning that people assign to *breaks in formerly strong relationships*. Breaks in strong ties are instances of social friction that reveal something beneath the surface level, that point to an underlying structure. These breaks in social ties lay bare the texture behind interpersonal bonds—a texture that is imbued with meaning, enriched with and fostered by normative orientations. Studying breaks offers insights into the values and commitments that people deeply care about. It affords a particularly rich perspective on the question of trust. As the discussion reveals, trust is closely intermingled with problems of solidarity, equality, and justice. To gain such a view, the analysis in this chapter brings two sociological methodologies into the conversation: combining the strengths of social network scholarship with those of cultural sociology.

On these grounds, the chapter reveals a final, elementary dimension of the moral framework: individuals harbor a sense of a deserving self—deserving in terms of a morality of work and economic outcomes, as well as in terms of strong, trusted social relations after 1989. People make sense of economic change by turning to those around them. From the perspective of those who lived through this period, the challenges of coping with economic change are inseparable from the need to rely on and to be esteemed by one's confidants. Trusted ties are critical sources of recognition, and individuals, above all, crave recognition for their struggles and achievements after 1989.

This allows us to illuminate conclusively our key problem: why do people stick to the principle of merit when drawing lessons from the transformation period? Why do they value individual agency and personal

THE SOCIAL EXPERIENCE OF THE TRANSFORMATION PERIOD

dispositions so greatly, despite having personally been confronted with the forces of chance, structural disadvantage, and a skewed distribution of opportunities after 1989? We can now see that the dynamic of relational recognition is at the heart of this conundrum. In it, the meaning of *work as a claim to social inclusion* is key. It rests on a specific idea of equality that is widely advanced by people and that does not contradict the belief in legitimate individual success and failure. Understood in this way, equality is inseparable from the problem of the deserving self: a person is regarded as worthy of social recognition based on his or her market agency after 1989. This has wide-ranging implications for popular justice reasoning. It is a decisive piece of the puzzle, contributing to our understanding of why the principle of merit has considerable salience—and why that of universal, unconditional solidarity, in turn, is relatively weak. But before unpacking these issues in detail, the broader context of the social experience of the transformation time must be explored.

PEOPLE ON THE MOVE

Moving Away

A defining element of the social experience of the period was the mass exodus that befell the region after the fall of the Berlin Wall. People emigrated en masse from the former East German territories. According to one estimate, around 3.6 million people left between 1989 and 2017, mostly resettling to the Western part of the country. Around 2.4 million—some of whom were returners—moved to the former East during the same time frame, mostly settling in urban areas. Rural and less densely populated areas in the former East German territories have been hit particularly hard by steady demographic decline. Yet this situation was not exactly new. it was already underway decades before the break-up of the Soviet Union. The German Democratic Republic (GDR) had always been a society of leavers, of citizens choosing to vote with their feet. That said, the militarized border prevented people from leaving en masse, and many lost their lives attempting to escape. After 1989, it was the ensuing labor market crisis—namely, the sudden shortage of jobs— that prompted a mass exodus to the West. Young, well-educated women were most likely to depart, leaving behind a dramatic demographic and economic gap. Some regions lost up to one-third of their population after 1989.[2]

Nearly all Central European societies suffered disastrous demographic decline during the 1990s. Political commentators Ivan Krastev and Stephen Holmes suggest that the process of "bleeding out," as they call it, was a population crisis of unprecedented proportions. Some countries were hit particularly hard. Between 1989 and 2017, Latvia lost 27 percent of its population, Lithuania around 22.5 percent, and Bulgaria 21 percent. Compared to these figures, East Germany's population loss of roughly 14 percent may seem like a moderate number. Still, as Krastev and Holmes assert, this is not merely about the loss of great numbers of people. The experience of massive population loss continues to be a source of social trauma today. It had a profound impact on the collective psyche of the newly emerging nation-states across the region, feeding fears of being abandoned, being subjected to processes outside one's control, and being relegated to the sidelines of history. Demographics, in this view, is politics: from the perspective of those who stayed, and perhaps also of some of those who returned, population loss after 1989 easily translates into a demographic angst with nationalistic undertones—a fear that can easily be exploited and weaponized by nativist politicians today.[3]

The Czech Republic, however, provides a counterexample. It stands out from most of its Central European neighbors because it has gained, not lost, population relative to 1989. When it departed from Slovakia in 1993, its population stood at 8 million, climbing to roughly 10.6 million nearly three decades later. People migrating to the Czech Republic frequently came from neighboring transitioning societies, with Ukrainians representing the largest group. Czechs also resettled within the country, abandoning poorer, deindustrialized rural areas in the northeastern and northwestern parts of the country to reside in richer, urban areas. This was a typical pattern all over Central Eastern Europe, which brought with it increasing regional disparities everywhere. Like most European societies, the Czech Republic also has an aging population and struggles with the prospect of long-term population decline. Still, the fact that Czechs lack a collective experience of out-migration after 1989 certainly shapes the memory of the transformation time in more positive ways today.[4]

Leaving and resettling somewhere else means different things to different people, but it always has an economic and social dimension to it. Sara

THE SOCIAL EXPERIENCE OF THE TRANSFORMATION PERIOD

is an elder-care professional in her early sixties. She received her training as a nurse in the GDR. She did not take up the profession out of conviction. She remembers that her only options were to become a hairdresser, a metal worker, or a health-care worker, so Sara took her first job in a hospital in 1985. About a year after the revolution, she moved with her family to Bavaria, in former West Germany, where she worked for the next eight years. She was thus among the first large wave of East Germans migrating in the early 1990s (the second wave took place about ten years later, shortly after the turn of the century). For Sara, resettling to Bavaria was like entering a new world. Taking a job at a Catholic hospital there, she was confronted with a problem that was entirely foreign to her: the role of religion at the workplace. Her Bavarian coworkers believed that a person's private faith was an important element of the quality of one's care—something that Sara, having grown up in one of the most atheist societies in the world, found hard to accept. She also had to cope with a rigid system of hierarchies between doctors and nurses in which people seemed to overemphasize formal interaction. Sara finds that they were less "socially inclined" than her former East German coworkers, "cold" even. None of the informal workplace rituals that she was accustomed to from back home, like having breakfast together in the ward, were practiced here.

Outside work, however, Sara succeeded in finding fulfillment in her social environment. She managed to forge friendships with people from "all over" and she also stayed in touch with her old friends in her East German hometown, traveling back and forth repeatedly. She considers herself very lucky in this respect because, as she asserts, not everyone managed to cope. She recounts the story of a former friend of hers from the East who also resettled in Bavaria after the revolution but who did not manage to forge meaningful ties there. The loneliness and the sense of social disconnectedness caused her great pain. First, she sought happiness in consumer consumption, spending money on useless things. As Sara saw it, this friend "did not stay true to herself" and became materialistic. Then, when things got worse, she took to drinking and got sick. Finally, she gave up and decided to return to her hometown. Sara reasons that her misfortunate was ultimately triggered by the fact that she was "torn out of her social environment."

Network researchers regard moving away as a primary cause for why social relations dissolve and new network ties are eventually formed.

THE SOCIAL EXPERIENCE OF THE TRANSFORMATION PERIOD

Increased spatial distance plays an important role in this process because it decreases the probability that two individuals will spontaneously run into each other. As is well documented in so-called foci of interaction research on how people form and maintain network ties, repeated encounters, whether planned or not, are vital for sustaining just about any type of relation but especially for nonfamilial relations. In fact, having *opportunities* to do so matters more than the *intention* to meet. The greater the logistical challenge or the costlier it becomes to get together regularly in terms of money and time, the more a friendship will be weakened by geographical distance.[5]

During an adult's life, losing ties is the rule rather than the exception. Network researcher Ronald Burt has summarized this finding by observing that relationships die of natural causes unless an effort is made. Next to moving away, relations also frequently end for reasons such as growing older, time constraints, diverging interests, or as a result of changes in network density and "structural embeddedness." The latter is a thought-provoking concept describing how single social ties often depend on constellations of other ties. For instance, when the relationship to a particular person who manages to connect different groups weakens, then there is a high chance that ties to other, less directly connected persons are also weakened or lost. This is common in a divorce, when the distinction between *your* friends and *my* friends is suddenly brought into relief. What these studies unambiguously demonstrate, in sum, is that social relations change when structures of interaction change—independent of whether people actually want this to happen or not.[6]

The language employed by network researchers is not accidental. Designating something a "structural" phenomenon suggests an absence of agency and responsibility for what happened. In this view, an outcome like tie dissolution is regrettable, but no one can really be blamed for it. It is simply the natural course of life. This, it turns out, is how some respondents think about this problem, too. As one East German engineer remarks, social relations after 1989 "followed the Gaussian normal distribution, just like any community does"—a pretty straightforward claim that these were simply normal external changes governed by natural laws. As we will see later in this chapter, however, the problem is actually much deeper: there are dimensions to it that are not reflected accurately by the concepts employed by network scholars or those coming from the engineering sciences.

Returning Home: The "Homophily of Experience"

The reason Sara returned to her hometown in the East after living in Bavaria for eight years was because she wanted to be close to her parents when having her first child. After relocating, she obtained a university degree in health-care work. After maternity leave, she took a job at a hospital. Resuming work in her old environment, she again experienced a degree of culture shock. Her new colleagues, all of them East Germans who had never moved away, took issue with the fact that she had spent such a "long time" in the West. The problem was multifaceted. First, Sara's qualifications became a point of contention. Some of her coworkers were suspicious of her academic degree, which had not existed before 1989. Did she perhaps think that she was something better now? Second, and even more important, her return triggered the question of whether she really belonged: there were traces of a Bavarian accent in her speech now. Was she really still one of them? Perhaps she had turned into a West German. Sara remembers: "The recognition of me, as a person, was contingent on them recognizing that 'she is one of us. She also experienced all of the things that happened here.' . . . Upon acknowledging, 'she did get her education here during GDR times,' that was when they finally gave in, accepted me."

Thus, for her to be truly reintegrated into this tight-knit community, she had to prove that she was one of them. Sara managed to do so, if only after some time. Sociologists studying the everyday symbolism of class have often argued that people tend to read differences in education as differences of social origin and class. Sara's story exemplifies the problem that comes with what is perceived as a transgression of existing, conventional social boundaries. The person who left returns to her old community, bringing a new set of skills and knowledge with her. The question, from the standpoint of the community, is whether these new competencies are of benefit to those who stayed behind. There's fear that her new skill set instead makes their knowledge look quaint or even worthless. This is one important reason for why these worlds can easily come into conflict. What is at stake here are the subtle ramifications of social upward mobility, or the "hidden injuries of class," to invoke Richard Sennett and Jonathan Cobb's famous phrase.[7]

Sara's account is striking for the fact that her colleagues, in order to accept her as a member of their community, want her to prove that she shares a particular experience with them—the experience of having lived

THE SOCIAL EXPERIENCE OF THE TRANSFORMATION PERIOD

through the breakdown of the GDR and the period after 1989. Let's briefly consider this from the perspective of social network research. One of the most widely used concepts in this literature is the concept of "homophily," which holds that shared traits and characteristics, such as socioeconomic status, race, gender, tastes, or religious and political views, tend to make people feel close to each other. Shared backgrounds and preferences make people more likely to form and sustain relationships with each other. *Birds of a feather flock together*, as the famous saying goes. How do the social claims made of Sara fit into this? The situation she is confronted with is something akin to a *homophily of experience*. This is not primarily about age, as Sara and her colleagues are more or less from the same generation, and they were all educated before the fall of the Berlin Wall. The crux of the matter is that Sara decided to leave right after the revolution and so she might have missed the experience of the changes wrought by this event. This comes down to her agency—the decisions she made after 1989. Why did she decide to leave? Did she perhaps wish to avoid the troubles that others who remained were forced to cope with? These are the types of questions she must respond to. In order to belong, Sara has to demonstrate that she understands and recognizes the hardships and uncertainties of the period of transformation. This is the price she has to pay given that she enjoyed, at least in the eyes of those who stayed behind, the luxury of leaving.[8]

Homophily of experience does not exist as a concept in network research because it cannot be expressed in terms of frequencies or probabilities. But this is a shortcoming of the mathematical modeling approach. Network scholars have not identified ways to delineate shared experiences, the *sense* of having participated in an event together, and to represent it in a set of variables that can then be used in a formal analysis. Yet feelings of social similarity rooted in the consciousness of sharing particular experiences might be a social force in their own right. It seems less illogical to make such a claim once we adapt the perspective of relational sociology and emphasize the historicity and context-specificity of social relations.

A REVOLUTION OF TRUST?

You can't get anything done without the right friends: this is a basic maxim of everyday life in postsocialist societies because informal relations are pervasive in this part of the world. Individuals rely on networks of family, kinship, and acquaintanceship ties for conducting their everyday business and gaining access to sought-after goods or opportunities. As anthropologists point out, provision networks are governed by the principle of reciprocity. To keep things going, favors must be returned, whether in the form of money or immaterial types of exchange.

The outsize role of informal arrangements in this region must be understood in part as a legacy of the relationship between the economy and society under state socialism. The economy of shortage, with its notorious unpredictability and scarcity of goods, forced individuals to find alternative channels by which to organize what they needed. People had to invent creative solutions, like bribing, stealing (*if you don't steal from the state, you're stealing from your family*, as the saying went), or hoarding goods. Unofficial practices of trade were so pervasive that they resulted in the emergence of a system of informal exchange, the so-called second economy. This is something that social scientists have observed for a long time: if the state has little capacity to distribute goods and services efficiently, and if the legal system cannot be trusted to ensure accountable procedures of provision, then people will rely on informal channels for subsistence and protection.

These arrangements continued to exist well after 1989. But now, with the introduction of markets and private property, they took on a new shape. In many places, a mixture of practices based on formal (based on institutions, and governed by the logic of supply and demand) and informal exchange (rooted in personal ties and sustained by reciprocity) emerged. Wherever the state was weak and wherever there was a scarcity of basic goods together with low wages (such in crisis-ridden Russia and Ukraine), informal relations continued to be vital, a decisive protection against poverty even. Even in places with less severe economic upheaval, the private, backyard garden plot for growing fruit and vegetables for one's personal needs also helped to sustain small-scale exchange networks and these remained a symbol of independence, family cohesion, and economic savviness. These are persistent legacies. Long after 1989, in many parts of the postsocialist world, the role of provision networks in everyday life remains more pronounced than elsewhere around the world.[9]

Informality is much weaker, however—and has always been weaker— in the East German and Czech cases than in the post-Soviet world. The two were already heavily industrialized societies with a relatively strong

THE SOCIAL EXPERIENCE OF THE TRANSFORMATION PERIOD

centralized state before 1989. In both, the second economy was more limited and was geared more toward luxury items than everyday goods compared to the more agrarian countries of Poland and Hungary, for instance. After the revolutions, Germany and the Czech Republic morphed into textbook market societies in which labor markets, wages, and prices soon functioned as the principal media of distribution and allocation of resources. People held on to their beloved garden plots but increasingly for symbolic reasons, and in stark contrast to, say, poverty-ridden Romania, Ukraine or eastern Poland during the same period. Informality certainly did not disappear from one day to the next, but it was arguably less important as a pillar of the emerging economic order than in many neighboring societies. Thus, in the East German and Czech cases, when studying the parameters of change to social networks, it is reasonable to view them in the context of market society.

We must now direct our attention to the specific problem of relations of trust in market society. How did people (re)organize their social networks in order to navigate these new capitalist labor markets? Sociologists refer to the kinds of relations needed in market society as "social capital." These are the ties that people sustain with others who they cooperate with, do business with, and are potentially sources of information about jobs or access to resources (with information, instead of goods of subsistence, as the prized good). Their primary function is to advance particular economic and career-specific goals—these ties are, in other words, typically instrumental in nature. What patterns of change can we find here? Perhaps unsurprisingly, it turns out that such ties really did gain relevance after the revolutions. The number of weak ties in East German networks increased after the fall of the Berlin Wall, if to a lesser extent than might have been anticipated. The way Czechs formed and organized business relations also shifted. These shifts were visible particularly among economic elites, as documented by studies of entrepreneurial networks that emerged during the 1990s. Here, social capital was a critical determinant of upward social mobility among business leaders. But even beyond elite environments, the overall trend was rather unambiguous: social capital relations increased in number and significance. Although instrumental, these relations, it should be noted, are also charged with meaning in the postsocialist world. To many, they signify freedom and independence. To some, sustaining business ties serves as a welcome reminder that the detested era of Communist

THE SOCIAL EXPERIENCE OF THE TRANSFORMATION PERIOD

Party rule, with its deep suspicion of connections to work contacts, friends, and acquaintances abroad, is a thing of the past.[10]

Trust, to be sure, is not merely a source of economic performance. It is also an index of the quality of democracy, civic life, and social cohesion. As outlined in the historical overview in chapter 1, the revolutions of 1989 are often primarily understood in precisely this sense—as moments of political liberation, democratization, and the emergence of a civic order across Central Eastern Europe. The end of political arbitrariness and a system of police surveillance (a particularly dense network of police informers was active in the GDR and Czechoslovakia) signifies a broader opening of society. People were able to form interpersonal connections that were not steeped in suspicion and fear of denunciation, and this in turn produced new possibilities for safely confiding in others. In this sense, 1989 was truly a revolution of trust.

American sociologist Robert Putnam famously argued that associationism is the essence of civic trust. When joining civil society associations or sports clubs and cultivating social ties with others in the pursuit of a common good, individuals come together on equal ground. Strangers may become friends. This fosters people's sense of trust in society, thus improving the quality of democratic life more broadly. By some accounts, however, civic trust in fact suffered greatly in the wake of the 1989 revolutions. During the 1990s, some scholars propose that, contrary to what one might expect, people did not join voluntary organizations but instead withdrew en masse from existing civic structures. More precisely, they left those organizations that often had *mandatory* membership before the revolutions. In East Germany, trade union membership dropped by more than half between 1991 and 1997, and membership in business organizations also declined. Compared even to Russia, the extent of withdrawal in former East Germany was dramatic. As one political scientist noted shortly after the turn of the century, "average membership appears to have dropped quite sharply in that short time span, as the average East German citizen belonged to 1.44 organizations in 1995–1997, but to only 0.78 in 1999." In West Germany, the decline was only marginal during the same time. This is remarkable because it was evidently not a problem of supply: unified Germany provided a well-functioning, diverse, and publicly funded landscape of civic and interest groups, especially when compared to civic initiatives in neighboring societies in the East, which were often plagued by lack of

THE SOCIAL EXPERIENCE OF THE TRANSFORMATION PERIOD

financing and by corruption. Commenting on these trends shortly after the turn of the century then, one could easily gain the impression that, "in postcommunist societies, many people are still invested in their own private circles, and they simply feel no need, much less desire, to join and participate in civil society organizations."[11]

The picture is not all that bleak, however; East Germans do, in fact, congregate in various associations. Gardening and fishing clubs, sport associations, and cultural organizations are everywhere to be found. In 2014, there was still a smaller percentage of individuals active in voluntary associations in the east than in the rest of Germany, but the difference, in particular, to other economically less prosperous regions (such as in the northwest) was rather small.[12] The East German reluctance to join voluntary associations is closely tied to the fact that some of these organizational structures— especially in the political and economic domain, like trade unions and interest groups—have long been perceived as being dominated by West Germans and thus as imposed from above.

In the Czech Republic, we can find some similarities but also some important differences in this respect. Here, too, people turned their back to some types of organizational life. Membership in labor organizations and unions, for instance, declined from 100 percent in 1989 to a mere 24 percent of the working population in 2000.[13] Sociologists also note that other forms of civil society and volunteering flourished after the revolution; many of these activities in fact also grew out of existing structures of civic life from before 1989. The notion that associational life was merely forced upon people and that voluntarism was therefore nonexistent in socialist Czechoslovakia is really a cliché. A wide range of "old" associations of people in sports, fishing, gardening, and voluntary firefighting existed before and also after 1989; many "new" types of organizations active in the fields of human rights, education, and social and health concerns emerged after 1989, especially in urban areas.[14] The number as well as diversity of nonprofit organizations in the Czech Republic grew continuously between 1990 and 2006. This new vitality of civic associationism was inspired to some extent by the allure of the Czechoslovak dissident movement and the avowal to "live in truth" as the basis for social and associational life, but it was also a continuation of existing practices and modes of sociality.[15] According to two Czech sociologists, membership levels in civic organizations today are "lower than in Western Europe, but the Czech Republic can

THE SOCIAL EXPERIENCE OF THE TRANSFORMATION PERIOD

be considered as quite engaged among post-communist countries." This is remarkable because it means that civil society grew despite the fact that trust in the democratic system, in government, and in political institutions has decreased between the early 2000s and today.[16]

Overall, we may note that after 1989 people preferred to avoid only a specific kind of associational life, namely, the kind that they associated with "politics," a label that designates social spaces in which rules and regulations are seen as imposed from above, as well those in which economic advantages are perceived to be distributed in nontransparent ways. This is what many detested under state-socialist rule, and it is what they—selectively, based on certain ideas and images about politics—came to associate with some areas of civic life after 1989, too. Still, people could maintain a rich associational life and pursue collaboratively whatever cause they thought of as worthwhile. For East Germans, of course, volunteering was overshadowed by a lingering sense of being treated as "second-class citizens" within the very organizations of civil society. The negative idea of a political bias in civic life was intertwined with a criticism of the inner workings of West German institutions; hence, the readiness to engage in and support these organizations voluntarily was and continues to be more fragile.

The perceived distance to government institutions became readily and tragically apparent during the COVID-19 pandemic. In most Eastern European postsocialist societies, the vaccination rate remained well below that of Western Europe, despite the widespread availability of vaccines after the spring of 2021. Within Germany, the rates also remained conspicuously lower in all of the East German states—by differences, in some cases, of more than fifteen percentage points—than in the rest of the country.[17]

While levels of trust in institutions continue to be very low in this part of the world, this isn't necessarily true for trust between people. In the latter case, trust can be defined in terms of how people think about those beyond the confines of their immediate social surroundings. Sociologists call this "generalized" trust and measure it as the belief that most people in society, even strangers, can be trusted. In a global comparison, postsocialist societies display low levels of generalized trust. To understand why, scholars point to a combination of factors inherited from state-socialist times, such as the dense network of secret police surveillance, a system of informality in political and economic life, lack of accountability, corruption, and arbitrariness of political rule. There is also evidence that the time after 1989 has

THE SOCIAL EXPERIENCE OF THE TRANSFORMATION PERIOD

shaken people's sense of generalized trust and fairness. Privatization was often accompanied by large-scale corruption. To large swaths of the population, the emergence of market society appeared as yet another example of how insiders (formerly the nomenklatura, now the capitalists) were taking advantage of the common good and pocketing tax money. That said, not every social arrangement deemed to be corrupt from an outside perspective is necessarily characterized by a lack of interpersonal trust. In fact, some scholars have raised the possibility that systems of informality are indicative of high levels of everyday trust between people, although the trust may be of a different kind than the one found in Western formalized institutions.[18]

In the Czech Republic, generalized trust did not suffer greatly after 1989 and has remained relatively stable over the past twenty years. In a global comparison, Czechs can be regarded as trusting "at the medium level." Compared to other postsocialist societies, Czechs are among those "with the highest level of trust in other people."[19] Findings for East Germany suggest that generalized trust was more negatively affected than in the Czech Republic, which is, again, illustrated by comparison to trends in West Germany. One study finds that, for the period between 1991 and 2000, East Germans show significantly lower levels of generalized trust than their West German counterparts, and that distrust increased—in both areas—during this time. Germans in both parts of the country perceived the years of transformation as a challenge to social solidarity. Another study on the topic presents a somewhat different evaluation, asserting that "with regard to generalised trust, convergence has occurred between East and West Germany in the period since reunification. . . . However, eastern Germans displayed greater particularised trust than their western countrymen." In other words, according to the authors of this study, the most consequential challenge to generalized trust comes from the significance of its opposite—particularistic trust, the belief that only those who are close to the self can be trusted. Particularistic trust is observed to be more important among East Germans than their Western counterparts. This is likely linked to the experience of the transformation of the labor market after 1989 given that particularistic trust gains greater relevance under conditions of uncertainty. In sum, generalized trust evidently suffered more in East Germany than in the Czech Republic after the revolutions.[20]

There is still a problem with how social scientists have conceived of the problem of trust in this context: they have predominantly regarded it as an instrument, as a means to an end. Trust has been understood in light of its possible effects, such as bringing about social cohesion, increasing market performance, or enhancing the quality of democracy, or it has been modeled as an element of individual deliberation, a calculation of the risks and benefits of relying on someone else. But relations of trust have rarely been observed as an end in themselves, as something that people pursue because they have an intrinsic need for it.

This is a serious shortcoming. Trust is a value in itself; it is the very texture that underlies relations of recognition. We must adopt such a genuinely relational view on the matter and examine social change after 1989 in this way.

SHIFTS IN STRONG TIES AFTER 1989

A good way to begin this inquiry is to ask what we know about patterns of change to strong ties, such as family, kin, and friendship relations, after the system transition. We have seen earlier that the 1990s brought extensive demographic ruptures to the region, for example, shrinking fertility rates, decreasing marriage rates, and increasing divorce rates. So what evidence do we have for concrete patterns of change in a person's immediate social environment—and how did strong ties fare after 1989?

Unfortunately, there is a lack of sound longitudinal data to answer this question conclusively. We can only gather bits of empirical evidence from different sources and stitch them together to draw a greater picture. Doing so affords the following insight: the period of transformation and the rise of social inequality across the region did indeed affect and recalibrate strong tie networks, if in more subtle ways than one might expect. Some ties were lost; others were reinforced. Significantly, these processes are not specific to the two cases studied here. Scholars looking at Croatia or Poland, for instance, have described how class dynamics increasingly affected friendship ties after the revolutions.[21]

Let's first review what we know about shifts in the East German case. As shown earlier, the German transformation was characterized by a deep labor market crisis, a radical dissolution of former industrial structures, and high rates of out-migration. Here, competition over jobs was much more widespread and bitter than in the Czech case, leading us to expect to find more instances of ruptures in social ties. Surprisingly, however, some scholars assert that there was *no change* whatsoever in East German strong tie networks after the fall of the Berlin Wall. How do they arrive at this claim? In an article published at around the turn of the century, demographers Bernhard Nauck and Otto G. Schwenk found that the size of both East and West German networks was roughly the same in 1990 and 1996. This allowed the authors to reject the hypothesis that political and economic changes engendered large-scale change in East German family networks and to conclude that there was no "transformation effect."[22]

This was an influential assessment. In a 2005 review of the topic of East German personal networks, one sociologist, with an eye to the article in question, claimed that existing findings on network change after 1989 are inconclusive and "contradictory." In fact, Nauck and Schwenk's key assessment—that there were no ruptures in East German networks after 1989—was contradicted by a number of studies that each drew on different data sets. In a seminal study on the afterlife of "niches" in GDR society after 1989, network researchers Beate Volker and Henryk Flap documented a sharp change in strong tie relations. They found that, after the revolutions, "many relationships were broken, especially those with people one did not trust or who were foes (on average, about three relationships were broken after the revolution)." Sociologists Martin Diewald and Jörg Lüdicke also found significant shifts. Differentiating between types of relationships and types of support, they revealed that there was great continuity—a boost in cohesion even—in family and kinship ties but that ties to former colleagues, superiors, and friends became weaker between 1989 and 1993. For friendship ties, the authors reported that the "losses clearly outweigh the gains." Two more studies struck a very similar tone, corroborating specifically the finding about the duality of select processes of strengthening and weakening. They similarly concluded that shifts should not be understood processes of all-encompassing change but instead as multifaceted and often rather subtle phenomena. Hence, with respect to strong ties—family, kin, and friends—the evidence appears ambiguous at first sight.[23]

It turns out, however, that Nauck and Schwenk's approach has severe limitations. The authors drew on a data set that is known for systematically underrepresenting nonfamily ties. According to network sociologist Rainer Diaz-Bone, the measure is characterized by a "kinship-bias." There are good reasons to assume that the types of ties most likely to be affected by negative changes after 1989—nonfamily ties—were marginalized in Nauck and Schwenk's study design. The authors themselves did not look further into this issue, asserting that "friends, neighbours, and work mates played at no time an important role in the networks of East German families, not even in the end times of the GDR." Such a view can hardly be sustained given what we know about the many interconnections between workplace and friendship relations in GDR society: people did sustain various social attachments outside the family. There's arguably a greater lesson to be learned here. We must be careful not to let our sociological concepts impose a limited idea of a person's web of affiliations. Just because the meaning of friendship is less straightforward than that of kinship, we cannot leave out nonfamily relations when studying trust. We can thus garner from the available evidence a good sense of the shifts in East German strong ties: after 1989, family and kinship ties were often reinforced, but friendship and workplace ties frequently weakened.[24]

Less detailed and reliable data are available for Czech networks after 1989. The key problem here is, as pointed out by one sociologist, is that the "measurement tools of social capital like the name generator, resource generator and position generator had not been applied [before 2007]." In other words, we lack systematic longitudinal studies to trace network change over the course of the 1990s; it is not possible to make sound inferences about trends and developments in personal networks during this period. Whatever data are available points to continuity in family and friendship ties. Of course, as noted earlier, societal shifts were extensive in these domains. Here, too, the transformation fundamentally reshaped family life, accelerating demographic trends such as a decline in marriage rates, the postponement of childbirth, a substantial decline in fertility rates, and a spike in divorce rates. As detailed by one Czech study, economic stress and insecurity in the early 1990s had a negative impact on marriages. Gender dynamics played a key role: the way husbands in particular would cope with workplace insecurities had a decisive effect on social relations. But there is no evidence that the composition of ties as such had shifted. We only know for sure that a certain pattern persisted. Czech sociologists studying friendship after the revolution predominantly from a social stratification perspective found much continuity in terms of a process of social closure along class and educational backgrounds. In general, however, research on social relations outside the family is sparse. There are not many empirical

THE SOCIAL EXPERIENCE OF THE TRANSFORMATION PERIOD

cues of either strengthening or weakening with respect to various types of strong ties after 1989.[25]

In sum, we can note that the transformation has not created extensive ruptures in interpersonal networks. There is no evidence that would lend support to an overarching story of the 1990s as one of *individualization* or *atomization*, not even in Germany, where the economic shock was greater and many more people moved away than in the Czech Republic. What the data on shifts in East German strong ties reveal can be understood as two countervailing processes: one of strengthening and one of weakening of select social bonds. And these two forces do not necessarily contradict each other. The time brought individuals in their core family network closer together. In contrast, negative developments can be found in the realm of nonfamilial ties such as friends, acquaintances, and coworkers. Because it was experienced as a period of insecurity, existing strong ties gained in importance. Other relations would not stand the test of time.

How does network change and continuity shape memory of the period? The remainder of this chapter gives space to the voices of individuals who struggled with these processes and the problems of social change. While at times appearing technical and deterministic in the language of social network sociology, the concept of social change here will be elucidated using a cultural, sociological, meaning-centered approach.

Tied Together: Associating with Others

Laura is a fifty-two-year-old East German cartographer and a mother of three. She found it challenging to balance family and professional life after the fall of the Berlin Wall. She also had to cope with a short episode of unemployment. Immediately after the transition, her company, which had produced maps for the now disintegrating East German military, was taken over by a West German entrepreneur and radically downsized. Laura was laid off. The departure was a bitter experience, mainly because of the way the dismissal was communicated. She only learned about the decision to lay her off after her colleagues already had. She spent a few months looking for a new job and went through retraining programs. Laura then decided to "take matters into [her] own hands." This moment is a key episode in her biographical account:

You've got to pick yourself up! In September 1989, I went back to work. In November, that story with the breakdown of the system started, and in this situation, the military cartographic service could not exist any longer! . . . And so I took matters into my own hands! . . . You're reorienting yourself, you're ready to do something new; this was true for a lot of people in our circle of friends as well. They did it in a similar way, taking the initiative. There's this nice little saying, 'the engineer can do anything!' That was our motto. We'll do it. Even if you had to learn something new. That was where we said, we can identify with those [who are ready to do so].

After the transition, Laura was ready to embrace change, despite all the challenges and difficulties it entailed. It was not an easy time. What mattered, above all, was that she committed to an attitude of perseverance. Her acquaintances struggled with similar problems: they all had to reorient themselves professionally. Laura could relate to those who, like her, decided to confront the challenges with an open mind. Sharing this approach brought them together, creating a lasting bond between them. Her close friends today, she proudly reports, are still the very same people who shared her conviction at the time.

Her story, in other words, is about how sharing a value gained from a common experience (or, in this case, a similar way of coping with that experience) can reinforce a feeling of social cohesion. To her, it is not an abstract value but something very concrete and tangible. She presents it as a personal quality, a mark of character.

This begs the question: when confronted with a process of *external, environmental* change, why is it that one would advance the argument that *internal, essential* traits matter all the more? The social psychological theory of "personality coherence" offers an answer. Social psychologists Avshalom Caspi and Terrie E. Moffitt argue that, paradoxically, "characterological continuity is most likely to emerge during periods of social discontinuity." In times of environmental ruptures and economic uncertainty, individuals emphasize internal dispositions because this provides them with a sense of continuity and cohesion, and thus allows them to better cope with change. As popular wisdom would have it, a person's *true self* comes to light during times of hardship and crisis. Ideas about personhood, consistency of attitudes, and individual moral qualities move to the foreground. The focus

THE SOCIAL EXPERIENCE OF THE TRANSFORMATION PERIOD

on personal qualities also allows individuals to derive positive lessons from unsettling and challenging experiences.[26]

As Laura's example shows, this emphasis on moral qualities also potentially provides the grounds on which social bonds are reinforced. Laura is not the only one who thinks like this. Many want their friends to relate to their opinions about the time after the revolution. As mentioned earlier, longitudinal research has demonstrated that East Germans strengthened some select bonds, especially family and kinship ties, after 1989. Relations of support (emotional support as well as information supply) were particularly important to those who experienced unemployment or income losses. Support networks could compensate for the loss of economic stability that many people experienced during this time.

Czech respondents similarly report that shared experiences tied them together. But they tell a somewhat different story. Many point to the unifying power of relations forged during state-socialist times. They frequently refer to feelings of solidarity that were nourished by shared sentiments of defiance and distrust for the state and the Communist Party. Jan, a seventy-two-year-old engineer and architect, for instance, remembers that "the aversion to the communist elite was what tied us together. Without doubt, it was like a common enemy." Like many other Czech respondents, he remarks that it was not the time after 1989 that reinforced his ties to others because he and his associates were "already" tightly knit together before the revolution. After the revolution, many found, they could generally count on others to support them. Feelings of cohesion and solidarity with others were not put to the test to the same degree as in the East German experience of the time. We can unpack this further by examining how people remember breaks in formerly strong ties.[27]

Broken Ties: Disassociating from Others

Laura, the cartographer portrayed above, is convinced that to cope, people must show a willingness to take matters into their own hands. To her, this is not just a lesson forged during extraordinary circumstances a long time ago. It is not merely a distant memory. It continues to inspire her today and still affects how she feels about other people. She recounts the story of an acquaintance who went through long periods of unemployment after the transition and has continued to have difficulties taking up regular

THE SOCIAL EXPERIENCE OF THE TRANSFORMATION PERIOD

employment ever since. Laura is principally empathetic toward him. In her view, he cannot be blamed for being laid off immediately after the system change. After all, back then, there were higher forces at play, and East German firms everywhere were forced to close down or radically downsize. After the dust had settled and a new normal emerged, however, she evaluates his choices more critically: she detects a lack of commitment on his part. In particular, she finds fault with his demanding and somewhat petulant attitude. It weighs on their relationship:

> This person has a degree in construction, and I couldn't understand [his choice] because there was always the possibility to work somewhere as a construction engineer. It's his mentality. Say, you don't manage to hold out long in one company, then you have to assess next time you're about to be employed, how often can you challenge [others], how often do you keep it to yourself at first, collect experiences before challenging others. This is about character. You can injure yourself! . . . The relationship is fraught . . . I think he's not satisfied with his situation either; he must be a bit ashamed. When you organize a larger gathering, then everyone would go, "So, what do you do?," and he doesn't want to talk about it. So he'd rather not show up.

From Laura's perspective, this acquaintance violates the one principle she holds dear: he fails to assume personal responsibility. She cannot accept this, especially because they both have a similar degree and she is thus well aware of his potential. Emphasizing this similarity is what allows Laura to draw a meaningful link between the *then* of the time after the system change and the *now* of the continuing relevance of the commitment to take matters into your own hands. At some point, he developed a "mentality" that effectively undermined the principle of maintaining active, engaging agency. This is what cost him dearly. As Laura concludes, he failed because he did not stay committed, an outcome for which he ultimately has only himself to blame. The distance creeping into their relationship seems to reflect precisely this problem.

Is it possible that the commitments people invoke in signaling that they feel close to some people, and that they want to keep a distance from others, are about more than just dyadic interpersonal relationships? Are these actually evaluations of society at large, imbued with overarching moral and cultural meaning?

THE SOCIAL EXPERIENCE OF THE TRANSFORMATION PERIOD

To address these questions, we must explore the meaning of acts of disassociating, of breaking ties and ending relationships. This phenomenon has not received much attention in the existing social science literature, with one important exception: there is extensive sociological and psychological scholarship on divorce. Yet divorce is also very specific in that the significance of splitting up is always determined by the fact that this is a (formerly) romantic relationship. Most social relations are not based on romantic affect, but they can still end.[28]

In adopting a broader perspective, we can incorporate findings from social network scholarship. The first thing that comes to our attention—and also constitutes a key analytical benefit of studying relationship breaks—is that, compared to the act of associating, that of disassociating is much more *straightforward* and much *less ambiguous*. Social network researchers studying homophily have always struggled with the numerous reasons why a person feels close to another, ranging from identifying a soul mate to a particular definition of the nature of a friendship bond; to similarities in race, class, gender, or age; to sharing a differentiated interest in activities such as art or sports. All of these might also apply simultaneously. In contrast, the reasons why a tie is broken are generally unambiguous. When breaks in ties are charged with *negative affect*, individuals are much more likely to attach a definite meaning to them. These moments provide unique insights into the—possibly tacit—foundations of the bond. Similar to what Harold Garfinkel famously called a "breaching experiment"—an intervention that lays bare the expectations and roles that actors carry into a situation—broken social ties can serve as a window into a deeper layer behind the surface, a normative and narrative texture beneath social bonds. Let's explore these facets step by step.[29]

Maria, today in her late sixties and retired, was trained as an engineer and worked as a technologist for a state-owned company with tens of thousands of employees in Communist Party–ruled East Germany. After the fall of the Berlin Wall, her firm was radically downsized. More than half of the employees were let go within the first months alone. Maria was dismissed and couldn't find work in her field. She took on different jobs, many of them unsteady and poorly paid, and experienced periods of unemployment throughout the 1990s. She remembers how a former friend set up a small business that sold automobile replacement parts during that time, an

THE SOCIAL EXPERIENCE OF THE TRANSFORMATION PERIOD

enterprise that turned out to be quite lucrative. Maria, however, was deeply troubled by how this affected her friend's personality:

> We used to be close, we used to be true girlfriends back then [before 1989]. I sewed her wedding dress so this was a deep friendship. We also went on a young tourist trip together around the Soviet Union and the Black Sea . . . At one point [after 1989] she came to my birthday, as a surprise, but only to acquire customers for her business! She occupied my guests, my friends, in this way! So we separated; we haven't been in contact for years . . . Once we had a school reunion . . . I remember how she bragged, "I don't need to work anymore, no additional jobs, I'm making that much." She was high up in the hierarchy. I don't know if she still does that, and I don't care. So that was a case when we said, "No, I don't want you around anymore."

An emerging status difference between Maria and her former friend, a troubling disparity growing out of a formerly equal relationship, informs her story. We will return to this substantive issue below. First, we must determine on what grounds we can classify her story as a broken tie. There are some formal characteristics common to stories like this one, and isolating them will allow us to better delineate the phenomenon in conceptual terms.

Maria notes that she and her friend had "separated" at some point. She uses a word that we would expect to find in endings to romantic relationships. "Separating," much like "breaking," denotes an active, forceful, and violent moment of change to a relationship. This is important because there are other ways to talk about such shifts that convey very different meanings. Language matters in the ways these changes are portrayed. If we talk about how a relationship, for instance, "fell asleep" or "drifted apart," then the passive voice implies there was less human agency involved. We can thus, in a first step, distinguish between more active and more passive phrasing in the way relationship endings are described.

Network scholars studying tie dissolution do not make this distinction. They rely on the paradigm that human ties dissolve, most of the time, for reasons that do not involve conscious human agency. We have already seen this in the ways network scholars think about moving away, namely, as a structural cause for why affiliations change. We also saw that personal networks commonly shrink as people grow older. Thus, in this view, the underlying reasons for network change are independent of a person's intentions. People develop diverging interests, spend less time together in the same physical space, enter new social contexts that make them abandon old ones, or lose contact to individual people that connect them to others. All of these are regrettable but unavoidable changes. Georg Simmel was one of the first network scholars to drive this point home. He maintained that form determines content in social relations. According to this view, if we want to understand how and why people's affiliations change over time, we must look to structural factors—in particular, the number and frequency of possible interactions, and the number of individuals who are potentially in touch with each other. In short, nonromantic relationships end when opportunities to meet decrease.[30]

Yet Maria's narrative reveals something else. In her story of a friendship turned sour, there was agency involved. The source of change stemmed not only from the circumstances but also from her friend's way of coping with them, that is, in something conscious, animated by human willpower and deliberation. This moment revealed new aspects of their relationship. It demonstrated to Maria that something about her friend's personality had shifted. She had developed new attitudes and orientations that contradicted or supplanted her earlier ones. What troubled Maria was not the external framework of change; for better or worse, everyone had to cope with the new reality of market society. It was, instead, the personal, intimate dimension. This quality of change only becomes apparent once we regard it as part of a structure of meaning growing out of the history of a relationship— as a history of mutual expectations.

To put it into conceptually sharper terms, Maria describes not a structural but a moral type of tie dissolution. In moral tie dissolution, people assign responsibility for why the relationship took a turn for the worse. This is why we can make a distinction between "natural" and "moral" endings. A relationship that ends for moral reasons is never entirely eradicated but rather transformed into something else. And it continues to hold meaning in the present. Ruptures of ties do not merely affect social bonds but also the texture of meaning attached to them; hence, there is a need to justify and narratively reconcile the act of disassociating. Table 4.1 summarizes this difference by classifying some of the language used by respondents.[31]

Numerous stories of ties broken for moral reasons are recounted by respondents. The issue is more salient among East Germans than among

TABLE 4.1
Examples of "Natural" and "Moral" Endings

"Natural" Endings	"Moral" Endings
"Relation falling asleep"	"Separating"
"Losing sight of each other"	"Breaking off contact"
"Drifting apart"	"Distancing yourself"
"Fading away"	"Don't want to spend any more time with . . . "
"Crossing paths less frequently"	"Don't want to be associated with . . . "
"Fall by the wayside"	"Turning away"
	"Torn apart"
	"Dropping someone"
	"Avoiding each other"
	"Withdrawing"
	"Relationship died"

Czechs. We will return to this difference later. In the next section, the goals are to explore what these acts of disassociating are substantively *about* and to investigate in greater depth the meaning of instances of broken ties.[32]

SEVERING TIES FOR POLITICAL REASONS: LEGACIES OF THE POLICE STATE

Many people living in postsocialist societies today experienced decades of authoritarian rule and state terror. The way the Communist Party wielded power was based on implicating wide swaths of society—through its propaganda apparatus but also through the mechanisms of forced cooperation, denunciation, punishment for symbolic aberration, and reward for loyalty. Party elites knew how to capitalize on citizens' fear and opportunism in order to maximize their stakes in the power game. Secret police surveillance constituted a central pillar of state power in the GDR and the Czechoslovak Socialist Republic (CSR) alike. In each case, the secret police recruited a large network of informers—civilians from all walks of life—so that the state's eyes and ears could penetrate the most distant corners of everyday life and all strata of society. Secret police activity was especially pervasive in East Germany because of the large number of so-called unofficial informants (citizens pressured or lured into collaborating).

THE SOCIAL EXPERIENCE OF THE TRANSFORMATION PERIOD

In the 1980s, according to one estimate, about one person in every 180 East German citizens was working for the secret police in some capacity. In Czechoslovakia, the rate was roughly one in every 867 citizens.[33]

Enormous as these numbers might seem, they do not really shed light on the real scale and scope of secret police activities. As a tool of power, deterrence was at least as important as active persecution. One aim of constant surveillance was to sustain a certain level of distrust so that people refrained from speaking freely, from developing ties of solidarity with others, and from envisioning political alternatives. As historians note, the secret police were also notoriously inefficient: unofficial informants often produced useless information, sometimes to sabotage the investigations and to protect the subjects they had been recruited to observe. Still, acts of informing on others could have disastrous consequences. Denunciations could mean that individuals would suffer severe economic damage or social ostracization (effects that also frequently extended to a person's family and friends). For some, it meant persecution and jail time, which regularly entailed exposure to physical violence and psychological torture, and sometimes even death.[34]

After 1989, people could ascertain, often for the first time, whether someone they knew personally had been in the service of the secret police. Unpleasant truths and compromising details about friends, family, or acquaintances could come to the surface. With the so-called lustration laws enacted in the early 1990s, the German and Czechoslovak governments prioritized granting former victims of state persecution access to their files, as in the film *The Lives of Others* (German: *Das Leben der Anderen*), a 2006 German film about the Stasi surveillance in East Berlin. It was a political but also an ethical decision: the idea was that people should have the opportunity as soon as possible to take account of their past and bring to light the injustices that had affected them personally. These secret police records, however, were often spotty, incomplete, and biased; even well-trained historians had trouble determining an individual's responsibility based on these sources. The files often raised more, and deeper moral questions than they could answer: was a person lured, perhaps threatened into cooperating? Was he or she acting voluntarily, out of conviction even?[35]

Jaroslav, a Czech construction engineer in his fifties, remembers how the "opening of society," as he calls it, could strain family relationships after the revolution. Sons would find out about their fathers' entanglement with

THE SOCIAL EXPERIENCE OF THE TRANSFORMATION PERIOD

the secret police—in some cases, as he recounts, making the discovery based on names that circulated through Czech media, such as the infamous document that circulated in the 1990s known as *Cibulka's list*, a collection of names of individuals who supposedly had some connection to the secret police but whose particular functions (as well as the reason for why their names appeared on the list) were not revealed. Personal discoveries were accompanied by heated public debate, guided by the moral desire to unambiguously attribute blame and responsibility, and to assign definitively the roles of victim and perpetrator in late socialist Czechoslovakia.

The shocking revelation that a trusted person possibly had dirt on his or her hands was a realization about how the private is always uncannily political. In a sense, here, history could unfold in intimate, interpersonal bonds. In such moments, the very meaning of the pre-1989 regime was negotiated: the meaning of the past and one's view of it became a matter of loyalty and social obligation in ties of trust. Sabine is an East German nurse in her late forties who went to work in the western part of the country for a few years and returned to her East German hometown after the turn of the century. She remembers that she was, for a very long time, consumed with one question: what do people really think—what are their genuine opinions on the GDR past? Clearly, not everyone subscribed to the official narrative that dismissed the old regime. For Sabine, there was no doubt that the GDR was a brutal dictatorship, but what if some people did not acknowledge this simple truth, and what if they continued to relativize the horrors of the regime? For this reason, Sabine remembers that "the time of the transition was a strange period, a time when you did not know for sure: Who's your friend, who's your enemy?" At some point, she wanted to know whether someone had been spying on her before the revolution, so she consulted her files. In this way, she learned about the activities of certain individuals in her circle of friends and acquaintances:

In 2000, I requested my "Stasi"-File and in 2002, I received the first materials after a long inquiry. So, I immediately went there, I had the code names translated. I remembered the names, and in fact there were some people among them from my circle, people I used to know . . . There was one very close friend among them. And so, a lot of private things came to light . . . I try to understand; I try to understand why someone would turn into a

THE SOCIAL EXPERIENCE OF THE TRANSFORMATION PERIOD

secret police informer. Whether I am willing to relate is a different matter, but I try to grasp why someone would denunciate another person.

Sabine explains that she decided to act and meet up with the individuals in question because she wanted to confront them with her discovery. She was curious how they would react. This was, to her, a way to signal her openness to reflect on the past together. She wanted to know whether they were ready to talk about their motives back then—which, to Sabine, is a way to understand how a person evaluates the state-socialist past, as a whole, today. Some conversations went well. Others did not. Her former friend was "intransigent," as Sabine recalls, and so she had to sever her relation to her. The break is fully justified for Sabine today because the person failed to acknowledge her wrongdoings. While this is a personal breach of trust (after all, her actions could have had disastrous consequences for Sabine), the break is also based on a genuine political concern in the present. Sabine claims that she did not want to judge this former friend's collaboration with the police as much as she wanted her to acknowledge the true meaning of the GDR past and to denounce its injustices today.

In this process of negotiating the meaning of the past, personal and political motives are inseparable. Sabine's story demonstrates the impossibility, or, at the very least, the profound challenge of remaining on friendly terms with those who contradict one's view of the true nature of the state-socialist regime. But it is also important to acknowledge that there are other ways in which people negotiate this problem today. For some, politics has always been something distant, something beyond the personal. Svetlana, a Czech nurse in her late fifties, is a case in point. Svetlana remembers a friend of hers who was in the service of the secret police in pre-1989 Czechoslovakia and continued to work as a police officer after the Velvet Revolution. To her, this is something rather ordinary—she states that the person was merely "doing his job," both before and after the system transition. She does not attach any political meaning to his activities, nor does she question their relationship on these grounds. Perhaps she would think about it differently if she had more or better information about his activities.

A person could become implicated in the regime in many ways. For this very reason, the personal can quickly become political in the memory of the pre-1989 past today. The terror might be long gone, but the ethical challenges of coping with its many political and social ramifications are still

THE SOCIAL EXPERIENCE OF THE TRANSFORMATION PERIOD

considerable. As Marci Shore writes, "the most poignant generational question brought about by 1989 was not who has the right to claim authorship of the revolution, but rather who was old enough to be held responsible for the choices they made under the state-socialist regime."[36]

SEVERING TIES FOR ECONOMIC REASONS: THE MORALITY OF WORK

There is this strong idea—a cultural narrative almost—that the transition of 1989 revealed some deeper truth about people's innermost thoughts and attitudes. And it is not just a political orientation that is at stake here. In fact, there is very often a sense that a person's *genuine attitude towards work* was revealed under these new circumstances, that it could somehow no longer be hidden from public view. This is another aspect that stories of broken ties frequently bring to light. Robert is a sixty-one-year-old East German engineer and entrepreneur who worked as a researcher and technician at a large GDR company called *Wismut* that specialized in uranium production before the revolution. *Wismut* produced thousands of tons of uranium each year, mostly for export to the Soviet Union, where the heavy metal was used for the production of nuclear weapons and in nuclear power plants. The company had a history of forced labor and a disastrous environmental record. When it was massively downsized after German reunification, it left behind poisoned soil and polluted lakes in the hills of Saxony bordering the Czech Republic.

After the transition, Robert left the sinking ship and set up his own construction firm. It soon grew, and today he oversees a couple of offices and around 100 employees. He never had to struggle with unemployment. As he sees it, however, he was well aware of how tough the circumstances were in the early 1990s and had personally known many people who struggled. Robert remembers this period as a time that brought to light the fundamental nature of people's attitude toward work:

> We had fierce debates in our circle of friends after 1989. I myself was not fond of German unification . . . And so I told my friends, "Well, if you really want unification, then we'll have it. I can do market economy. But then we all have to move ourselves, right? Things can't continue the way they were." So some people were breaking away . . . Those who remained, they share your values. They know that you have to more or less take matters into your hand. There's

no one among them who says: "Well I got unemployed here and there, and now they should pick me up and better take care of me."

Robert broke off his ties to those who, in his eyes, failed to take responsibility for their own fate. Doing so was justified because, as he sees it, the time after 1989 offered great opportunities if one only took advantage of them. He believes that, at the time, it was imperative to "move yourself," and he mocks those who claimed that someone else should "pick up" and "take care" of them—as if it was their choice to be dependent on others. This, to him, is a deeply immoral stance; it reeks of victimization. He contends that if he had ever lost his job, he would have pulled himself up by his bootstraps by "going out and stocking shelves" at the supermarket. Robert derives a certain satisfaction from the fact that the lazy attitude of his former associates had evidently harmed them in the long run, thus proving that he had been right all along. His belief in merit is retrospectively affirmed, both by his own success as an entrepreneur and by the relative failure of those he has since removed from his circle of friends.

Robert also notes that he and his former friends never openly fought about these issues. The process of keeping oneself apart had a subtle and creeping quality to it: "After some time you gather the person has such and such views . . . and then you drop it." But the fact that he chose to let them go still informs his stance today. It is a matter of principle. Breaking ties allowed him to purify his social environment, to rid himself of the nagging sense of moral ambiguity in his circle of associates. The readiness to take matters into one's own hands is the critical lesson drawn from his personal experience of the transition time. He does not wish to have someone among his trusted ties who casts doubt on this position because this would undermine the biographical narrative that Robert has crafted for himself.

According to Robert, what justified the break was the fact that his patience and goodwill were exhausted. We already encountered this motive in Laura's story, the cartographer who successfully coped with the loss of her job after the revolution. We can see how, in both cases, a value derived from a rupturing experience in the past can continue to inform a social orientation today. Individuals ask themselves, Whose interpretations of the transformation time am I ready to endorse or, at a minimum, tolerate? Feelings of similarity or difference to other people's views are voiced and reaffirmed in this way. To use Pierre Bourdieu's language, positions

THE SOCIAL EXPERIENCE OF THE TRANSFORMATION PERIOD

are assumed in a social space, in a field of relations. For Robert, distancing himself from former friends and turning them into weak ties are symbolic acts that affirm his own position in society.

There is, however, more to this problem than the wish to affirm one's status relative to others. A logic of valuation becomes apparent here: a sense of what the right way to live after 1989 looks like. This moral grammar is laid bare in the broken tie. In the process of justifying the break, valuations of work are turned into an index of personal qualities, of character.

Talk of individual character is a moral grammar because it comes with assumptions about the nature and the legitimacy of inequality in the wider society. The act of translating economic differences into questions of character rests on two assumptions. First, according to this view, some people are inclined toward work while others are not. It posits a binary distinction between people who embrace work (people of *good* character) and those who would rather avoid it (those who allegedly *lack* character). Through this distinction, the societal dimension of this problem is radically simplified. Factors such as the different availability of work for different groups of people, the fact that different kinds of tasks have varying qualities that affect a person's health and well-being, or the various meanings a person can derive from these activities are ignored. The idea of a hardworking attitude posits that all variants of work principally have similar and comparable elements and that there is invariable substance to any kind of labor.

Second, behind the idea that some people are naturally committed to a hardworking attitude, we can find the belief that work expresses and affirms community bonds. Embracing productivity for its own sake functions as a claim to social membership, a sign that a person is not advancing egotistic motives but cares about the flourishing of others. *Not* subscribing to a hardworking attitude could come across as disregard of social obligations, as questioning fundamental values of the community. This issue is not just prevalent in this particular historical context where, until 1989, it seemed only natural that nearly every adult person, male and female, was employed full-time. Sociologists studying the social meaning of economic transactions have long argued that our ideas about the economic realm are shaped by social obligations and commitments. Economic activities—working, consuming, householding, or investing—never aim at only efficiency and performance but are also driven by social considerations, in particular, the wish to maintain social attachments. "Processes that underlie the formation, negation, reparation, or dissolution of economic relations," writes sociologist Nina Bandelj, are always codetermined by "emotions, meaning, power asymmetries." When people consciously disassociate from each other by invoking a morality of work, this intertwinement of economic expectations and moral commitments reveals itself in full force.[37] Thus, there is one elementary *social* value that surfaces in the majority of stories of broken ties charged with economic meaning: the value of equality.

Returning to Robert, for example, we can see how the meaning of equality is contested. Robert believes in hard work, and he wants all those he trusts to do so, too. Doesn't the fact that he dropped certain people from his circle of friends reveal that he esteems difference over similarity and that he embraces inequality on these grounds? This, however, is a superficial reading. Looking closer, we can see that he is really concerned with equality. The gist of his story is not that he is superior to them but instead that he is disappointed that they did not live up to their own values. They—not him—are the ones who violated a supposedly shared principle. Robert suggests that, while he was initially skeptical, it was they who embraced German unification and market society. He then followed suit: "If you really want unification, then we'll have it." Together, in this moment, they had agreed on leaving the past behind. They all wanted something new. The market was where they were going to find it. Thus, Robert's entrepreneurial success in the present is really an expression of his commitment. He managed to stay true to his ideals and to himself. Yet instead of recognizing this, his former associates began to harbor negative feelings toward him, regarding his fortunes as illegitimate and questioning his moral integrity in this way. By doing so, it was they who broke the former bond of trust and equality.

Talk of an attitude extolling hard work embraces equality in private and work relations. Sociologist Michèle Lamont has found that whenever people draw boundaries between themselves and others based on this notion—regarding themselves as hardworking, and others as deviant from this norm—other types of social differentiation, such as those based on status or taste, become less important. For this reason, according to Lamont, working-class individuals are prone to draw moral boundaries while high-status individuals tend to foreground refined manners and taste as markers of difference. The decisive element in boundaries based on a commitment to hard work is an assumed equality, not an assumed difference, between individuals.[38]

THE SOCIAL EXPERIENCE OF THE TRANSFORMATION PERIOD

It is a powerful and dynamic way of reasoning. The underlying idea is that there is, in principle, a fundamentally equal condition with regard to an individual's *disposition to work*. A person either subscribes to a hard-working attitude or fails to do so. Although this notion is an attribution of character—intrinsic and invariable—it is still based on the claim that one must *choose* to commit oneself to it. At first glance, this seems contradictory. Doesn't the idea of a deterministic predisposition of character exclude agency and voluntary choice? Thanks to the assumption of equality, these two dimensions are in fact intertwined. Hard work is a normative discourse concerned with how a person's character is formed. It requires consistency of attitudes; a person's commitment to it is not just evaluated once or at a single point in time but as part of a longer-term process. Because one can always stray or lose one's way, there is a need for continued dedication. This very fact that a person is seen as responsible for *staying true to oneself* constitutes the equally shared condition, the common ground. The idea that choice makes a difference, in the moral sense employed here, suggests that the circumstances of choosing are equal.

This way of thinking is prevalent among East Germans and Czechs, as well as among engineers and health-care workers, alike. Most respondents in this study who invoke merit and an attitude extolling the value of hard work base their reasoning on some variant of this understanding of equality.

Equality can easily be undermined. Often, the root cause of a conflict breach over economic issues is found in sentiments of envy. Verena is an East German health-care worker in her late forties who was trained as a nurse in East Germany before the fall of the Berlin Wall. Today, she heads an elder-care facility. To Verena, the experience of change in social relations after 1989 is the decisive theme in her memory of this period: "Like in a movie," she asserts, she can still see others around her at the time in rich and vivid detail, "in the very way they were dressed." It was a time of great enthusiasm, but one also had to be on the lookout. Not everyone could be trusted. Like many East Germans and Czechs, Verena's understanding of equality is informed by the experience of working in social arrangements like the *collective* before the fall of the Berlin Wall. This is a very positive memory. In her work today, she still wants to retain as much as possible the spirit of the cooperation and solidarity that the *collective* once nourished. In the way she reflects on her experience of disassociating herself from someone who used to be close to her, however, it becomes evident that

THE SOCIAL EXPERIENCE OF THE TRANSFORMATION PERIOD

there are limits to her feelings of solidarity with others. Verena remembers the loss of a former friend shortly after the Berlin Wall came down:

> I had a very good friend from school, we went through thick and thin together, then came the Wende, and then it started. She went, "You got new sneakers again!" But it was . . . really based on hard work and not just like that . . . She couldn't afford anything; she had to make every penny count at home because her parents weren't working . . . This friendship was broken by envy. I couldn't bear her always complaining anymore at some point. In the beginning I said, "Well then take my sneakers." I gave her my old sneakers so we could keep it up for another two years or so, but then I said, at some point, I don't have to do this to myself; she finally has to go and do some hard work herself, and so I quit. I never saw her again, never!

In this recounting, Verena's friend lacked initiative and failed to seize opportunities after the revolution. After trying to help her to no avail, Verena lost patience with her. Thus, ultimately, the friend has only herself to blame. The fact that their relationship had been terminated and that it is unlikely they will ever reconnect seems justified. Verena claims that this friendship was "broken by envy." This is a revealing judgment. We generally think of envy as the desire to have something that other people have. And, on the surface, this is what Verena's account of how they initially fought over an object of consumption is about—fashionable sneakers. Consumer goods such as these weren't available in the state-socialist days of queuing and rationing, and they were much sought after when the Berlin Wall came down. But the conflict seems trivial. Why risk a human relationship over an object?

Her story is arguably deeper than the problem of who gets to purchase what after 1989. It is about the violation of a value that Verena holds dear. The friend was taking advantage of her by refusing to "do some hard work herself," as she declares. She failed to show that she was ready to take matters into her own hands. The fact that she became "envious" of Verena's material possessions signals this deeper problem and violates the bond of equality that was predicated on a shared understanding of what one can legitimately expect to receive in return for one's efforts. Her lack of recognition for this value and for Verena's commitment to it is what effectively undermined the relationship. Just like in Robert's example then, the moral gist of the story is that the other person failed to live up to an expectation considered to be reasonable and right by their friend.

Envy is widely considered a morally refutable emotion, and not just in societies that have recently transitioned into market economies. To deem a person as "envious" has a powerful effect. It effectively removes the legitimate basis of a critique of inequities. Because envy is understood as rooted in the desire for things that one is not truly entitled to have, it is considered an illegitimate motive for criticizing status differences. Thus, when Verena singles out envy as the root cause of the rift in her friendship, it serves to justify the break in the relationship and to cast the outcome as the other person's failing.[39]

There is a weighty status difference at play here. Verena, the higher-status person, can level a charge against her lower-status friend. Sociologists studying culture and inequality have long been interested in how people negotiate status differences through rejecting, naturalizing, or neutralizing particular affects. This is often how people experience social inequality in their everyday lives. Pierre Bourdieu, writing at the end of the twentieth century, offered what is perhaps the most radical theoretical contribution to this problem, arguing that a person's sensuous life is determined by their position in society. For Bourdieu, engrained beliefs and dispositions— always a fusion of the affective and cognitive dimension of experience that determines a person's habitus—are shaped by struggles of status confirmation and demarcation in the social field. More recent approaches to subjective perceptions of inequality have presented a less deterministic picture by insisting that a range of sentiments can be intertwined with status dynamics. Andrew Sayer, for instance, notes that moral-economic sentiments such as benevolence, gratitude, compassion, pride, shame, envy, selfishness, vanity, sense of justice, prudence, and propriety might be charged with class and status differences—but they do not have to be, nor do they, by themselves, necessarily signal difference. While Bourdieu holds that the principal motive in status demarcations is an individual's interest in feeling better about oneself, we should embrace the possibility that a greater number of motives play a role. Among them, for instance, might be a sense of obligation toward others, rooted in the need for mutual respect. Relational sociologists and some economic sociologists concur with this position. They posit that we must study the meaningful dimension of social relations to understand how people perceive and evaluate inequality in everyday life.

Affective dispositions, they note, are always nourished in concrete webs of everyday relations.[40]

To examine how individuals link quotidian experiences and their perception of broader, society-wide disparities, we must look to how they assign meaning to their webs of social ties. Such a perspective was already elaborated in part in chapter 3, where moral grammars of deservingness were found in the stories people tell about other people's experiences after 1989. Now, we can go one step further and ask how these issues affect relations of trust. Exploring breaks in formerly strong ties offers a window into how perceptions of inequality are attached to trusted social relations.

In theorizing the moral framework in the introduction to this book, we encountered Axel Honneth's theory of social recognition, which posits that a subject's consciousness—the idea of the self—is made possible only through the bond of mutual recognition sustained to another subject. A sense of a worthy self, one capable of being valued, is expressed and affirmed through the relation to another person. People derive different types of recognition from different sources: the kind of recognition that we can gain from those who we feel *equal* to is the highest, most profound kind to be found in the social world. "Nothing that a subordinate says or does toward the dominant can match the recognition in words and deeds that an equal can give," as Sayer notes.[41]

The bond of equality is one of indispensable, vital social recognition. This is why it is gravely endangered by status differentiation. Whenever people assumed that there was a degree of equality in their relations in the past, emerging and growing asymmetries of status are perceived as singularly hurtful. When a strong tie of recognition breaks, a reinforcing source of the sense of self is lost. People feel deeply threatened by such experiences—and in coping with them, they struggle, above all, to defend their sense of self-worth.

So far, the voices of individuals who have severed ties to perceived lower-status individuals have gained the bulk of our attention. But many also tell the opposite tale—that of breaking off contact to those who experienced social upward mobility after 1989. For many, this came with the enormous cost of having negatively affected these individuals' personality. These accounts reveal the hidden injuries that come with diverging status trajectories in societies that were largely unfamiliar with social mobility before 1989. Arguably, these cases are even more multilayered than the ones

THE SOCIAL EXPERIENCE OF THE TRANSFORMATION PERIOD

discussed so far because here, individuals must protect themselves against a particularly powerful and damaging cultural charge: that of having somehow failed to master the massive redistribution of life chances after the system change of 1989.

Lenka is a Czech health-care worker in her late forties who works at the pediatric ward of a hospital specializing in plastic surgery. She was trained as a nurse in state-socialist Czechoslovakia. She remembers how the health-care system had changed dramatically after the revolution: money could suddenly be made in this field. With the rise of a profitable market for cosmetic surgery, the logic of capitalist commodification entered into her work. Soon, however, it became obvious that only some individuals—in particular, doctors offering private services—were able to profit in this market. Working at a city hospital, Lenka could only wonder about the enormous rise of wages occurring in some pockets of her field. She was also deeply troubled by the rise of competition that came with the marketization of the Czech health-care system. She saw how relations of trust among coworkers suffered from it because it became harder to rely on each other in a more competitive environment. She proudly counts herself among the "normal" people—those who stayed true to themselves and refused to join the capitalist rat race. The negative shifts not only affected her work; she could also feel these tensions in her circle of close friends. In this realm, her principled commitment was profoundly tested, as she recounts in the story of a lost friend:

> I had this very close friend twenty years ago. She suddenly—it's not that she got so rich—she started to have opinions, opinions that I could not agree with at all . . . So we separated . . . I can easily be with a friend who is doing better and better, who is successful. I can stay friends with such a person if she wants to. But the question is: will she feel like a "pleb" when she's with me, and will she treat me like that, show it also in public . . . I'm staying normal. It doesn't bother me if someone is doing better . . . but if that person shifts around, that's a problem for me.

By arguing that she does not want to make another person feel like a "pleb," an ordinary person of humble origin, she conjures a powerful class indicator. But it is Lenka, of course, who is afraid of feeling inadequate, something that other people's behavior can arouse in her. In relation to her former friend—who shares her past, who used to be close—there is a danger of feeling shame and humiliation for not having attained a comparable level of economic success after 1989. This imbalance raises the unsettling question, Was there something wrong with the choices made by her, Lenka? She insists, however, that the problem does not rest with the fact that her former friend makes more money than her today. It is not the financial difference that bothers her. Instead, she claims that this is really about an inner shift in this person's beliefs and values; specifically the fact that this former friend was apparently ready to abandon her earlier self. Lenka's critique is grounded in genuinely moral concerns. But while this allows her to fend off the charge that she is merely envious of her friend's success, the burden of proof still lies with her—she is the one who has to justify her views. She is vulnerable, and the tools of defense at her disposal are limited. The one thing she can do is to craft a narrative that protects herself from the charge that she did not put enough effort into her work after 1989.

Money corrupts a person's character, as the old adage has it. Many people with firsthand experience of the advent of market society in Central Eastern Europe would certainly agree. But what is it about money that makes it so contentious in close, trusted social ties? It is not simply the fact that some people have more of it than others. Money reveals moral boundaries; it is a sign that distinguishes beliefs and practices that are viewed as acceptable from those that are not. This is what economic sociologist Viviana Zelizer, who devoted much of her career to exploring the tension between the sphere of the market and that of intimate social relations, describes in rich detail in her work. Zelizer finds that a great number of social dynamics are unleashed wherever these two seemingly contradictory worlds collide. Historically, these were always two overlapping domains: money was never just a material quantity, never just exchangeable, impersonal, and cold, but always also a symbolic medium used to negotiate social attachment, belonging, and identity. Consequently, Zelizer writes of money not in the singular but in the plural: there exists a range of special "monies" that are earmarked for particular social purposes, such as insurance payments, allowances, inheritances, dowries, or pocket money. These different modes of monetary exchange attribute identities to their participants. They are bound by negotiated and socially accepted meanings for how money may or may not be legitimately used in the interpersonal realm. Thus,

THE SOCIAL EXPERIENCE OF THE TRANSFORMATION PERIOD

when we say that money corrupts a social relationship—such as a friendship or love relation—what we mean is that it violates something about
the specific order of meaning attached to it. We must read contestations of
money as indicative of deeper normative grammars, as surface-level conflicts that point to the depth, and the fragile texture of meaning, of social
arrangements.[42]

The bottom line, for Lenka, is that of equality. The larger relevance of
her former friend's fortunes is that they denote a kind of change she finds
challenging to grapple with. By breaking the tie, she can thus negotiate
the overarching problem of change and continuity after 1989. Some things
can be changed and surely will have to change, but there must be a substance to the relationship that should not be abandoned or dismissed.
A stable, unwavering core to a friendship tie must be preserved in order
to preserve the friendship. A sense of fundamental, unconditional equality
is indispensable—not in terms of the possession of material goods but in
terms of the possibility of mutual recognition. This understanding is what
the friend had violated. Not only did the person shift her opinions but she
also failed to acknowledge the shift in her personality and her views, thus
rejecting this idea of the substance of the relationship. She lacked respect
for the shared past, acting out of ignorance for the very grounds on which
the relationship was built. It is the act of misrecognizing the common bond
of equality in the past that Lenka ultimately cannot bear.

The wages of Czech health-care workers have increased only marginally
since 1989. As we have seen in the historical discussion in chapter 1, the
promise of social upward mobility did not materialize for individuals in
this group—except perhaps for those lucky enough to have a partner with
a well-paying job. Lenka's decision to break off the bond with her former
friend must be seen in this context. It is about her own professional aspirations after the revolution, her struggle to attain a decent standard of living.
She wants others to respect her choices, her autonomy, and her success,
which she defines as something intrinsic, as a moral type of growth. In
this sense, the break in the friendship is a genuinely personal issue charged
with economic meaning. But it is also possible to see it from the opposite
angle, as a problem of societal inequality viewed from the standpoint of the
subject living in a web of thick relations. Both readings are arguably valid
and important. A person's perception of the rise of diverging life chances
after 1989 cannot be separated from the problem of trust.

THE SOCIAL EXPERIENCE OF THE TRANSFORMATION PERIOD

There are numerous episodes similar to the one recounted by Lenka. The experience of losing contact with individuals who climbed the social ladder after the revolutions is widespread—so much so that it might well be labeled a cultural trope, a widely shared narrative about the very meaning of the transformation. In part, this already became evident in the widespread criticism of undeserved wealth after 1989 discussed in chapter 3. But as accounts of broken relationships reveal, this problem is much deeper. It is a profoundly personal issue, affecting strong and trusted ties. In observing how the unequal distribution of life chances plays out in one's immediate social environment, it is one's sense of self-worth that is at stake.

Ursula, sixty-three, whose story we have encountered in chapter 2, was educated as a technician in a large industrial combinate in state-socialist East Germany. After the system transition, she was laid off and could not find a job in her area of expertise nor could she find permanent employment. For the past thirty years, she had gone through consecutive phases of precarious employment, retraining, and periods of long-term unemployment. Today, she is close to her retirement, facing a final period of joblessness. Hers is what some German media commentators have come to call a *broken biography* after the fall of the Berlin Wall.

Yet this is not how she sees things herself. Her narrative is filled with agency, resilience, and even irony. Tongue in cheek, she reports how she was among the first recipients of an infamous welfare program introduced in Germany in the early 2000s, the so-called 1-Euro-Jobs aimed at reintegrating people into the labor market (and into low-skilled work) by heavily subsidizing their wages. To Ursula, the social experience of the transformation time was overwhelmingly positive. Still, the fact that some fared better than others in the long run did in fact put a strain on her relationships. The case of her relationship to one friend, in particular, is illustrative:

A friend of mine engaged in flights of fancy a bit after the Wende. Her husband earned some money and she received a little something through her grandma, only a bit, but you do realize how this person forgets what it was like not to have it, and how she used to be . . . These really are new types of behavior; at the restaurant she suddenly calls over the waiter three times, just because something isn't right and she's complaining, and goes like, "I deserve good things for my good money!" So that is exaggerated, because she really used to be—she comes from a poor background . . . So I stopped meeting up

THE SOCIAL EXPERIENCE OF THE TRANSFORMATION PERIOD

with her because it was unpleasant. But today, it's better because she only has a few friends left and now she is coming to her senses . . . You know, I am not like that . . . I don't begrudge others if they have work. Some get angry about it, like "Oh, these people have work and make money!" But I am not like that.

Her friend found herself with "a little something," but this is not what bothered Ursula. Instead, she was annoyed at her comportment—her haughtiness and pretension—which was hard to bear given that Ursula was more than well aware that her friend was merely performing a new role, that this was not who she really was. Just like Lenka's, Ursula's critique is based on values, not material arguments. She wants to avoid, at all costs, being seen as envious of her friend's fortune. This is why she draws a distinction between herself and people who "get angry" about the fact that others have work. That Ursula and her friend eventually managed to repair their relationship was only possible because the friend returned one step closer to her former self.

Ursula respects her friend's work ethic. Why would she make this concession in light of her own deeply disturbing experience with the labor market? Evidently, she must protect herself. Ursula must keep the risk of being personally blamed for the dire situation in which she found herself after 1989 at bay. It is one thing to be shamed by society, but it is quite another to be blamed by someone to whom one maintains a trusted relationship. There is nothing as humiliating as being held individually responsible for misfortune by a close friend. This is the moment the bond of recognition is effectively shattered. Cognizant of this problem, Ursula adds, "I must say, when you have work yourself, it is so easy to forget what it is like to be jobless. Talk is cheap! You tell yourself, well I got work, why doesn't she? And you forget that it is precisely not the case that anyone gets work if they just want to. In fact, I have to remind myself again and again. You have to be careful not to jump on the bandwagon."

This bandwagon effect is another formulation of the idea of merit. Ursula has come to accept that it is an illusion. She cannot, however, reject the very foundations on which it is grounded: the idea that economic outcomes ultimately result from inner forces, from causes that are rooted in a person's character. Ursula herself invokes moral arguments, as we have seen earlier. It is the moral change, not the material change, that bewilders her. What is more, she, too, needs recognition for what she went through—unemployment, retraining, precarious work—and the immeasurable patience that all of this required of her. This is why she cedes to the logic of hard work, the culturally dominant language of success valued by society and by her friend. To recognize her friend's economic accomplishments is the only way for her to remain committed, to acknowledge her own place in the societal game of recognition after 1989, and to write a legitimate biography for herself.

Stories like Ursula's—we might call them bottom-up breaks—are multifaceted. But they reveal one thing above all: individuals seek to retain their dignity in light of rupturing experiences at work. In the face of economic crises and hardship, this means emphasizing one's inner forces and narrating the self as an autonomous subject; for many, in means tacitly accepting the assumption that there must be a link between one's economic status in society and one's inner qualities and disposition.

To be sure, people follow different strategies to salvage their worth vis-à-vis former confidants who were lucky enough to rise socially after 1989. Some choose to call this into question, lowering the value of their qualifications, competencies, or tastes. Others present a more nuanced assessment, thus clarifying their own values, priorities, and commitments. What is common among all accounts is that they suggest a complex set of motives. Respondents are usually quick to reject the idea that their critique is driven by materialist motives. They maintain that it is not because they wanted what others had, not because of envy or frustration with another person's status advantage, that they chose to part ways with them. The sentiments involved here are multidimensional.

This is something that large swaths of sociological scholarship, which draw heavily on Bourdieu's proposition that people signal distance to others on the basis of instrumental concerns, fail to appreciate. Bourdieu contends that people use moral language to conceal their interest and that lower-status individuals follow their natural inclination to make a virtue out of a necessity. The actual content of moral sentiments is relatively unimportant in this view. But the present examples suggest that such sentiments, in and of themselves, must be taken seriously. They are real, not made-up, superficial, or dispensable, because they are nourished in existing relations of social obligations, commitments, and attachments. To theorize them as mere expressions of something else would mean discounting them and thus ultimately misrepresenting people's subjective experience of inequality.

THE SOCIAL EXPERIENCE OF THE TRANSFORMATION PERIOD

Instead, it is precisely the *power of moral worldviews* to which we need to direct our attention. What we must focus on is the vexing insight that people's strategies of retaining dignity in such conflicts is inseparable from their ability to define structural, societal problems as problems of character. To study cultural constructions of individual character is essential for understanding perceptions of inequality, but we cannot even begin to grasp it if we assume that articulations of moral sentiments are primarily a strategy for deflecting attention from material motives.

If one listens closely to stories of breaking ties to those who thrived after 1989, an identical pattern is repeated. It is the departure from *similar and equal backgrounds*, not the amount of wealth or money that others have accrued, that people find truly distressing. Experiencing the "flights of fancy," as Ursula calls it, of a former friend with similarly humble beginnings is confusing and unsettling. Differences in the present are pronounced because people measure themselves and others against a baseline condition of similarity, the idea of a more symmetrical, more balanced relationship in the past. One is forced to ask oneself: do I really want this person's recognition if his or her standards have shifted so dramatically? Was I wrong to want to be esteemed by this person in the first place? Because the departure from equality is charged with a cultural grammar of economic success or failure, it has another deeply troubling ramification: the value of personal choices made after the revolution is easily at stake. Shame and anger, as well as defiance and pride, result from this.

The loss of equality sits at the heart of strong tie ruptures. The episodes depicted reveal a desire to restore a sense of equality or, more accurately, to create a new form of equality in the relationship by establishing distance, by disassociating the self from the other. This new bond of equality is based on disregard, on the conscious withdrawing of recognition. It is a form of negatively derived but well-justified and deserved balance in the present. Avoiding or maintaining distance from another person is an act with much symbolic power. Consequently, the message conveyed must also be unambiguous: rejecting a person becomes a rejection of a moral worldview.

In comparing East German and Czech experiences, it becomes evident that the problem of disassociating and breaking ties is less aggravated in the latter case. This raises questions that concern the method of analysis: are we recording a difference in experience, or do we perhaps merely observe a difference in people's memories of the time? All in all, the disparities in

THE SOCIAL EXPERIENCE OF THE TRANSFORMATION PERIOD

structural changes in people's networks documented in the interviews for this study do reflect what information we have from representative surveys on this topic, even if, as pointed out in the beginning of this chapter, the data available for the Czech case are incomplete. By gathering the evidence available from various sources, including information about trends in "generalized trust," interpersonal trust, and demographic change discussed earlier, it is possible to infer that the transformation period was perceived less as a crisis of trust in the Czech Republic than it was in Germany. Remember also that East Germans had to cope with a deeper economic crisis, the near-total dissolution of industry, and a mass exodus of the population. They also faced a profound challenge to their very identity—the threat of being *taken over* by West German culture. None of this was true for Czechs after the Velvet Revolution. In sum, then, the greater salience of breaks among East Germans arguably reflects the more tumultuous conditions of the transition.

GENDER AND BROKEN TIES

As we have seen at several points throughout this book, a person's experience of the transformation period was decidedly shaped by gender, whether in terms of labor market opportunities, the value of one's skills after 1989, or the shifting norms in family life. Privatization, financialization, and the stratification of skills and incomes allowed the more traditional male breadwinner model to gain hold. Numerous facets of social life that make up the social—even *private*—experience of the transition are inseparable from gender dynamics. In the domains of reproductive work, such as child care and caring for the elderly, the introduction of market society after 1989 has only recalibrated existing gender inequities.

Perhaps it comes as a surprise, then, to note that episodes of broken ties can be found among both male and female respondents in this study. The way people remember breaks and imbue them with meaning really only captures a small slice of the convoluted experience of this time. Still, there are very similar patterns in how people recount these episodes. The morality of work in particular is a crucial theme in accounts of broken ties for female and for male respondents alike. How can we make sense of this?

The fact that every individual depends on others as well as the fact that autonomy can be gained only from the quality of being supported by a web of trusted social relationships are arguably universal human traits. What is often explicitly marked by gender in the realm of social relations, as American sociologist Allison Pugh argues, is that men and women may develop different styles of attachment to others. Pugh, who studies romantic partners, finds that, above all, the idea of sacrifice and duty, of signaling care for others through a commitment to work, emerges as a male trait in American society. Perhaps we can accordingly distinguish gendered styles of *detachment*?[43]

This is possible, but this is not quite what the present material reveals. Here, in the historical context of the departure from a (purportedly) emancipated, gender-equal society, an interesting similarity becomes evident: upholding the importance of a strong work ethic is not exclusively male. Women, both engineers and health-care workers, regularly emphasize their image as productive members of society. Work is a principal source of worth for them, too. We can see them fighting over these very issues in episodes of broken ties. The reality of labor market change after the revolutions has pushed women raised in Communist Party–ruled East Germany and Czechoslovakia into more traditional roles, yet they continue to draw on the discourse of work as social value that transcends the realms of the private.

SOLIDARITY

As we have seen, some were able to reinforce their bonds in the aftermath of the revolutions and often valued particular principles derived from the time as an ongoing source of social cohesion today. Others highlight the troubled experiences of friends and acquaintances after 1989, turning them into a cause for solidarity. Frank is a sixty-six-year-old East German engineer who has worked at a large optics company for more than four decades. He had experienced the transition of this company on the shop floor. It was once one of the GDR's largest state combines—with some 68,800 employees; it went through a process of massive downsizing and a West German takeover in the 1990s, eventually morphing into the global conglomerate that it is today. Frank has never experienced unemployment himself, yet he is convinced that he was just lucky to have been able to remain in his position. More generally, he believes that the capitalist labor market does not reward individual effort as much as it unequally distributes life chances in a game of bitter competition.

THE SOCIAL EXPERIENCE OF THE TRANSFORMATION PERIOD

Frank speaks on behalf of his friends, some of whom were laid off in the early 1990s and have since had to struggle with the consequences to this day. When recounting systemic changes in the post-1989 East German labor market, such as the scarcity of jobs in particular technical fields, he incorporates their experience into his own account. They are still his associates, and he takes pride in having assembled such a "diverse" set of people. But it requires great effort to sustain these ties, as he explains, "Our group of regulars consists of nine guys. Four of them did well. One only has about 800€ in pension payments . . . so we get along well, but we can't talk about money! . . . The one likes to talk about his travels, the other one can barely get by and of course he feels stupid! So I told the guy, 'You can keep that story with your travels to yourself; we've got to focus on the past and not on your travels.'"

Frank is acting on behalf of another person: he is actively mediating, or brokering, between different parties. Maintaining these bonds is by no means an easy task. Again, moral evaluations of work and the problem of having one's work biography after 1989 recognized as deserved are at the heart of the conflict he struggles with. Differences in wealth and status that emerged only after 1989 but continue to weigh on them today threaten to create rifts in their group at any moment. Frank claims that "we can't talk about money" because money symbolizes this very process of differentiation among individuals who used to be equal. Equality, again, refers to a value to which this particular group was and still remains committed. Making the disparities explicit—whether talking of travel or other pleasant retirement activities as the fruit of one's labor—is humiliating for the person who struggles to get by financially. Talk of money is intricately bound with the problem of recognition.[44]

Maintaining social relations today requires renegotiating the bonds of recognition in the present, and this in turn requires tact and consideration. The imperative to "focus on the past" in the conversations is part of this concern to reconstruct, and salvage, the former space of equality. It is different from pure nostalgia because it is concerned with practical consequences in the present, with maintaining social cohesion to facilitate smooth, unburdened interaction among friends. To do so, it is absolutely necessary to ward off stigma for those who have experienced hardship. Frank recalls that, at some point, some members of the group considered financially supporting this friend in need. They soon abandoned the idea because it would have only made explicit the asymmetry that they work so hard to conceal. Frank thinks that if they would have done so, the very offer would have questioned their friend's autonomy, in which case "he would have gone, and he wouldn't have come back."

The danger of blaming the effects of the transformation time on each other is still real and immanent, as Frank knows all too well. To him, these are really "systemic effects," but it remains challenging to negotiate them in one's everyday relations to others. For Frank, solidarity requires ensuring that this person does not feel that his confidants regard him as individually responsible for his economic hardship while still finding a way to respect his autonomy. It remains a balancing act.

Solidarity has a very specific meaning in this example. It entails avoiding breaks, salvaging social cohesion, and counteracting disintegrating forces. Solidarity here functions as a protective gesture, and it is bound to the private realm. As argued earlier in this chapter, there are other ways to think about trust and solidarity, such as generalized trust or trust in strangers, or the idea that norms of trust function like a noncontractual basis of contracts (to invoke Emile Durkheim's formulation). Situating the present example in context, it is helpful to remember that, in postsocialist societies, civic types of solidarity suffered greatly after 1989. As we saw earlier in this chapter, in East Germany, membership in civic associations such as unions and professional interest groups declined on an enormous scale in the mid- to late 1990s. The trend was less pronounced in the Czech Republic, but here, too, associational life only began to emerge decades after the Velvet Revolution. Taking stock of the postsocialist dilemma, shortly after the turn of the century, one scholar published a famous book entitled the *Defeat of Solidarity*, in which he diagnosed an extraordinary weakness of labor representation in this part of the world at the time. Today, the situation is again improving in some areas of civic life because membership rates in unions are on the rise. But it is certainly not an exaggeration to say that a key element of the transformation experience was a near-complete delegitimization of traditional leftist, universalist ideas of solidarity.[45]

Thus, it seems all the more justified to explore small social arrangements in order to illuminate how people apprehend, practice, and remember solidarity in these spaces. As we have seen, this allows us to examine the interconnection between social relations and norms of trust, and it also enables us to ask: what values do individuals make their ties to others conditional

THE SOCIAL EXPERIENCE OF THE TRANSFORMATION PERIOD

upon? What kind of commitment do they think is needed to sustain the relationship, without which it might otherwise disintegrate? These questions touch on the very fiber of an underlying moral grammar, one that is arguably not limited to a single specific tie. The normative conflict key to many of the examples discussed here—the question of assigning individual responsibility for economic failure or success—is a pattern, a set of recurring forces affecting trusted relationships. As such, it extends beyond single, isolated instances, and beyond the private realm. It is a moral problem, nourished by the social experience of the transformation time.

FRIENDSHIP AND CLASS BETRAYAL

Why is it that ties of friendship are so central in many of the accounts documented here? Friendship has a unique status among all social relations. It is impossible to define it exhaustively. Philosophers, cultural historians, and sociologist alike agree that there is at least one element common to all friendship relations: two friends choose, out of their free will, to commit themselves to each other. Unlike kinship ties, friendship ties are acquired instead of ascribed. The friendship is entered into voluntarily. This decision, summoned and symbolized in a bond of mutual recognition, serves as the basis for the commitment to one another over time. Friendship, Aristotle argued, is characterized by equality and reciprocity. These qualities are rooted in the mutual decision to form a bond in the past. And from this follows a quality that is unique to a friendship tie: because it is imagined as chosen, it can also be dissolved or lost, unlike, for instance, the bond that is based on sharing a parent with a sibling.[46]

The ideas of choice and equality give friendship a quality of freedom that is unknown even to love relations: "in friendship, friends set the term of communication; in love these are prescribed." The principle of equality creates moral symmetry, allowing each party to derive a sense of self from the relation. This is the dynamic moment of recognition—the idea that a person can approximate a higher form of consciousness of the self through the bond to another subject. A sense of self-worth is expressed and affirmed by another person. In friendship, respect and esteem are based on equal footing.[47]

Philosopher Avishai Margalit asserts that friendship is bound up with memory like no other social relation. He claims that the strength of such ties derives primarily from their "historical depth." Friendship relations are durable. Engaging with a friend provides us not so much with a specific purpose; it is a purpose in its own right: "In friendship you don't act for your sake or for your friend's sake, you act for the sake of the friendship." This goal transcends the single moment. In caring about the other person, we care about the trajectory of the relationship. This temporal dimension—evidenced, for instance, by the fact that friends do not have to prove their worth anew to each other every time they meet—provides the self with feelings of consistency over time. By engaging with a friend, we are reminded of who we used to be, who we have become, and why this change is in accord with who we want to be.[48]

According to Margalit, this special status of friendship is most clearly brought to light in instances of rupture. This is the meaning of "betrayal." The term might sooner conjure grand political associations of treasonous acts inflicted on nations, kingdoms, or communities of fate. But it also exists at the level of ordinary interpersonal relations, where it is of no less moral and cultural meaning. In the accounts of breaks we encountered in this chapter, we could see precisely the symbolic power of this ordinary level. It is marked by the unpredictability of human relations. Like surrender, betrayal is a "temporal interval," an "ending" and a "return" at the same time, a space to observe identities in transition.[49] Unlike surrender, however, it is not an exchange. Instead, betrayal starts out as a one-sided violation of a mutual commitment; it is not the other person that is violated but the relation between two persons. Only a strong tie, understood as a tie of mutual commitment, attachment, and recognition, can be betrayed. Such ties are found in family relations but especially in friendship relations. And only a tie that never had an external goal as its purpose can be betrayed. That tie must have been treated as an end in itself; it had no other goal than the flourishing of each of the two persons or, more precisely, the flourishing of the relation itself. Betrayal is the blow to the relation of commitment, which comes with a profound shock to the status of recognition of the other as a person: "the shocking discovery in betrayal is the recognition of the betrayer's lack of concern, the issue is not one's interests, but one's significance."[50]

In fact, two specific dimensions to betrayal make it particularly grave in friendship ties, and the cultural and philosophical framework allows us to see most clearly. First, it can, be understood as shattering the meaning of a shared past. Two individuals in a friendship tie engage in a mutual commitment to care about each other's past, to accept each other's past as part of their own; "you cannot stop remembering someone and continue to care for her," writes Margalit. Two friends' understandings of their past—the past of the self and the past of the other—are mutually entangled. Because it is constitutive of the relation, the shared past is "colored by the betrayal." The shared past is the source of a sense of belonging. In betrayal, something is out of place. The sense of belonging is questioned by the threat of replacement, whether "replaced by a lover, replaced by an enemy state, replaced by another god. Replacement is the nemesis of belonging." We could see this most clearly in Lenka's story, and earlier too in Maria's, in which both recount a former friend who climbed the social ladder after 1989 and began acting in a way that was perceived to misrecognize the very foundations and the uniqueness of the bond.[51]

Second, betrayal can be conceived of as an epistemic rupture in the relation. Evidence for the power of the past comes from the need to *reevaluate* the meaning of a strong tie after it has been broken. The betrayed person is left only with this option. Again, we saw this in numerous examples in this chapter in which the singular quality of the bond was retrospectively diminished, and the former friend was sometimes reduced to the status of a mere acquaintance. Reclassifying the relationship in this way is an act of exercising justice. To devalue the relation in the past, to convince oneself that someone had not been the right friend all along, is an attempt to salvage the dignity of the self.

More generally, the reevaluation of the past is a critical cultural agency after moments of loss and surrender. Indeed, when a friendship breaks, the need to reevaluate the bond of recognition and equality points to an epistemic dependency on the other person in the past. Betrayal shatters a relation and a source of knowledge about the world, transforming epistemic grounds along with the relation. It is precisely this reevaluation of the past that is taboo in maintaining friendship ties. If a person was to situationally reevaluate the significance of a friendship, it would call into question its historical gravity and consistency. In these relations, rapid turnover must be kept at bay.

Shifts in social status and different social mobility outcomes among friends engender the problem of class betrayal. Sociologists have long known that social inequalities, in particular, inequalities of class and race,

THE SOCIAL EXPERIENCE OF THE TRANSFORMATION PERIOD

are inimical to the formation of friendship ties. Cross-class friendships are hard to form and challenging to sustain. Education plays a weighty role in this. Societies with educational institutions that allow for less integration of working-class individuals, who often come from immigrant communities, also foster fewer cross-class connections. Unlike in the dramatically stratified, former Soviet Russia or Ukraine, this problem is alleviated in postsocialist Central Eastern Europe. Here, we still find, in a global comparison, relatively equal societies, with many of the cultural practices and institutional frameworks of egalitarianism in place. One the other hand, the issue is aggravated. Because the changes after 1989 were extensive and rapid, social mobility trajectories diverged greatly within a few years after the revolutions. This process unfolded against the background of a collective point of departure—the breakdown of state socialism and its given social order—in 1989. The subjective experience of societal differentiation is more concrete and tangible in this context than it is in Western societies, where structures of reproduction have been in place for many generations. This is why, in our context, the sense of change in friendship relations is read against the sense of change in wider society, and vice versa.

As discussed earlier, there is empirical proof that social mobility threatened friendship bonds during the East German transformation. We know from longitudinal studies that relations of upwardly mobile East Germans, in particular, those between coworkers and friends, suffered after 1989. Those who thrived financially and who focused on advancing their careers were likely to lose or weaken ties to former confidants. Emotional closeness decreased as society became increasingly differentiated and life chances became more unequally distributed. This was due in part to the historically specific context of a departure from GDR society, with its neat, orderly system role definitions in family and work life. Back then, everyone knew his or her place in society; now, there were suddenly many possible identities. Overall, this is a story of system change as much as one of rising social inequality. Still, it underscores that the tension between friendship and social mobility is not just a subjective feeling; it is grounded in objective, social structural patterns.[52]

Unfortunately, less conclusive evidence is available for the Czech case. There, as we have seen, sociologists have determined that friendship patterns were strongly shaped by factors such as education, gender, and age already soon after the breakdown of state socialism. The tendency toward social closure along socioeconomic factors has persisted ever since. Again, the crisis of trust was less grave in the 1990s Czech Republic than in East Germany—and this might, at least in part, explain why diverging social mobility trajectories are also perceived as less damaging here.

To be sure, the problem is not limited to these two cases. Today, across the postsocialist world, there is mounting evidence that processes of social differentiation by education, income, and wealth have affected the ways in which people conduct their friendships after the system transition.[53]

THE DESERVING SELF AS ROOTED IN NOTIONS OF EQUALITY

Frictions in formerly strong ties demonstrate that people do not treat their relationships lightly. They do not think that such ties are interchangeable or replaceable. People care deeply about bonds of trust. They want others to affirm their sense of self—this is the dialectical dynamic of social recognition. Breaks in relationships reveal this in rich detail, laying bare a normative texture of orientations that people make their strong ties conditional upon. Sociologists have often focused on how people erect boundaries between themselves and those who are different from them, particularly in terms of racial or ethnic background, income levels, or social mores and cultural tastes. In the work of Bourdieu, the perceived *distance* to another person, and the group they allegedly represent, is the very reason that social boundaries are drawn. Yet in the present case, something else became evident: these boundaries are in fact based on a condition of *similarity* and *proximity*. The very fact that people are alike—or at least used to be alike—informs the meaning of these social demarcations. This is what makes them socially consequential and imbues them with "thick" moral meaning far beyond the moment when the first cracks appeared in the relationship.[54]

As we saw, the yardstick of equality applied here is a shared bond of similarity in the past. The history of the relationship is a source of belonging; according to Margalit, "the shared past is constitutive of the relation. It is the shared past that is colored by the betrayal." What values and deeply held beliefs do they feel they must safeguard, so much so that, when these norms are violated, they feel there is no choice left but to dissolve the tie?

This commitment to the bond of equality, as we saw, is often nourished by moralized ideas of work, by values such as individual responsibility, grit, and perseverance.[55] It is a specific idea of equality. Here, the attitude

THE SOCIAL EXPERIENCE OF THE TRANSFORMATION PERIOD

toward work is seen as a genuinely social orientation, a duty toward one's community. Through it, one's membership in a given social ensemble is grounded in a principle: each and every person is on an equal footing because he or she *gains access* to this community in an identical way. Anyone can, in theory, mobilize their physical and intellectual forces to engage in productive activities, thereby signaling their readiness to be part of a social arrangement and thus to be recognized by others as a valued member of society. It is, in principle, an emancipatory, even self-transcending idea because it promises to overcome the potentially negative, harmful effect of differences between individuals. Differences might exist, but they are irrelevant for the status and the quality of social belonging. Equality makes possible social inclusion.

This is in part a legacy of egalitarianism and the "social integration through work" that shaped people's lives in East Germany and Czechoslovakia before the breakdown of state socialism. Those societies, as we saw, sacralized work, above all "productive labor." People draw on these ideas today. But it does not lead them to claim that each and everyone deserves the same outcomes. The dominant assumption is that people can *become* equal through work, that respect and social membership must be *earned* on the basis of one's contributions. This is where, as we see in people's stories, meritocratic thinking comes in. Its many unfulfilled promises and contradictions after 1989—the fact that not everyone could become a full member of society through work, that contributions were not equally valued—produces the terrifying sense that people have only themselves to blame. Those who have only themselves to blame in turn are unworthy of respect. Recognition suffers or is withdrawn altogether. Trusted relationships cannot bear this profoundly demoralizing aspect of meritocracy. As an overarching logic of social inclusion, it exerts its power over the realms of work as much as that of social relations.

ECONOMIC CHANGE AS A MATTER OF CHARACTER

Moralized ideas about work are often at the heart of these intimate conflicts. As we saw, people attach these ideas to others. There is a widespread assumption that a person's economic status after 1989 is also a reflection of his or her character. In theory, this is not what meritocratic achievement is about. People can claim to be esteemed only for what they have done,

THE SOCIAL EXPERIENCE OF THE TRANSFORMATION PERIOD

not for who they are. Yet in practice, this differentiation is obscured in the moral framework. Respondents actively made sense of other people's economic choices after 1989. Evaluating someone's agency in this way was really a statement about the quality of one's relationship and about the kind of social obligations inherent in it. We could see how, from the standpoint of the evaluating subject, the distinction between *what a person does* and *who a person is* was blurred. Because people's ideas about economic agency rest on cultural images and narratives in the moral framework, it becomes possible to treat individual dispositions and personality traits as a source of meritocratic esteem. The choices a person makes in terms of what and how to work, in particular, are regarded as an index of his or her inner qualities. Here, we encounter a notion of equality that does not contradict the principle of merit but instead can easily coexist with or even be rooted in the idea that there are some inherent traits in people that also explain and justify their economic fortunes.[56]

Social psychologists note that, in times of rapid social change, people want clarity and consistency in their relationships. They want others *to be* a certain way. Frequently, they want them to stay true to themselves—a claim that the condition of equality underlying a relationship must be maintained. "Working through the why of negative events" and "assigning responsibility for the stressful circumstances" provide narrative stability and autobiographical coherence, externalizing blame for negative developments.[57] We saw this in episodes of disassociating, in broken ties. Here, the act of asserting a moral self by invoking autobiographical consistency has a social dimension: the other person embodies an ambiguity that potentially undermines order. Recounting the act of disassociation ensures that the coherent story of the self is not polluted by this person. But we could also see how this issue transcends the realm of the psychological, how there is a profoundly cultural dimension to it. Personal dispositions, as this chapter has demonstrated, function like signs that people use to communicate something about the world. They are literally read in acts of social semiotics. In evaluating personal dispositions, people invoke moral grammars available in society and imbue an interpersonal conflict with justice ideas. They make sense of economic change through ideas of character.

Individuals cultivate the idea of a deserving self. Similar to the notion of "respectability," the concept of the deserving self treats external economic facts—both achievements and failures—as indicative of a person's internal

THE SOCIAL EXPERIENCE OF THE TRANSFORMATION PERIOD

life and character. Striving for the deserving self is to exalt those inner forces because, as Andrew Sayer puts it, "internal goods" (such as character, personal qualities, and social relations) are regarded as more fundamental than "external goods" (such as money and fame) because "we want the latter, but we also want to deserve them."[58]

We can now add a final piece to the moral framework: it is shaped by the quest to construe a deserving self, by the need for recognition as such by others, and thus by the overarching goal of social inclusion. Social relations and moral values are intertwined. The fact that people can make their attachments to others conditional on the conviction that others are personally responsible for their economic fate demonstrates that this value is inseparable from the meaning of social ties. And this sense of normative cohesion comes at a price. As evident in the narratives of individuals who disassociate themselves from others, a propensity to practice a form of *purification* of one's trusted circle—a kind of conditional solidarity—results from strong tie breaks. We could see how the feeling of similarity to some select others is predicated on excluding those who threaten or undermine one's notion of the deserving self.

The deserving self, as the gist of the moral framework, can therefore be found in relationships of trust after 1989. Individuals seek recognition for their economic achievements; they want their biographical choices to be regarded as legitimate by others. They extend this moral claim to their larger social environment and thus expect others to share and support their notion of worth in society. People want to associate with those who share their normative orientations, and they want to disassociate from those they believe cast doubt on themselves. They strive for balance, for a harmonious relationship between economic memories and their social attachments. They want to ensure that both their economic outcomes and their trusted social relations after 1989 are deserved.

EPILOGUE

How Right-Wing Populists Capture Deservingness

CULTURAL GRAMMAR

In this book, I examined how people remember momentous shifts in the realms of work and social relations in two postsocialist societies: East Germany and the Czech Republic. A key finding was that, in both of these societies, people's reasoning about change is guided by the problem of social inclusion. This is what social memory is centrally about: the way we represent the past directs our sense of where we belong; who we feel close to; and, conversely, whose life-worlds are alien to us, who we reject. The book's contribution was to show that economic memories are also informed by a cultural grammar of social inclusion and recognition.

The post-1989 period was a "restless" crisis event.[1] It was a time of sweeping political, economic, and social change, a historical juncture of the forces of democracy and soaring social inequalities. Ideas about *who deserves what* and *why* haunt people's imagination about this time today. These are moral judgments about how others coped with economic change and what they can legitimately expect in return. As we saw, people act on their sense of economic deservingness in their social network—they make the choice of who they want to associate with dependent on these ideas.

Notions of deservingness, I argued, are part of overarching meaning structures of social memory—narratives about economic agency that promote or reject certain cultural tropes about economic victimhood in the past. I call them economic memories in this book. Because they are concerned with social inclusion, economic memories are intertwined with the cultural dynamics of repair—the struggle of coping with a "tear in the social fabric," as Ron Eyerman and Jeffrey Alexander elegantly put it in their theory of cultural trauma.[2]

There is a disquieting aspect to deservingness. Our world today is profoundly uprooted by the rise of populist, authoritarian right-wing parties. Around the globe, these political movements threaten the foundations of open societies. Hostile to minorities and immigrants, they traffic in nativist ideologies and stir racist violence. They question the legitimacy of their political opponents. Once they are in government, they frequently follow words with deeds, undermining democratic institutions, the media, and the rule of law.

In postsocialist Central Eastern Europe, these movements have been thriving for some time. In Hungary and Poland, the two most prominent cases, the ascent to power of right-wing groups began after the financial crisis of 2008. In a very short time, they have become a role model for aspiring authoritarians around the world. As thinkers such as Ivan Krastev and Stephen Holmes, and Timothy Snyder have noted, when Donald Trump was elected president of the United States in 2016, the world was remade in the image of Eastern European experiences.[3]

Social scientists and the larger public continue to argue over why people vote for these parties. What makes their divisive agenda attractive to broad swaths of society? Experts have maintained that support for these parties is either rooted in cultural concerns (such as demographic angst; anti-immigrant sentiments and racism; or opposition to multiculturalism and LGBQT+ rights) or economic conditions (such as economic deprivation or fear of status loss).[4] As a growing number of observers concede, however, this binary opposition is rather limited. In everyday life, culture and economics are interlinked. Drawing on the sociology work of Emile Durkheim, Noam Gidron and Peter Hall argue, for instance, that right-wing populists exploit a popular desire for social recognition, whereby recognition is a cultural force that is not independent of economics, but it is also not determined by it.[5]

But we may ask, recognition of what, exactly? A person can feel recognized or misrecognized in various ways. Recognition does not exist in the abstract; it is always *about* something. It is sustained in concrete social relations. This is where this book's findings about the power of notions of

EPILOGUE

deservingness come in. We saw that the lack of recognition for the claim to be seen as a productive member of society is potentially a source of resentment. The contradictions of meritocracy may breed demoralization, disappointment, and a sense of social exclusion.[6] People articulate such sentiments against the background of a particular horizon of change—for example, as memories of the post-1989 period—and with reference to a meaningful web of social relations.

Scholars have often struggled to make sense of right-wing populists' economic profile. Are they for or against the market? Does their attack on globalization lead them to embrace more extensive social policies and a more encompassing, risk-channeling welfare state? In terms of policies, there are contradictions—in Donald Trump's America, tax cuts benefitted the wealthy; in authoritarian-ruled Poland, the government enacted a popular program to support poor Polish families. In terms of these actors' ideas about justice, however, their vision of *who deserves what in society* is not a paradox: the purported solutions they offer for capitalism's problems are themselves firmly rooted in a market logic, if one undergirded by conservative orientations such as family values.[7] Right-wing populists give voice to a widespread sense of disappointment with the promises of meritocracy. But they do not abandon meritocratic ideals. Instead, they claim that merit needs to be *restored* and that this can be achieved only by *purifying* the realm of the market of the negative influence of politics. Despite their anti-elitist rhetoric, these actors in fact cherish technocratic values and deploy the language of skills, competences, and practical solutions as the only legitimate forms of governance.[8]

If we look to contemporary Germany and the Czech Republic, we can see that right-wing populists invariably promote such ways of reasoning. In Germany, the nativist, authoritarian Alternative for Germany Party (AfD) has won between about 20 percent and 28 percent of the vote in the five East German regional parliaments in 2019, which is greater than its success in Western regional elections by far; in the federal elections of 2021, it has again triumphed in the East. Founded only in 2013, the party has emerged as the "populist tribune for eastern Germans."[9] AfD accentuated its anti-immigration stance during the 2015 European migrant crisis, when it could capitalize on stirring nativism and racism in the German public. But the party has never focused exclusively on either cultural or economic grievances; it has always consistently combined the two. In the Czech Republic,

CULTURE AND ECONOMY LINKED

EPILOGUE

businessman Andrej Babiš's populist Association of Dissatisfied Citizens Party (ANO; *ano* means "yes" in Czech) is the dominant political force today. ANO was founded in 2011, and after first entering parliament in 2013, the self-proclaimed "movement" grew steadily, winning an impressive 29.6 percent of the vote in 2017 and entering a governing coalition as the strongest party. While it was later defeated in the 2021 elections by a center-leftist bloc, it remains the dominant political force in the country. Babiš's business empire as well as his political career are based on oligarchic power concentration. While ANO is usually seen as more moderate than AfD in terms of its nativist agenda, it is also hostile to migrants and refugees.[10]

Politicians from both parties depict citizens as hard-working and resilient. In party programs and speeches, they deem the work of "ordinary" people as the site where value is created in society. In 2019, AfD Thuringia announced, "We are proud of the outstanding motivation and performance of our workers, engineers, scientists, employees and entrepreneurs. Their productivity is particularly commendable as Thuringia is still struggling with massive structural deficits, resulting from four decades of socialist SED [Communist Party] rule as well as a partly misguided process of reunification."

Striking a similar tone, ANO's Andrej Babiš praises Czech "resilience," "inventiveness," "creativity," and the "golden hands" of Czech workers. His vision is to "run the state like a firm." He likes to fashion himself as an "ordinary citizen" in contrast to politicians. In a defining speech, he claimed, "I offer my managerial competences . . . [My approach] will be based on consulting, on offering solutions to the economic and social problems as an alternative to the solutions sought after by political parties."[11]

AfD and ANO promote narratives that contrast the space of economics with the sphere of politics. They portray the latter as the domain where nothing of value is ever produced, where existing value is merely redistributed. Politicians from these parties regularly invoke a historical analogy between the rule of the Communist Party and post-1989 liberal democracy on these grounds: they assert that both social orders do not in fact reward *genuine* economic performance. They portray the realm of politics as inefficient, corrupt, and plagued by irrational bureaucratic regulation. They draw on memories of the 1990s, in particular of privatization. In their narrative, privatization was a disaster, not because it introduced markets but because it was plagued by corruption, mismanagement, and incompetence

EPILOGUE

on the part of politicians. In their view, it was plagued by *too much* political regulation.[12] The idea that the state grew too powerful during this period is, of course, a fantasy. As we saw, the state was in fact retreating from citizens' lives as a consequence of deregulation, financialization, and privatization after 1989. These actors are promoting in reality a cultural logic in which corruption is understood as an act of polluting the purity of the market by political action, not the other way around. This is in fact an older trope in reasoning about justice. As Robert Lane argued, "market justice" can be weaponized against "political justice" based on the assumption that the market is the *natural* way of resolving problems of redistribution, whereas politics is *artificial* and prone to reward morally undeserving individuals.[13]

To be sure, there are numerous and varied reasons why right-wing populists appeal to voters around the world today. But from our analysis of the East German and the Czech transformations and memories of both today, we can derive one proposition: when these populist actors talk about the economy, they speak the *language of deservingness*. They do so by referencing the disruptive experiences of change during the 1990s, asserting that their constituents have a moral economic right—finally, after all this time—to have their work properly valued by society.[14] Moralizing ideas of work, as we saw, also structure people's experience of the overarching processes of deindustrialization, labor market change, and revaluation of skills during the turbulent 1990s. To the extent that political actors unambiguously define who or what counts as deserved after 1989, their rhetoric resonates with the moral framework.

This analysis leaves us with many questions but also with a set of concrete implications for sociological analysis. How people experience economic change and what lessons they draw from these experiences are not predetermined. Cultural scripts that are available steer their imagination of the past—and with it, their sense of what is possible in the future.

METHODOLOGICAL APPENDIX

In qualitative research, the ways in which we approach and delineate social reality also give shape to the social ensemble that we study. Our methods must be justified in relation to the theoretical frameworks that we employ and toward that which we seek to describe, explain, and understand. In the following, I discuss the reliability of the data used in this research. I revisit issues that were already touched upon in the introduction (regarding the sample), in chapter 1 (the historical comparison), as well as in chapters 2 (personal narratives) and 4 (the memory of ruptures in social ties) from a systematic angle.

This book started out as my PhD dissertation in sociology at Yale University. The intellectual project that inspired it goes back much further. I grew up in Vienna: famously, a West European city located farther east than Prague, a place where one can overhear a multitude of Slavic languages on a typical day on the tram. In Vienna, I picked up a sense that there was an element of grand history in the lives of ordinary people in Eastern Europe. My work as an educator at a Czech memorial site and a guide for school group visits to Polish sites commemorating the victims of Nazism fostered this impression. As Marci Shore writes, "Eastern Europe is special. It is Europe, only more so. It is a place where people live and die, only more so. In these lands between Russia and the West, the past is palpable, and heavy."[1]

METHODOLOGICAL APPENDIX

I was particularly drawn to the most recent example of society-level change in the region, the dissolution of state socialism and the transition to democratic market society during the 1990s. I soon discovered, however, that most sociological and political science scholarship on the post-1989 period was primarily concerned with elites and institution building. I wanted to reconstruct these shifts from a bottom-up perspective while also keeping the bigger picture in mind. Hence, I began to immerse myself in oral history and anthropological research. These writings inspired me to elaborate a genuinely sociological perspective that relies on comparative, theory-driven analysis of everyday experiences of economic change in this book.

I employ a multidimensional research design. I compare a single, macro-level process in two cases: the transformation of society in East Germany and the Czech Republic after 1989. As I elaborate in the introduction and in chapter 2, one reason why I study these two societies is that they display numerous political and economic similarities before 1989, but they embarked on varying pathways of change after 1989. This juxtaposition allowed me to focus on the question of how the 1990s affected people's lives in different ways. My goal is not to offer a detailed account of life in the late-socialist period—this would be a different book—but to provide a more encompassing, historically anchored understanding of economic and social experiences of the transformation. My analysis is theoretically and methodologically devoted to examining the aftermath of 1989 as a critical period in history in its own right.

As I argue in the introduction, by focusing on East Germany, I depart from much of the literature that analyzes this case in relation to developments in West Germany after 1989. This comparison is sometimes based on the assumptions that the two Germanies are identical in cultural terms and that state socialism constituted a deviation from this pattern. Yet such a view downplays the extent to which four decades of Communist Party rule have decidedly shaped East German society and culture. In fact, while researching and writing this book, my conviction that we need more systematic comparisons of the German experience with that of its Central East European neighbors grew only stronger.

Why focus on the Czech Republic, but not Slovakia—after all, the two societies emerged from a single political entity, the federation of Czechoslovakia, only in 1993? This choice rests on three considerations. First, the

Slovak experience of the 1990s is somewhat closer to the East German—Slovaks went through deeper labor market shocks than did the Czechs, and, not unlike East Germans, they found themselves in a subordinate position vis-à-vis their economically more powerful neighbors in the West, in this case, the Czechs. Because the Czech and the East German experiences vary after 1989 in this respect, and because this difference is theoretically pertinent, it is the preferred lens for the comparison. Second, East Germans and Czechs share a common historical legacy of industrial society, epitomized by the manufacturing heartlands in Saxony and northwestern Bohemia. As I lay out in chapter 2, this allows me to trace how differences in the departure from an older social contract of industrial society emerge from this shared trajectory. Third, to reconstruct the Slovak transformation would have exceeded the practical boundaries of this study, which, to be sure, is an unfortunate methodological constraint because Slovak history and culture has for a long time been sidetracked, ignored, or reduced to an appendix of Czech history. This also became apparent during my fieldwork: in my interviews with Czech respondents, the Slovak perspective almost did not feature at all.

THE SAMPLE

Against the background of this historical juxtaposition, I narrow the level of analysis and trace patterns of how people make sense of economic change during the 1990s. Here, I tackle a classic sociological problem: how do personal and relational micro-level experiences of change relate to large, macro-sociological forces? Early in the project, this was the question that aroused my sociological imagination, and I kept returning to it again and again with different conceptual glasses. To explore it empirically, I draw on a sampling design that allows me to embed personal stories into a body of social science knowledge about the institutional determinants of life-course trajectories after 1989. Existing studies have demonstrated that skills and educational qualifications crucially determined individual outcomes during the turbulent period of labor market change during the 1990s in these two cases. Therefore, as I elaborate in chapter 3, respondents were drawn from two professional groups, engineers and health-care workers, whose skills were differently valued on the reconfigured labor market after 1989. The professional context also provides a common language for evaluating

METHODOLOGICAL APPENDIX

economic change because individuals who share a profession also share, to some extent at least, elements of a common practical and theoretical knowledge of the world.

Individuals who have experienced the transition as young adults were selected for this research. After running a few test interviews that helped me to refine my questionnaire, I sat down for a conversation with sixty-seven individuals from East Germany and the Czech Republic (see table A.1). Respondents were between forty-five and seventy-four years of age at the time of the research in 2016 and 2017 (fifty-eight years on average; with 82 percent of respondents between fifty and sixty-nine years of age). Respondents had finished their education, and most already had a few years of work experience by the time the revolutions arrived. Thus, they come from a generation that was somewhat advantaged relative to the one before them, whose lives were unsettled in the middle of their work biographies by the rupture of 1989.[2] The people surveyed in this book are part of the emerging middle class, which means that their experience is likely different from that of the marginalized, dispossessed, and/or racialized communities that anthropologists of postsocialism typically study. The social framing of my respondents' perspective without doubt also shapes the ways in which I link my empirical findings back to theories of morality and justice in this book.

The sample is marked by a gender disparity (see table A.1). From sixty-seven respondents, among health-care workers, all thirty respondents are female with the exception of one male health-care worker; among engineers, twelve of thirty-seven respondents are female. Because gender and profession are largely collapsed in this sample, and because this is a qualitative analysis, the implication is that these two dimensions of social identity cannot be substantively disentangled in the analysis. In narratives about

TABLE A.1
Overview of Sample, *n* = 67

		East German Respondents	Czech Respondents
Engineers	Male	15	10
	Female	8	4
Health-care Workers	Male	1	0
	Female	17	12
Total		41	26

METHODOLOGICAL APPENDIX

economic change, however, gender is a powerful cultural force, and I thus pay close attention to the gendered dimensions of language and meaning making in this book.

I contacted respondents by getting in touch with engineering offices and hospitals as well as health-care facilities (Google Maps was used to locate the facilities; individuals were contacted by sending emails, then calling). I also recruited some respondents through snowball sampling. These were predominantly cases characterized by particularly difficult economic biographies after 1989. This step, aiming at better saturation of data, was taken after it became clear that a tendency prevails for those with more successful outcomes to respond positively to interviewing requests. Not everyone was ready to talk to me, but many did respond favorably.

INTERVIEWING AND DESIGNING A SURVEY, AND ANALYZING EPISODES FROM THE PAST

In an interview study, our own identities as researchers also shape the process of data collection. We cannot leave them at the door once we enter the field. One issue that my respondents regularly inquired about was whether I was born before or after 1989. This, to many, seemed like an elementary difference. Because I was a child when state socialism still existed, there was a vague sense that I was able to relate and that I possessed a quasi-generational understanding stemming from this time—even if I, as an Austrian citizen, did not experience the dissolution of the old social order around me. Talking to East Germans of an elderly generation (many of whom still harbor negative feelings toward West Germans) perhaps fostered in me, as a person from Austria, a sense of connection. Some respondents commented on my position as that of a somewhat "neutral" observer in this constellation. Coming from a renowned U.S.-American university helped to gain access, too. In the Czech Republic, some respondents initially expressed surprise about my interest to talk about the 1990s and not to focus on the topic of migration. At the time, the refugee crisis of 2015 was a salient political issue. But once we started the interview, they, too, had many stories to tell about the transformation.

Pursuing interviews as a research instrument comes with advantages and disadvantages. One advantage is that this method potentially allows researchers to read, in Clifford Geertz's sense, "social life as a text":

interviews are powerful tools to reconstruct the meaning of the past in lived biographical experience. Interviewing can provide access to narrative accounts of social life and allow for great hermeneutical depth in the analysis. But there are also challenges that come with this method. When talking about the past in an interview, a researcher is interested in multiple things at the same time: what happened; how, and why, is it remembered; and how does the present affect respondents' memories? Some understand this multiplicity of methodological dimensions as a weakness of the method; others regard it as an opportunity for social science because it mirrors the complexity and meaning-centeredness of social life.

I combine elements of the narrative-biographical interview with the episodic interview. In narrative-biographical interviewing, we are interested in how people craft their personal story. Accounts of the past are interlinked with trajectories of the self over time; "narrating is a speech activity that involves ordering characters in space and time."[3] Hence, in the first part of the interviews, I used open-ended questions to allow respondents to generate a comprehensive biographical account. I left it to respondents to identify critical landmarks and turning points in the story.[4] Overall, this method is guided by the assumption that pathways of decisions and agency in the past ("roads not taken") can be reconstructed through the analysis of sequences in meaning structures (distinguishing the "lived life" and the "told life" with a focus on biographical agency).[5]

In the episodic parts, I focus on economic justice and social relationships.[6] How do I justify foregrounding these issues? As a general rule, in biographical interviewing, we must be careful not to impose particular interpretations and researcher-induced meanings; otherwise, we run the risk of reading preexisting theoretical assumptions from our data. When I first began this project, I was aware of a small pocket of existing research—notably, Adam Mrozowicki's 2011 monograph "Coping with Social Change" on Polish workers—that employs open, unstructured biographical methods and finds that two domains of everyday life, work and social relationships, were particularly salient for people's sense of biographical agency during the 1990s. Drawing on these insights, I felt confident about focusing on these issues in the episodic parts of the conversations because this approach allows interviewees to explore them systematically and comparatively. More recently, after I had concluded my fieldwork, a range of new oral history studies appeared that prove this assumption right, such

METHODOLOGICAL APPENDIX

as Joanna Wawrzyniak and Alexsandra Leyk's *Cuts: An Oral History of the Transformation*, Kaja Kaźmierska and Katerian Waniek's *Telling the Great Change* on Poland, and Miroslav Vaněk and Pavel Mücke's 2016 *Velvet Revolutions* on the Czech Republic.[7] Using in-depth biographical interviewing, these studies determine that the issues of economic and social change figure prominently in people's memories of the period.

Hence, I use episodic interviewing to examine these issues in depth. The episodic interview, drawing on Robert Merton's focused interview tradition,[8] carries a thematic focus into the interview process in order to document different perspectives on a specific topic (assuming that a person's perception of a topic is rooted in particular episodic experiences). Here, the researcher also takes rich narrative, experience-based accounts as the point of departure but assumes that they form the basis for processes of classification and evaluation. The goal of the episodic interview is to understand how respondents form abstract concepts around experiences, how they move from episodic to semantic knowledge.[9] I prompted respondents to share accounts of experiences and decisions of other people in their social network after 1989, thus generating accounts of classification and moral evaluation by which they position themselves vis-à-vis others.[10]

This strategy also reflects a methodological commitment that resonates with the overarching theoretical ambition of this book. Sociologists often study morality and social recognition through attitudinal surveys. Yet it makes sense to foreground people's relational experience of these phenomena. As the work of authors such as Mario Small or Matthew Desmond suggests, our methodologies must mirror the fact that social recognition is nourished in concrete, tangible networks of interpersonal connections.[11] On these grounds, I pursued a relational approach in interviewing, encouraging respondents to create accounts and explanations by comparing, contrasting, or synthesizing their own experience with others in their environment.

Asking people to share stories about what happened in the past and analyzing memories comes with additional challenges. A key issue is the retrospective nature of the data, particularly as such data are subject to recall bias.[12] I took a number of safeguards to alleviate this problem. My goal is to look into the black box of remembered economic and social change ideographically, not to derive probabilistic or nomothetic statements from it. The post-1989 transformations are times of overdetermined change.

METHODOLOGICAL APPENDIX

Seen from the perspective of retrospective event history, "causal determinants of change are not wholly predictable in their effects because the unmeasured determinants of change might be changing simultaneously."[13] In my approach, I do not try to isolate causal variables but rather to learn how participants interpret the social forces of change after 1989. The original event of, for instance, a broken friendship tie cannot retrospectively be explained by testing external causes. Instead, in the analysis, I trace how external or internal factors (such as "moral" and "natural" tie dissolution, as I discuss in chapter 5) are assigned as meaningful, life-world categories by the respondents themselves.

In addition to the interviews, I employed a closed-ended, standardized survey with an explicit focus on social relations. The survey was designed to generate comparable data in case interview data were missing or ambiguous. Its purpose is to cross-read the interview material. I use the survey data to contextualize the qualitative analysis in chapter 5. Using an online tool, I sent this survey to participants typically two weeks after the conversation to ensure that the specifics of the interview situation did not enter the survey. It was answered by sixty-one of the sixty-seven respondents.

THE POLITICS OF MEMORY AROUND
CRISIS INTERPRETATIONS

My theoretical framework took shape while developing the book and its core argumentative thrust further. *Deserved* is a book about the power of culture and social relationships in guiding our interpretations of economic change. This insight allowed me to read some of my respondents' accounts in a new light at a later stage in the project. At the same time, I came to realize, in very practical terms, that interpretations of crisis events and their aftermath are never inherently stable—that events are "restless," in Robin Wagner-Pacifici's terms.[14] The meaning of the 1990s is subject to political contestation. Right-wing populist movements in Central Eastern Europe know how to exploit the many ambiguities inherent in the memory of this period, but the full-scale Russian attack on Ukraine in 2022 arguably brought the significance of the politics of memory into full relief. Russian memory politics is obsessed with the 1990s, crafting a propaganda narrative of geopolitical *humiliation* around it while also silencing the voices of those who suffered under the decade-long Soviet terror that preceded it.

METHODOLOGICAL APPENDIX

If we are interested in the transformation period, we need to keep in mind that the process of coming to terms with the consequences of Soviet rule is not in fact over. Many societies in Europe, and certainly not just Eastern European societies, are still struggling to make sense of the legacies of political repression, ethnonationalism, social conservatism, and the complexities of interpersonal guilt and trauma left behind by the pre-1989 regimes.[15] We must continue to examine these forces. We also need rich, multidimensional accounts of the 1990s that do not equate politics and economics but that take economic inequities and their social consequences, as well as cultural interpretations of economic change, seriously. This is what animated me to write this book. In the end, I hope it is a contribution to the social science debate on culture and inequality as well as to the larger intellectual endeavor to understand the social roots of the politics of interpreting and remembering difficult pasts.

ACKNOWLEDGMENTS

I am grateful, above all, to the individuals who agreed to be interviewed for this research and who shared episodes from their life, often very personal ones, with me. They remain anonymous, but this project would not have been possible without their openness and their trust. This book grew out of my dissertation at Yale University. There, living in crisp and sun-drenched New Haven, I was lucky to have a tremendously supportive committee: Jeffrey Alexander, Julia Adams, Emily Erikson, and Marci Shore. At Yale, I was fortunate to benefit from the intellectual environment of the sociology department. Conversations at the Friday Center for Cultural Sociology workshops, made possible by Nadine Amalfi; at the Tuesday Comparative Research Workshop meetings; at the Thursday Center for Empirical Research on Stratification and Inequality; as well as at the supper club, all found their way into these pages. I am indebted to Phil Smith and Ron Eyerman in particular, to my graduate colleagues, and numerous visiting scholars for sharing their perceptive insights and allowing me to assemble ideas for this project throughout these years of scholarly and friendly exchange.

In Germany, where I was able to do research thanks to a Deutscher Akademischer Austauschdienst (DAAD) grant, I want to thank Chris Hann, Lale Yalçın-Heckmann, and Sylvia Terpe at the Max Planck Institute in

ACKNOWLEDGMENTS

Halle/Saale. Karl Ulrich Mayer, who had already left New Haven by the time I got there, welcomed me in Berlin and shared data from the East German Life History Study with me. Luise Tönhardt provided guidance in dissecting the complexities of East German identity, always in a humorous and eye-opening way. At Bremen University, where I took up a post-doctoral position in 2019, I was lucky to work with Patrick Sachweh, who supported me in countless ways. There, in this enchanting north German city, I was able to deepen the inequality angle of this book thanks to the exchanges with my wonderful colleagues in the sociology department and also the wider social science community at SOCIUM (Research Center on Inequality and Social Policy).

In the Czech Republic, my research was supported by a MacMillan International Dissertation Research Grant. I wish to thank Petr Kubala, who accompanied me to the interviews, shared his observations, and assisted me with much administrative work; and Lenka Vávrová, who helped me spice up my Czech and provided me with excellent transcriptions. Werner Binder, a fellow Yale Center for Cultural Sociology soulmate, greatly enriched my project, as did Hana Czajkowska. Muriel Blaive gave me some very valuable advice. When I returned to northeastern Bohemia, where I used to work as a *dobrovolník* (volunteer) many years ago, Jana Šmolová and Karel Rožec again, like many times before, embraced me with open arms.

I am also indebted to many individuals who supported me before I came to New Haven. In Vienna, Dieter Segert's seminar comparing the East German and Czech transition after 1989 inspired the analytical framework of this book. Heidemarie Uhl at the Austrian Academy of Sciences and my former colleagues at the nongovernmental organization Gedenkdienst sparked my interest in the forces of social memory in society.

My editors at Columbia University Press (CUP), Eric Schwartz and Lowell Frye, were truly ideal collaborators. Responsive, encouraging, and pragmatic, they were close allies in the cause of refining the manuscript. Three anonymous reviewers at CUP made invaluable suggestions that helped me to improve it further. Carly Ottenbreit, Lena Krian, and Nathan Taylor helped me to navigate the intricacies of the book-writing process in so many ways. In New Haven, and far beyond the East Coast, the friendship and companionship of Mustafa Yavas, Dana Hayward, Dicky Yangzom, and Shai Dromi held it all together. My friends in Vienna, Mainz, and Bremen

ACKNOWLEDGMENTS

deeply shaped the kinds of questions that I pursue; in fact, they only made it possible for me to become a sociologist.

Thanks go to Tom and Ren, for their lightheartedness and their love; to my brother Jan and his family in Vienna; to Liesl in magical Wachapreague and the family on the Eastern Shore. And my deepest gratitude and my love to my partner, Daniela Berner, for her sharp mind, her sincerity, and her laughter.

COPYRIGHT ACKNOWLEDGMENTS

Some parts of this book have already appeared, in abridged versions, in journal articles and book chapters. Parts of chapter 3 of this book were published in the chapter "Economic Change and the Value of Skills: East German and Czech Care Workers Remember the 1990s," Remembering the 1990s and Economic Change, edited by Veronika Pehe and Joanna Wawrzyniak (New York: Palgrave MacMillan, 2022), as well as "Economic Memories" of the Aftermath of the 1989 Revolutions in East Germany and the Czech Republic, East European Politics and Societies 35, no. 1 (2021): 89–112, https://journals.sagepub.com/doi/10.1177/0888325420902248. Segments of chapter 4 were published in the article "The Temporal Logic of Deservingness: Inequality Beliefs in Two Post-Socialist Societies," Socius: Sociological Research for a Dynamic World 5 (2019): 1–16, https://doi.org/10.1177%2F2378023119864231. Parts of chapter 5 are taken from "Culture in Network Breaks: Tie Dissolution as a Vehicle of Justice," Poetics 87 (2021): 101528, https://doi.org/10.1016/j.poetic.2020.101528. Parts of the epilogue appeared in the article "Restoring Economic Pride?: How Right-Wing Populists Moralize Economic Change," Journal of Contemporary European Studies, https://doi.org/10.1080/14782804.2022.2056729.

NOTES

INTRODUCTION

1. Quotes are taken from Allan Sekula, *Photography Against the Grain. Essays and Photo Works 1973–1983* (Halifax: Nova Scotia College of Arts and Design, 1984).
2. Jonathan B. Mijs, "The Paradox of Inequality: Income Inequality and Belief in Meritocracy Go Hand in Hand," *Socio-Economic Review* 19, no. 1 (2021): 7–35.
3. There is growing in interest in the power of narrative in economic life; see Robert J. Shiller, *Narrative Economics. How Stories Go Viral & Drive Major Economic Events* (Princeton, NJ: Princeton University Press, 2019). In relation to the historicity of social inequality, see Mike Savage, *The Return of Inequality: Social Change and the Weight of the Past* (Cambridge, MA: Harvard University Press, 2021). The concept of economic memories speaks to both strands and combines them from a cultural sociological perspective; see Jeffrey C. Alexander, "Market as Narrative and Character: For a Cultural Sociology of Economic Life," *Journal of Cultural Economy* 4, no. 4 (2011): 477–488.
4. Marci Shore, "(The End of) Communism as a Generational History: Some Thoughts on Czechoslovakia and Poland," *Contemporary European History* 18, no 3 (2009): 303–329, 319; Alexei Yurchak, *Everything Was Forever, Until It Was No More: The Last Soviet Generation* (Princeton, NJ: Princeton University Press, 2006).
5. Nina Bandelj and Christopher W. Gibson, "Contextualizing Anti-Immigrant Attitudes of East Europeans." *Review of European Studies* 12, no 3 (2020): 32–49, 32.
6. Hilary Appel and Mitchell A. Orenstein, *From Triumph to Crisis: Neoliberal Economic Reform in Postcommunist Countries* (Cambridge: Cambridge University Press, 2018), 61.
7. Ivan T. Berend, *From the Soviet Bloc to the European Union: The Economic and Social Transformation of Central and Eastern Europe Since 1973* (Cambridge: Cambridge University Press, 2009), 163.

INTRODUCTION

8. Philip Ther, *Europe Since 1989: A History* (Princeton, NJ: Princeton University Press, 2016), 82, 88.

9. Margit Tavits and Natalia Letki, "When Left Is Right: Party Ideology and Policy in Post-Communist Europe." *American Political Science Review* 103, no. 4 (2009): 555–569.

10. See Ther, *Europe Since 1989*, 120.

11. Kristen Ghodsee and Mitchell A. Orenstein, *Taking Stock of Shock: The Social Consequences of the 1989 Revolutions* (New York: Oxford University Press, 2021), 32. Particularly drastic, and in many ways far beyond what was imaginable in Central Eastern Europe, was the social shock that accompanied the Russian transformation. In Russia, around a third of the population was threatened by poverty, and life expectancy dropped by more than five years between 1990 and 1994; see Ghodsee and Orenstein, *Taking Stock of Shock*, 83. On the comparison to the United States, see Lawrence King, Gábor Scheiring, and Elias Nosrati, "Deaths of Despair in Comparative Perspective," *Annual Review of Sociology* 48 (2022): 299–322.

12. See Alexander, "Market as Narrative and Character." Here, I also draw on the rich sociological perspectives offered on emotions in the economy by Viviana A. Zelizer, *The Social Meaning of Money* (New York: Basic Books, 1998); Nina Bandelj, "Thinking About Social Relations in Economy as Relational Work," in *Re-Imagining Economic Sociology*, ed. Patrik Aspers and Nigel Dodd (Oxford: Oxford University Press), 227–251; and Fred F. Wherry, *The Culture of Markets* (Cambridge: Polity, 2012). Important contributions also come from economic anthropologists such as Stephen Gudeman and Chris Hann, *Economy and Ritual: Studies in Postsocialist Transformations* (New York: Berghahn, 2017).

13. Elisabeth C. Dunn, *Privatizing Poland: Baby Food, Big Business, and the Remaking of Labor* (Ithaca, NY: Cornell University Press, 2004); Chris Hann, "Moral(ity) and Economy: Work, Workfare and Fairness in Provincial Hungary," *European Journal of Sociology* 59, no. 29 (2018): 225–254; Martha Lampland, *The Object of Labor: Commodification in Socialist Hungary* (Chicago: University of Chicago Press, 1995); and Andreas Glaeser, *Divided in Unity: Identity, Germany, and the Berlin Police* (Chicago: University of Chicago Press, 2000).

14. The notion of individual achievement emerges against the backdrop of the dissolution of working-class milieus and the decline of solidarity, as chronicled by Eszter Bartha, *Alienating Labour: Workers on the Road from Socialism to Capitalism in East Germany and Hungary* (Oxford: Berghahn, 2013). For Hungarian society, see Gábor Scheiring, "Left Behind in the Hungarian Rustbelt: The Cultural-Political Economy of Working-Class Neo-Nationalism," *Sociology* 54, no. 6 (2020): 1159–1177. I argue in this book that certain ideational resources—such as moralized ideas of work—that existed before 1989 inform people's normative ideas about market society after 1989.

15. For instance, Grigore Pop-Eleches and Joshua A. Tucker, *Communism's Shadow: The Effect of Communist Legacies on Post-Communist Political Attitudes* (Princeton, NJ: Princeton University Press, 2017), find that individuals in postsocialist societies prioritize community obligations over individualistic achievement. At the same time, solidarity seems to be a scarce resource. Johanna Kallio and Mikko Niemelä, "Who Blames the Poor?: Multilevel Evidence of Support for and Determinants of Individualistic Explanation of Poverty in Europe," *European Societies* 16, no. 1

INTRODUCTION

(2014): 112–135, determine that citizens in this part of the world have a strong inclination to hold others individually responsible for their misfortune.

16. A classic account is Svetlana Boym, *The Future of Nostalgia* (New York: Basic Books, 2008), who distinguishes between "retrospective" (a more complacent) and "reflexive" (a more critical) form of nostalgia. In the approach I develop here, I concur with Veronika Pehe, *Velvet Retro: Postsocialist Nostalgia and the Politics of Heroism in Czech Popular Culture* (New York: Berghahn, 2020), and Joanna Wawrzyniak, "Hard Times but Our Own: Post-Socialist Nostalgia and the Transformation of Industrial Life in Poland," *Zeithistorische Forschungen/Studies in Contemporary History* 18 (2021): 73–92, who emphasize that a majority of citizens in Central Eastern Europe today do not express the wish to return to the state-socialist past because they strongly reject the politics associated with it. Consequently, we must ask, What aspects of life before 1989 people seek to salvage, selectively, and how do those references shape the experience of the transformation? Pehe and Wawrzyniak raise the possibility that people may in fact be nostalgic for the 1990s. Nostalgia is typically associated with deindustrialization (understood as the decline of manufacturing) and working-class identities. The experience of service-sector employees (in this book, I examine the experience of health care workers) has have not received much attention in the literature on deindustrialization, with the notable exception of a study by historian Gabriel Winant, *The Next Shift: The Fall of Industry and the Rise of Health Care in Rustbelt America* (Cambridge, MA: Harvard University Press, 2021).

17. Ivan Krastev and Stephen Holmes, *The Light That Failed: A Reckoning* (London: Allen Lane, 2019).

18. See, for example, Wendy Brown, *In the Ruins of Neoliberalism: The Rise of Antidemocratic Politics in the West* (New York: Columbia University Press, 2019).

19. Claus Offe, *Varieties of Transition: The East European and East German Experience* (Cambridge: Polity Press, 1996), 140.

20. For the methodology of studying shared historical trajectories and a "negative case," see Ann S. Orloff, *The Politics of Pensions: A Comparative Analysis of Britain, Canada, and the United States, 1880–1940* (Madison: University of Wisconsin Press, 1993), 30.

21. See Adam Mrozowicki, *Coping with Social Change: Life Strategies of Workers in Poland's New Capitalism* (Leuven: Leuven University Press, 2011); Miroslav Vaněk and Pavel Mücke, *Velvet Revolutions: An Oral History of Czech Society* (Oxford: Oxford University Press, 2016); Alexandra Leyk and Joanna Wawrzyniak, *Cięcia: Mówiona historia transformacji* (Warsaw: Wydawnictwo Krytyki Politycznej, 2020); Kaja Kaźmierska and Katarzyna Waniek, *Telling the Great Change: The Process of the Systemic Transformation in Poland in Biographical Perspective* (Łódź: Wydawnictwo Uniwersystetu Łódzkiego , 2020). See also Scheiring, "Left Behind in the Hungarian Rustbelt," who demonstrates that negative health outcomes as well as destabilizing political outcomes are rooted in economic experiences of change.

22. Winant, *The Next Shift*, 17.

23. See the methodological appendix for details.

24. Emile Durkheim, *The Division of Labor in Society* (New York: Simon and Schuster, 1997).

INTRODUCTION

25. Axel Honneth, *The I in We: Studies in the Theory of Recognition* (Cambridge: Polity, 2012).

26. Maurice Halbwachs, who was Jewish, was killed in the Nazi concentration camp Buchenwald in 1944. For Halbwachs, memory had a socially integrative function: recalling was to "place ourselves in the perspective of [the] group," thus viewing the "totality of thoughts common to a group." See Maurice Halbwachs, *On Collective Memory* (Chicago: University of Chicago Press, 1992), 52, 120–166. Sarah Gensburger rightly calls for a more genuinely relational reading of his work; see Sarah Gensburger, "Halbwachs' Studies in Collective Memory: A Founding Text for Contemporary 'Memory Studies'?," *Journal of Classical Sociology* 16, no. 4 (2016): 396–413.

27. For approaches to social memory studies, see Jeffrey C. Alexander, *Trauma: A Social Theory* (Hoboken, NJ: John Wiley, 2012); Ron Eyerman, *Memory, Trauma, and Identity* (New York: Palgrave, 2019); Christina Simko, "Forgetting to Remember: The Present Neglect and Future Prospects of Collective Memory in Sociological Theory," in *Handbook of Contemporary Sociological Theory*, ed. Seth Abrutyn (New York: Springer, 2016), 457–475; Jeffrey K. Olick, "Collective Memory: The Two Cultures," *Sociological Theory* 17, no 3 (2000): 333–348. For an East European theory perspective, see Michael H. Bernhard and Jan Kubik, "A Theory of the Politics of Memory," in *Twenty Years After Communism: The Politics of Memory and Commemoration*, ed. Michael H. Bernhard and Jan Kubik (New York: Oxford University Press, 2014), 7–34.

28. Howard Schumann and Amy Corning, "The Conversion of Generational Effects into Collective Memory," *International Journal of Public Opinion Research* 29, no. 3 (2016): 520–532, 526, 529. The sociological concept of generation was famously developed by Karl Mannheim, who proposed that a generation is not primarily defined by quantitative characteristics—such as being born at the same time—but rather by the shared experience of critical events.

29. See Bin Xu, "Intragenerational Variations in Autobiographical Memory: China's 'Sent-Down Youth' Generation," *Social Psychology Quarterly* 82, no. 2 (2019): 134–157.

30. Life-course researchers and economists describe cohort-specific, long-term negative labor market effects of economic crises as "scarring." Already in noncrisis times, a powerful temporal lag exists between how structural factors, such as the demand for certain skills and the availability of jobs at the time of labor market entry, affect a person's economic outcomes years later. In the wake of severe economic upheaval, fortunes of entire cohorts are upended. Long-term fallouts include blocked social upward mobility, relatively low pay, and prolonged unemployment for particular groups in society. Glen H. Elder, in his *Children of the Great Depression: Social Change in Life Experience* (Boulder, CO: Westview Press, 1999), was among the first to describe this link: a small difference in age at the time economic shock hit (the two cohorts studied by Elder were merely seven to eight years apart) made a major difference in the long-term effects on the life course. This finding has again been confirmed for the Great Recession of 2007–2009—with outcomes such as lower pay and lower chances of employment observed at the cohort level nearly a decade after the onset of the crisis. Those graduating into a turbulent labor market at the time suffered compounded and persistent disadvantages, as did those

INTRODUCTION

who happened to live in regions that were particularly badly hit by unemployment at the time. Both groups are scarred by a continuing recession hangover. Scarring, to be sure, is not about social memory; it is about legacies of institutional disadvantage; see, for instance, Danny Yagan, "Employment Hysteresis from the Great Recession," *Journal of Political Economy* 127, no 5 (2019): 2505–2558.

31. This expression was coined by Ann Swidler, "Culture in Action: Symbols and Strategies," *American Sociological Review* 51, no. 2 (1986): 273–286.

32. Isaac A. Reed and Julia P. Adams, "Culture in the Transitions to Modernity: Seven Pillars of a New Research Agenda," *Theory and Society* 40, no. 3 (2011): 247–272; Jeffrey C. Alexander, *The Meanings of Social Life. A Cultural Sociology* (Oxford: Oxford University Press, 2003); William H. Sewell, "Three Temporalities: Toward an Eventful Sociology," in *The Historic Turn in the Human Sciences*, ed. Terrence McDonnell (Ann Arbor: University of Michigan Press, 1996), 245–280. The quote is taken from Robin Wagner-Pacifici, *What Is an Event?* (Chicago: University of Chicago Press, 2017), 10–11; Mabel Berezin, "Events as Templates of Possibility: An Analytic Typology of Political Facts," in *The Oxford Handbook of Cultural Sociology*, ed. Jeffrey C. Alexander, Ronald Jacobs, and Philip Smith (New York: Oxford University Press, 2012), 613–635.

33. Edward P. Thompson, *The Making of the English Working Class* (New York: Vintage, 1963); Karl Polanyi, *The Great Transformation: The Political and Economic Origins of Our Time* (Boston: Beacon, 2001).

34. Thompson, *The Making of the English Working Class*, 63; Polanyi, *The Great Transformation*, 48. On contemporary sociological applications of this tradition, see Marion Fourcade and Kieran Healy, "Moral Views of Market Society," *Annual Review of Sociology* 33 (2007): 285–311. The concept was further developed in the realms of migration, state power, and policing by Didier Fassin, "Moral Economies Revisited," *Annales: Histoires, Science Sociales* 64 (2009): 1237–1266. Economic anthropologist Chris Hann, who has long worked on theorizing the link between morality and economy in the postsocialist context, criticizes this concept for lacking a clear application and suggests that, for the sake of consistency, we should refrain from using it altogether and instead analyze the value dimension of economic action within a Weberian framework; see Hann, "Moral(ity) and Economy." Here, I do not aim to settle the controversies around the concept; however, I contribute a new perspective by studying perceived ruptures in the social texture in an empirical way—not merely as a metaphor of the social—and reading the meanings that arise from them in light of theories of economic justice.

35. This quote is taken from Thomas C. Arnold, "Rethinking Moral Economy," *American Political Science Review* 96, no. 1 (2001): 85–95, 86.

36. The debate between Nancy Fraser and Axel Honneth systematically reveals the many interconnections between these two domains; see Nancy Fraser and Axel Honneth, *Redistribution or Recognition?: A Political-Philosophical Exchange* (London: Verso, 2003).

37. Isaac A. Reed, *Power in Modernity: Agency Relations and the Creative Destruction of the King's Two Bodies* (Chicago: University of Chicago Press, 2020).

38. See, for example, the work by Wim Van Oorschot, "Making the Difference in Social Europe: Deservingness Perceptions Among Citizens of European Welfare States," *Journal of European Social Policy* 16, no. 1 (2006): 23–42; Bart Meuleman, Femke

Roosma, and Koen Abts, "Welfare Deservingness Opinions from Heuristic to Measurable Concept: The CARIN Deservingness Principles Scale," *Social Science Research* 85 (2020): 102352. On solidarity, see Patrick Sachweh and Sebastian Koos, "The Moral Economies of Market Societies: Popular Attitudes Towards Market Competition, Redistribution and Reciprocity in Comparative Perspective," *Socio-Economic Review* 17, no. 4 (2019): 793–821.

39. See J. Stacy Adams, "Inequity in Social Exchange," *Advances in Experimental Social Psychology* 2 (1965): 267–299; and Brenda Major, "From Social Inequality to Personal Entitlement: The Role of Social Comparisons, Legitimacy Appraisals, and Group Membership," *Advances in Experimental Social Psychology* 26 (1994): 293–355.

40. As Karen Hegtvedt and Deena Isom explain, the classic example is Samuel A. Stouffer's *The American Soldier*, a study about the U.S. military conducted in the 1940s. When asked about their satisfaction with the army's promotion system, Stouffer found that solders articulated feelings of deprivation not with respect to their assessment of objective upward mobility chances but through the subjective and relative comparison to others who apparently fared better. Commenting on Stouffer, they note: "Emphasis rested on the comparison group, not rewards in the larger system." See Karen Hegtvedt and Deena Isom, "Inequality: A Matter of Justice?," in *Handbook of the Social Psychology of Inequality*, ed. Jane McLeod, Edward J. Lawler, and Michael Schwalbe (Dordrecht: Springer, 2014): 65–94, 70.

41. See, for instance, Morton Deutsch, "Equity, Equality, and Need: What Determines Which Value Will Be Used as the Basis of Distributive Justice?," *Journal of Social Issues* 31, no. 3 (1975): 137–149; Stefan Liebig and Carsten Sauer, "Sociology of Justice," in *Handbook of Social Justice Theory and Research*, ed. Clara Sabbagh and Manfred Schmitt (New York: Springer, 2016): 37–59; and the works by Daniel Miller, *Social Justice* (Oxford: Oxford University Press, 1979) and *Principles of Social Justice* (Cambridge, MA: Harvard University Press, 1999). In practice, these principles can be articulated together, so we must ask how they are weighted when related to each other.

42. Compare, for instance, the findings by Marie Duru-Bellat and Elise Tenret, "Who's For Meritocracy?: Individual and Contextual Variations in the Faith," *Comparative Education Review* 56, no. 2 (2012): 223–247, as well as Mijs, "The Paradox of Inequality."

43. Miller, *Principles of Social Justice*, 50.

44. See, for example, Van Oorschot, "Making the Difference in Social Europe," and Meuleman et al., "Welfare Deservingness Opinions."

45. Celeste Watkins-Hayes and Elyse G. Kovalsky, "The Discourse of Deservingness," in *The Oxford Handbook of the Social Science of Poverty*, ed. David Brady and Linda M. Burton (Oxford: Oxford University Press): 193–220.

46. Alexander, *Trauma*, 18–19. See also Eyerman, *Memory, Trauma, and Identity*, 5, on the notion of cultural trauma as a "tear in the social fabric," an idea that profoundly shapes my approach in this book.

47. Honneth, *The I in We*, 41.

48. On the notion of the "niche," see Beate Volker and Henk Flap, "Weak Ties as a Liability: The Case of East Germany," *Rationality and Society* 13, no. 4 (2001): 397–428, 419.

INTRODUCTION

49. Catherine Wanner, "Money, Morality and New Forms of Exchange in Postsocialist Ukraine," *Ethnos* 70, no. 4 (2005): 515–537, 531.
50. Katherine S. Newman, *Falling from Grace: The Experience of Downward Mobility in the American Middle Class* (New York: Free Press, 1988), 102–112, 135. Newman found that friendship relations were deeply affected by economic dislocation. Those who had experienced downward mobility tended to withdraw from regular meetups with friends because they were ashamed of their economic plight. Contacts dissipated because individuals no longer had the financial means to afford certain rituals of meeting up and getting together, such as hosting a dinner party or going on vacation together. Feelings of shame also entered the retrospective interpretation of these changes. As one person recalled, "Everybody stops talking to you" when economic hardship hit. Crucially, Newman showed that this was especially true among middle-class, white-collar respondents, for whom a strong expectation not to talk about one's economic troubles, including a sacred rule never to ask friends for money, prevailed. In contrast, in working-class contexts, people were more open about talking about money and economic hardship, and a certain division of labor and financial support among friends was considered normal. See Newman, *Falling from Grace*, 59, 222. The Czech study is from Joseph Hraba, Frederick O. Lorenz, and Zdeňka Pechačová, "Family Stress During the Czech Transformation," *Journal of Marriage and Family* 62, no. 2 (2000): 520–531, 529.
51. Relational sociologists emphasize the historical embeddedness of ties. In this view, individuals sense how a relationship is developing, evaluate relationship trajectories, and act on these understandings. I draw on the seminal work by Ann Mische, "Relational Sociology, Culture, and Agency," in *The Sage Handbook of Social Network Analysis*, ed. Joan Scott and Peter J. Carrington (Los Angeles: Sage, 2011): 80–97; as well as Mustafa Emirbayer, "Manifesto for a Relational Sociology," *American Journal of Sociology* 103, no. 2 (1997): 281–317. Novel and innovative approaches to culture in networks are provided by John Mohr et al., *Measuring Culture* (New York: Columbia University Press, 2020): 94–127. The links between social memory and social ties that I explore in this book also resonate with Francesca Polletta's research about how *imagining* social relationships into being in many ways drives social action and connectedness; see Francesca Polletta, *Inventing the Ties That Bind: Imagined Relationships in Moral and Political Life* (Chicago: Chicago University Press, 2020).
52. Pierre Bourdieu, *Distinction: A Social Critique of the Judgement of Taste* (Cambridge, MA: Harvard University Press, 1984). On social boundaries, see Michèle Lamont and Virag Molnár, "The Study of Boundaries in the Social Sciences," *Annual Review of Sociology* (2002): 167–195.
53. Michal Buchowski, "Property Relations, Class, and Labour in Rural Poland," in *Postsocialist Europe: Anthropological Perspectives from Home*, ed. Peter Skalnik and Lázló Kurti (New York/Oxford: Berghahn Books, 2009), 51–75; Jennifer Patico, "Spinning the Market: The Moral Alchemy of Everyday Talk in Postsocialist Russia," *Critique of Anthropology* 29, no. 2 (2009): 205–224.
54. See Emirbayer, "Manifesto for a Relational Sociology."
55. The notion of "thick" and "thin" moral concepts and quotes are from Gabriel Abend, *The Moral Background: An Inquiry into the History of Business Ethics* (Princeton, NJ: Princeton University Press, 2014), 38, 39.

INTRODUCTION

56. See, for instance, George C. Homans, *Social Behavior: Its Elementary Forms* (New York: Harcourt, Brace and World, 1974), on ideas of social balance. See also Liebig and Sauer, "Sociology of Justice," 50–51. Notably, justice research reveals that comparisons are more likely to be inspired by perceived social similarity than by social difference: There is a tendency to compare the self to those who are similar in attitudes, values, or personality traits. See Andrew Clark and Claudia Senik, "Who Compares to Whom?: The Anatomy of Income Comparisons in Europe," *The Economic Journal* 120 (2010): 573–594. Individuals look to those whose experiences they can relate to, who are proximate, and who they tend to interact with frequently rather than to distant groups. Local comparisons to colleagues or former high school friends as well as temporal comparisons to one's personal situation in the past are known to be particularly powerful in income comparisons.
57. This quote is by Wagner-Pacifici, *What Is an Event?*, 25.

1. HISTORICAL TRAJECTORIES

1. Tony Judt, with Timothy Snyder, *Thinking the Twentieth Century* (New York: Penguin, 2012), 278.
2. "Stasi in die Produktion!" "Stasi" is short for the secret police.
3. The quote is taken from Jill Massino, *Ambiguous Transitions: Gender, Everyday Life, and the State in Socialist and Postsocialist Romania* (New York: Berghahn, 2019), 3.
4. Konrad H. Jarausch, "Care and Coercion: The GDR as Welfare Dictatorship," in *Dictatorship as Experience: Towards a Socio-Cultural History of the GDR*, ed. Konrad H. Jarausch (New York: Berghahn, 1999), 47–69. For an account of state socialist modernity, see Stephen Kotkin, *Magnetic Mountain: Stalinism as a Civilization* (Berkeley: University of California Press, 1997).
5. This was the subtitle of a volume that espoused the institutionalist approach. Jon Elster, Claus Offe and Ulrich K. Preuss, *Institutional Design in Post-Communist Societies: Rebuilding the Ship at Sea* (Cambridge: Cambridge University Press, 1998).
6. The small size of its population, the Slavic traditions, and the eastward orientation in Czechoslovakia stands in contrast to the German westward orientation, its imperialist ambitions, and its perpetual condition of being "too small for the world, but too big for Europe," an expression credited to Henry Kissinger.
7. See Vladmír Macura, *The Mystifications of a Nation: "The Potato Bug" and Other Essays on Czech Culture* (Madison: University of Wisconsin Press, 2010).
8. U.S. president Woodrow Wilson had proclaimed that the future prospect of peace on the continent would rest on the principle of ethnic self-determination. The newfound Czechoslovak state at the time was a maximally heterogenous political entity: It was home to Czechs, Poles, Slovaks, Hungarians, Ruthenians, Roma, and a sizable German minority. As a truly multiethnic space, much like Central Europe as a whole, it was also a minefield for the politicization of ethnic identities. German and Austrian ethnic (*völkisch*) nationalism was on the rise. German ethnic nationalists, drawing on nineteenth-century ideologies of anti-Semitism, racism, and social Darwinism, understood how to exploit the collective sense of loss that the German public increasingly associated with the Treaty of Versailles of 1919.

1. HISTORICAL TRAJECTORIES

Hitler's rise to power—his appeal to German conservatives, who often still clung to a Prussian identity—was in no small part due to his effectiveness in denouncing the treaty as a historical injustice to Germany and as an orchestration of Jews, Communists, and capitalists who, in Hitler's fantasy, all bonded together to keep Germany deprived of power. On the multifaceted history, see Mary Heimann, *Czechoslovakia: The State That Failed* (New Haven, CT: Yale University Press, 2011).

9. The antagonism was particularly stark in the Sudetenland, the part of former Bohemia and Moravia that was home to a German-speaking minority. There, in the 1935 elections, the Nazi-friendly party *Heimatsfront/Sudetendeutsche Partei* won the largest share of the vote. Czechoslovak prime minister Edvard Beneš tried to contain tensions, counting on the support from Western allies. After Hitler annexed Austria in March 1938, the danger of a Nazi takeover of the Sudeten territories became clear to the world. At an infamous meeting in Munich in late summer of 1938 to which Beneš was not even invited, world leaders failed to protect Czechoslovak sovereignty and instead handed the Sudeten territories to Hitler. The Munich Accords, known as the "Munich betrayal" (*zrada v Mnichově*) or the "Munich dictate" in Czech, was a formative moment for Czech identity. The political unit administered by Nazi leaders and Czech collaborators in the remaining Czech territories was known as the *Protectorate Bohemia and Moravia*. After the Munich Accords, Slovakia set up its own Catholic fascist state led by Jozef Tiso under German tutelage.

10. After the beginning of the war on September 1, 1939, Jews and Roma were persecuted and imprisoned, and their possessions plundered, and tens of thousands of Czechoslovak Jews were murdered before the end of the war. Czechs were subjected to political terror, and the resistance movement was crushed. Then, after the war, as retribution for Nazi terror, the government of the third Czechoslovak Republic targeted ethnic Germans, labeling them as traitors to the nation and holding them collectively responsible for Nazi crimes. Thousands of Sudeten Germans were murdered and hundreds of thousands expelled to Germany and Austria in an act of historical retaliation.

11. While a cornerstone of Czech nationalism has long been the struggle for independence from imperial powers—Austrian, German, and later Russian—contemporary German national political mythology is organized around key events of the twentieth century, in particular the year 1945 as the beginning of democracy in this country.

12. The Czechoslovak labor movement was emboldened by the victory over Nazi Germany. The Czechoslovak Communist Party came to power by illegitimate means, but it could rely on an impressively strong electoral base. It gained around 40 percent of the vote in the first free elections in 1946 and soon turned into the largest communist party (relative to the population size) in the state-socialist world. see Bradley F. Abrams, *The Struggle for the Soul of the Nation: Czech Culture and the Rise of Communism* (Lanham, MD: Rowman & Littlefield, 2005), 53–57.

13. On differences to Poland and Hungary, see, for instance, Christoph Boyer, "Sozialgeschichte der Arbeiterschaft und Staatssozialistische Entwicklungspfade: Konzeptionelle Überlegungen und eine Erklärungsskizze," in *Arbeiter im Staatssozialismus. Ideologischer Anspruch und Soziale Wirklichkeit*, ed. Peter Hübner, Christoph Kleßmann, and Klaus Tenfelde (Cologne: Böhlau Verlag, 2005), 71–86.

1. HISTORICAL TRAJECTORIES

14. The numbers are taken from Charles Maier, *Dissolution: The Crisis of Communism and the End of East Germany* (Princeton, NJ: Princeton University Press, 1999), 20; Catherine Epstein, "The Stasi: New Research on the East German Ministry of State Security," *Kritika: Explorations in Russian and Eurasian History* 5, no. 2 (2004): 321–348; and Pavel Maškarinec, "Komparace systémových projevů totalitního panství NDR a Československa v letech 1953–1968 v rovině politického pluralismu a způsobů jeho potírání," *Slovenská politologická revue* 1 (2010): 39–58. Maškarinec argues that there was a greater toleration of "limited pluralism" in the Czechoslovak Socialist Republic (CSR). These numbers alone do not provide an exhaustive picture of the role of the secret police in everyday life. While extensive, the network of East German unofficial informants by which colleagues, friends, and even family members would snoop on each other was often far less effective than the secret police had hoped for.

15. Claus Offe notes that we may think of this, in one sense, as another similarity between the two regimes. "Both countries exhibit a low degree of national integration, if for opposite reasons. What was involved in the case of the GDR [German Democratic Republic] was less than a nation and in the CSR more than one nation, namely the coexistence of two titular nations, the Czechs and the Slovaks." Claus Offe, *Varieties of Transition: The East European and East German Experience* (Cambridge: Polity Press, 1996), 140.

16. Offe, *Varieties of Transition*, 140.

17. See Boyer, "Sozialgeschichte"; Michael Brie, "Staatssozialistische Länder Europas im Vergleich: Alternative Herrschaftsstrategien und divergente Typen," in *Einheit als Privileg: Vergleichende Perspektiven auf die Transformation Ostdeutschlands*, ed. Helmut Wiesenthal (Frankfurt: Campus, 1996), 39–104; as well as Ariane Hegewisch, Chris Brewster, and Josef Koubek, "Different Roads: Changes in Industrial and Employee Relations in the Czech Republic and East Germany Since 1989," *Industrial Relations Journal* 27, no. 1(1996): 50–64.

18. On the history of this border region, see Caitlin Murdock, *Changing Places: Society, Culture, and Territory in the Saxon-Bohemian Borderlands, 1870–1946* (Ann Arbor: University of Michigan Press, 2010). The river Labe/Elbe, which continues to the North Sea, connected the region to global shipping routes. Bohemia was known as the most industrialized part of the Austrian Empire and Saxony was, for a time, the German Reich's center of industry. Trade flourished in this tightly interconnected, multilingual, and multinational social and cultural space. The strength of the industrial sector also allowed for the emergence of an organized working class. High standards in education and medicine (a legacy of imperial rule) as well as high literacy rates created favorable conditions for political mobilization. Here, in the late nineteenth century, workers fought for collective bargaining rights, limited working hours, and basic social insurance and security schemes. For more about the nascent Bismarck-type conservative welfare state, a model that rests on profession-based social insurance schemes and conservative family politics in the form of the male breadwinner model, see Steve Saxonberg, "Eastern Europe," in *The Routledge Handbook of the Welfare State*, ed. Bent Greve (London: Routledge, 2012), 171–182. This model helped cushion some of the social shocks of industrialization in the nineteenth century. Comparatively low levels of social inequality in this region, as in other parts of Central Europe, can be understood as a longtime

1. HISTORICAL TRAJECTORIES

outcome of the success of the labor movement as well as a socially integrative force of strong public institutions such as public schools, hospitals, railroads, and roads.

19. Industrial production, long the source of private wealth of the bourgeoisie of the nineteenth and early twentieth centuries, was now controlled by the state. In Czechoslovakia, the first wave of nationalization happened right after the war and before the Communist Party takeover. Major enterprises in the mining, metallurgy, and banking sectors were nationalized in 1945. After 1948, as a general rule, any firm that employed more than fifty workers was to be owned by the state. See Jiří Večerník, *Markets and People: The Czech Reform Experience in a Comparative Perspective* (Avebury: Aldershot, 1996), 146. In the GDR, large firms were managed by the state early on, while many medium-sized and smaller firms were nationalized in the early 1970s.

20. See Anna Pollert, *Transformation at Work in the New Market Economies of Central Eastern Europe* (London: Sage, 1999), 177.

21. For Czechoslovakia, see Jaroslav Krejčí and Pavel Machonin, *Czechoslovakia 1918–92: A Laboratory for Social Change* (New York: St. Martin's Press, 1996), 199–120. For the GDR, see Holle Grünert, "Das Beschäftigungssystem der DDR," in *Arbeit, Arbeitsmarkt und Betriebe*, ed. Lutz Burkhardt (Opladen: Leske & Budrich, 1996): 19–68, 32.

22. See Brie, "Staatssozialistische Länder;" Offe, *Varieties of Transition*.

23. This rigid economic policy was an important backstory to the 1953 uprising in East Germany and the reforms attempts of the Prague Spring that were crushed in 1968. Many reform fights were, in fact, fought on the factory floor, with workers demanding more autonomy.

24. Historian Paulina Bren devotes a chapter of her book on late socialist CSR culture to this series. See Paulina Bren, *The Greengrocer and His TV: The Culture of Communism After the 1968 Prague Spring* (Ithaca, NY: Cornell University Press, 2010), 171–172. On the status of engineering, see also Ivan T. Berend, *From the Soviet Bloc to the European Union: The Economic and Social Transformation of Central and Eastern Europe since 1973* (Cambridge: Cambridge University Press, 2009), 160.

25. See Martin Kohli, "Die DDR als Arbeitsgesellschaft?: Arbeit, Lebenslauf und Soziale Differenzierung," in *Sozialgeschichte der DDR*, ed. Hartmut Kaelble, Jürgen Kocka, and Helmut Zwahr (Stuttgart: Klett-Cola 1994), 31–61.

26. In the postwar years, this resonated with wide swaths of the population. Many Czechoslovaks still had vivid memories of mass unemployment during the 1930s and embraced the creation of jobs and the promise of security on these grounds. See Miroslav Vaněk and Pavel Mücke, *Velvet Revolutions: An Oral History of Czech Society* (Oxford: Oxford University Press, 2016), 118–119.

27. See Kohli, "Die DDR als Arbeitsgesellschaft," 41.

28. Jacqui True, *Gender, Globalization, and Postsocialism: The Czech Republic After Communism* (New York: Columbia University Press, 2003), 30–31.

29. On these contradictions, see the work by Dierk Hoffmann, "Leistungsprinzip und Versorgungsprinzip. Widersprüche der DDR-Arbeitsgesellschaft," in *Sozialstaatlichkeit in der DDR: sozialpolitische Entwicklungen im Spannungsfeld von Diktatur und Gesellschaft 1945/49–1989*, ed. Dierk Hoffmann and Michael Schwartz (Munich: Oldenbourg Verlag 2005), 89–113. Incentivizing workers was the only way to increase productivity because firms were structurally immune to pressure.

1. HISTORICAL TRAJECTORIES

There was no way to sanction firms that generated low output because competition did not exist, and prices could not be used as an indicator for productivity. Plant directors knew how to simulate efficiency in order to acquiesce their supervisors. They would often request more resources than needed and strategically report under- and overvalued production capacities.

30. Kohli, "Die DDR als Arbeitsgesellschaft," 46.

31. See Dorothee Wierling, "Work, Workers, and Politics in the German Democratic Republic," *International Labor and Working-Class History*, 50 (1996): 44–63. On consumer identities and schooling, see Kerstin Brückweh, Clemens Villinger, and Kathrin Zöller, eds., *Die lange Geschichte der Wende: Geschichtswissenschaft im Dialog* (Berlin: Ch. Links Verlag, 2020). Stefan Walter compares West and East German poetry albums and finds that the materialist values of diligence and hard work were always—but notably also after the 1960s movements in the West—more pronounced among East German citizens; Stefan Walter, " 'Arbeit und Fleiß, das sind die Flügel . . ': Die Thematisierung von Arbeit und Leistung in Poesiealben der DDR und der Bundesrepublik zwischen 1945 und 1989," *AIS-Studien* 11, no. 2 (2018): 7–24.

32. Hoffmann, "Leistungsprinzip," 102.

33. A 1956 law decreed that benefits for jobless citizens could be distributed only if all means of forcing an individual into a state of regular employment were exhausted. Arnd Bauerkämper, *Die Sozialgeschichte der DDR* (Munich: Oldenbourg Wissenschaftsverlag 2005), 7.

34. True, *Gender, Globalization, and Postsocialism*, 32.

35. This is discussed by Rosie Read, "Caring Values and the Value of Care: Women, Maternalism, and Caring Work in the Czech Republic," *Contemporary European History* 28 (2019): 500–511, 501.

36. Kohli, "Die DDR als Arbeitsgesellschaft," 46, as well as Cordula Schlegelmilch, "Zwischen Kollektiv und Individualisierung-Gemeinschaftserfahrungen im Umbruch," in *Vergesellschaftung und Frauenerwerbsarbeit im Ost-West-Vergleich*, ed. Sabine Gensior (Berlin: Edition Sigma, 1995): 27–49.

37. Jiří Pokorny, "Die Betriebsklubs in der Tschechoslowakei 1945–1968: Zur Organisation sozialistischer Erziehung, Kultur und Erholung der Arbeiterschaft," in *Sozialgeschichtliche Kommunismusforschung. Tschechoslowakei, Polen, Ungarn und die DDR 1945–1968*, ed. Christiane Brenner and Peter Heumos (Munich: Oldenbourg Verlag 2005): 263–275, 265, 268.

38. The quotes are taken from Wierling, "Work, Workers, and Politics," 55, 47, as well as Bauerkämpfer, *Die Sozialgeschichte*, 14. The collective was characteristic of GDR work culture. It was supposed to foster "proletarian prowess." Members of a collective sustained relatively egalitarian relations among themselves. Collectives had a range of social and cultural functions, such as care in the private realm (elder care, and care for the sick), education, and the organization of common free-time activities. Collectives also sometimes negotiated higher wages. Based on a strong sense of loyalty and group cohesion, they could function as a "counter-milieu" to politics.

39. In the postwar years, this was a monumental achievement. Children from poor families could enter primary and secondary education. In Czechoslovakia, the policy of "leveling" wages between 1948 and 1955 resulted in the growth of the

wages of coal miners by almost 80 percent; those of ore miners by around 100 percent; while so-called intelligentsia, white-collar wages (including education, health care, and culture) declined, as documented by Richard K. Evanson, "Regime and Working Class in Czechoslovakia 1948–1968," *Soviet Studies* 37, no. 2 (1985): 248–268, 251. So-called intelligentsia work was considered inferior to that of workers and farmers. The party deemed manual labor to be the most "productive" type of labor—in the sense of usefulness to society. Male manual labor was—in symbolic terms, at least—at the top of the hierarchy (social groups were generally defined politically, not economically or sociologically, which generated many ambiguities). Overall, while the education system was heavily geared toward the priorities of industrial politics and "bureaucratic socialism," it did produce remarkable achievements: Shortly before the breakdown of state socialism, the Czechoslovak and East German workforces had achieved very high levels of education, even in a global comparison. In Czechoslovakia, the share of individuals with vocational secondary education was greater than in Poland, Hungary, or Romania. See Martin Kreidl, "Socialist Egalitarian Policies and Educational Inequality in Central Europe After World War II," *Sociologia/Slovak Sociological Review* 38, no. 3 (2006): 199–221, 205–206.

40. See Heike Solga, "The Rise of Meritocracy?: Class Mobility in East Germany Before and After 1989," in *After the Fall of the Wall: Life Courses in the Transformation of East Germany*, ed. Martin Diewald, Anne Goedicke, and Karl Ulrich Mayer (Stanford, CA: Stanford University Press), 140–169, 150.

41. On the Czechoslovak situation, see Lenka Kalinová, "Mythos und Realität des 'Arbeiterstaates' in der Tschechoslowakei," in *Arbeiter im Staatssozialismus. Ideologischer Anspruch und Soziale Wirklichkeit*, ed. Peter Hübner, Christoph Kleßmann, and Klaus Tenfelde (Cologne: Böhlau Verlag 2005), 87–107.

42. Shortly before 1989, the percentage of students in the humanities was a mere 1.2 in Czechoslovakia and 2.1 in East Germany (compared to about 8.8 in Poland), as noted by Aviezer Tucker, *The Legacies of Totalitarianism: A Theoretical Framework* (Cambridge: Cambridge University Press, 2015), 183. After 1968, in Czechoslovakia, party functionaries were no longer recruited from the working class but from well-connected and well-educated families, often with academic credentials. The expansion of higher education, characteristic for Western industrial societies of the 1960s and 1970s, never happened here: while the number of students per 10.000 inhabitants nearly tripled between 1965 and 1980 in West Germany, it grew only marginally in East Germany during the same period; see Steffen Mau, *Lütten-Klein: Leben in der ostdeutschen Transformationsgesellschaft* (Berlin: Suhrkamp, 2019), 56.

43. Vaněk and Mücke 2016, *Velvet Revolutions*, and Mau, *Lütten-Klein*, 37.

44. This quote is taken from Michal Pullmann, " 'Ruhige Arbeit' und Einhegung der Gewalt. Ideologie und Gesellschaftlicher Konsens in der Spätsozialistischen Tschechoslowakei," in *Ordnung und Sicherheit, Devianz und Kriminalität im Staatssozialismus: Tschechoslowakei und DDR 1948/49–1989*, ed. Volker Zimmermann and Michal Pullman (Göttingen: Vandenhoeck & Ruprecht 2014), 39–59, 39.

45. The punitive measures did not just target individuals but also their families and friends. Families of politically suspect persons were systematically punished, for instance, by restricting a child's access to higher education, see Kalinová, "Mythos und Realität," 105.

1. HISTORICAL TRAJECTORIES

46. The period of normalization in Czechoslovakia is often understood as society's withdrawal into the private sphere. Challenging this notion of an opposition between politics and the private realm, historian Paulina Bren labels the social contract of the time a "privatized citizenship." In her view, the two domains were connected in subtle ways. Normalization, she argues, "did not leave the private sphere alone; and in addition, it sought to domesticate the public realm" (Bren, *The Greengrocer and His TV*, 163). In particular, the meaning of female work had changed. The Stalinist proposition that the private sphere was the realm of petit-bourgeois interests was now virtually forgotten. Instead, now, in addition to being celebrated in their role as active and diligent workers in the public sphere, women were also defined as good mothers in the private sphere. The post-1968 socially conservative vision centered on the image of a traditional, healthy family that could only flourish under the conditions provided by the Communist Party. In this understanding, it was female workers who brought the principles of domesticity, harmony, and care as well as an absence of political conflict to the worksite. This was not a "return" to the private sphere, as Bren notes, but rather an "expression of the private life endorsed by the state as a cornerstone of party policy and normalization's political culture." See Bren, *The Greengrocer and His TV*, 174.

47. Compare Bartha, *Alienating Labour*, 7; and Maier, *Dissolution*, 60.

48. In the early GDR, socially conservative norms had already informed the way homosexuals were discriminated against. See, for instance, Jennifer V. Evans, "The Moral State: Men, Mining, and Masculinity in the Early GDR," *German History* 23, no. 3 (2005): 355–370.

49. See Thomas Lindenberger, "'Asoziale Lebensweise': Herrschaftslegitimation, Sozialdisziplinierung und die Konstruktion eines 'Negativen Milieus' in der SED-Diktatur," *Geschichte und Gesellschaft* 31, no. 2 (2005): 227–254, 245. Prostitution was counted among these offenses on the theory that it resulted from an "unwillingness to work." The measures often targeted the youth, who were also often charged with "unruly behavior."

50. See historian Michal Pullmann's work on social stigma in late socialist Czechoslovakia: Michal Pullmann, *Konec experimentu: Přestavba a pád komunismu v Československu* (Prague: Scriptorium 2011). See also Pullmann, "Ruhige Arbeit," 50; as well as Vaněk and Mücke, *Velvet Revolutions*, 120, on "asocial behavior."

51. In the early 1970s, a law instituted the creation of a branch of social work that aimed at the resocialization of "socially deviant citizens." A handbook for social workers issued in the mid-1970s defined the goal of "resocialization" as "a condition of deepening social integration, which is marked by a change in values of the client, the easing of troubled interpersonal relations, stabilization of employment, discipline in civil and family life, as well as the readiness to address obligations born out of the antisocial attitude." Pávlok 1947, quoted in Martina Špiláčková, *Soziale Arbeit im Sozialismus: Ein Beispiel aus der Tschechoslowakei (1968–1989)* (Wiesbaden: Springer-Verlag, 2014), 178.

52. In Czechoslovakia, legal violence based on these charges also targeted the Roma minority. Female Romni were subject to forced sterilization, a measure that, as noted by Pullmann, "Ruhige Arbeit," 51, also found support among the general population. Depoliticization also meant that leftist political activity—coded as "reformist"— was strongly sanctioned, and many regarded "unruly" intellectuals—notably also

1. HISTORICAL TRAJECTORIES

those who had signed the Charta 77 that called on Czechoslovak authorities to respect human right standards—in moral terms as "troublemakers." See Kevin McDermott, *Communist Czechoslovakia, 1945–89: A Political and Social History.* (New York: Macmillan International Higher Education, 2015). Dissidents were regularly charged with "parasitism."

53. Lindenberger, "Asoziale Lebensweise," 253.

54. Anthropologist Martha Lampland describes the effects of social divisions in her study of Hungarian villagers in the 1980s. The villagers, as Lampland observes, are decidedly utilitarian. They believe in individual interest, hard work, and individually deserved economic outcomes. They find that those who work for or in any way rely on the state for their livelihood are either naive or are willful agents of a system that has betrayed them. Lampland writes: "Villagers did not dispute the general principle of personal aggrandizement . . . their quarrel was not with boutique owners. It was with the rhetoric that framed and justified actions taken by local and national leaders. It was the rhetoric of the socialist state that villagers found truly offensive." Villagers believe themselves to be part of the "truly productive labor force," as opposed to "administrative personnel, who it was said, spent long afternoons polishing their nails or drinking at the pub." See Martha Lampland, *The Object of Labor: Commodification in Socialist Hungary* (Chicago: University of Chicago Press, 1995), 268, 316.

55. See Maier, *Dissolution*, 60. In East Germany and Czechoslovakia, the macroeconomic outlook was plagued by the notorious inefficiency of the large plants. State-owned companies, structurally resistant to reform, often engaged in resource hoarding. In some high-profile sectors of the economy, political embargoes left firms without access to Western technologies. These industrial giants also had a terrible environmental record, producing lasting environment damage as well as health emergencies in their communities.

56. Jonathan R. Zatlin, "Scarcity and Resentment: Economic Sources of Xenophobia in the GDR, 1971–1989," *Central European History* 40, no. 4 (2007): 683–720.

57. See Scheiring, "Left Behind in the Hungarian Rustbelt," 1162.

58. The quote is taken from James Krapfl, *Revolution with a Human Face: Politics, Culture, and Community in Czechoslovakia, 1989–1992* (Ithaca, NY: Cornell University Press, 2013), 4. Protests intensified after riot police attacked a crowd of students on November 17, 1989. After the resignation of party functionaries and a general strike later that month, the KSČ had lost its grip on power. It had lost the support of its administrative class as well as of large swaths of the police, who had no intention of saving the regime.

59. Between August 1989 and April 1990, more than 2,500 demonstrations, rallies, and sit-ins in factories took place. The number of participants in the *Montagsdemos* in Leipzig increased from about 5,000 in late September to about 200,000 during November and December, with protests peaking in late October and early November. See Donatella Della Porta, *Mobilizing for Democracy. Comparing 1989 and 2011* (Oxford: Oxford University Press, 2014), 36. The opposition movement, backed by groups like *Neues Forum*, articulated a diverse set of claims, but there was a consensus that one-party rule must be abolished. Carol Mueller observes that claims shifted from reform to revolution only in the last three months of 1989: "Earlier in the year, demonstrators made reactive demands for rights that were

legally guaranteed, but only erratically honored, if at all; to leave the GDR after seeking permission; to expect a fair election count; and to expect policing that was neither violent nor capricious. As the year progressed, these reactive claims were replaced by calls for non-violence, party reform, and finally, for preservation of the GDR by a few dedicated socialists in the face of massive demands for unification." See Carol Mueller, "Claim 'Radicalization'?: The 1989 Protest Cycle in the GDR," *Social Problems* 46, no. 4 (1999): 528–546, 543.

60. There was another strong element of similarity in the mode of political. Unlike in many neighboring societies, in Prague and Berlin, the revolutions of 1989 led to a radical break with the past. After a first few rounds of negotiations with former leaders, the model of a negotiated transition that was applied elsewhere—notably in Warsaw and Budapest, in the form of roundtable talks—was abandoned. Old elites were ousted. Soon, they would also be held accountable in what became the most expansive transitional justice ("lustration") programs in the postsocialist world. Katherine Verdery provides an excellent comparative overview in "Postsocialist Cleansing in Eastern Europe: Purity and Danger in Transitional Justice," *Socialism Vanquished, Socialism Challenged: Eastern Europe and China, 1989–2009*, ed. Nina Bandelj and Dorothy J. Solinger (Oxford: Oxford University Press, 2012), 69–82. In Germany, transitional justice was administered in the context of the West German takeover and radical elite change, and it was particularly wide-ranging. Here, individuals could be charged not only because of their actions in the past but also based on positions they had held in the old system. In this way, tens of thousands of individuals were disqualified from public office, and from professions such as parliamentarians, judges, and local councilors. They also couldn't become teachers, postal workers, government secretaries, and even janitors in public buildings. In the Czech Republic, individuals could be charged because of criminal actions in the past. In practice, here, the efforts remained largely symbolic.

61. See Anne Goedicke, "A 'Ready-Made State': The Mode of Institutional Transition in East Germany After 1989," in *After the Fall of the Wall: Life Courses in the Transformation of East Germany*, ed. Martin Diewald, Anne Goedicke, and Karl Ulrich Mayer (Stanford, CA: Stanford University Press, 2006), 44–64.

62. See Abby Innes, *Czechoslovakia: The Short Goodbye* (New Haven, CT: Yale University Press, 2001).

63. In early 1990, there were two options for unification on the table: Article 146 of the West German constitution envisioned the redrafting of the entire constitution; article 23 foresaw the possibility that additional territories would be incorporated into the Federal Republic without any changes to the body of law. Conservatives' decisive victory in the first free elections of the East German parliament in the spring of 1990 created the facts on the ground: The model of incorporation was applied. The civic movement and former dissident groups overwhelmingly rejected reunification on the terms of article 23—they had long advocated for a reformist "third way socialism" and they saw the moment as a chance to rewrite the German constitution in this spirit. However, these groups did very poorly the first free elections. It quickly became clear that such ideas remained on the sidelines. As Dieter Segert outlines, West German chancellor Helmut Kohl's brilliant strategic move in this situation was to push for an early monetary union, which suffocated attempts to imagine political alternatives to the incorporation into the West German system.

1. HISTORICAL TRAJECTORIES

See Dieter Segert, *Das 41. Jahr. Eine andere Geschichte der DDR* (Cologne: Böhlau Verlag, 2008).

64. *Treuhand's* operating model was based on the principle of bidding. The agency would, within a limited time frame, auction off the former East German people's property. The rationale for speeding up the process as much as possible was particularly consequential. Offering all property at the same time created an oversupply of companies, which meant that investors were in an excellent position to bargain or simply wait until prices would fall. *Treuhand* staff handed out bargains to investors with little credentials and in some cases relied on empty promises, failing to ensure a proper contractual basis in advance. Because everyone was under the impression that the state desperately wanted to sell, a veritable spiral of devaluation of former East German property ensued. In total, the agency controlled over 12,000 firms that employed around 4 million people, or around two-fifths of the East German workforce. See Goedicke, "A 'Ready-Made State,'" 28–49. The agency was thus, before it ceased its activities in 1994, the world's largest public employer. Of those firms, around 53 percent were privatized, 13 percent reprivatized, and 30 percent liquidated.

65. Philip Ther, *Europe Since 1989: A History* (Princeton, NJ: Princeton University Press, 2016), 88.

66. Counting those that were not based on some type of labor market measures. These data are taken from Burkart Lutz and Holle Grünert, "Der Zerfall der Beschäftigungsstrukturen der DDR 1989—1993," in *Arbeit, Arbeitsmarkt und Betriebe. Berichte der Kommission für die Erforschung des sozialen und politischen Wandels in den neuen Bundesländern*, ed. Burkart Lutz, Hildegard M. Nickel, Rudi Schmidt, and Arndt Sorge (Wiesbaden: VS Verlag für Sozialwissenschaften, 1996): 69–120, 71. If we consider government-subsidized welfare jobs, around 4 million workplaces were lost in the first years after 1989. According to another estimate, 80 percent of the working population of the GDR lost their workplace either temporarily or permanently between 1989 and 1995. These numbers are reported by Paul Windolf, "Die Wirtschaftliche Transformation: Politische und Ökonomische Systemrationalitäten," in *Der Vereinigungsschock. Vergleichende Betrachtungen zehn Jahre danach*, ed. Wolfgang Schluchter and Peter Quint (Weilerswist: Velbrück Wissenschaft, 2001): 392–413, 411.

67. This quote is from Offe, *Varieties of Transition*, 153.

68. Martin Diewald, and Anne Goedicke, "Unusual Turbulences—Unexpected Continuities: Transformation Life Courses in Retrospective," in *After the Fall of the Wall: Life Courses in the Transformation of East Germany*, ed. Martin Diewald, Anne Goedicke, and Karl Ulrich Mayer (Stanford, CA: Stanford University Press, 2006), 293–318, 300–302.

69. See Reinhard Pollak and Walter Müller, "Soziale Mobilität in Ost-und Westdeutschland im ersten Jahrzehnt nach der Wiedervereinigung," in *Sozialer und politischer Wandel in Deutschland*, ed. Rüdiger Schmitt-Beck, Martina Wasmer, and Achim Koch (Wiesbaden: Springer 2004), 69–95, 85. This was notably the opposite of labor market dynamics in West Germany, where more people experienced upward rather than downward mobility in the early 1990s, as noted by Rainer Geißler, *Die Sozialstruktur Deutschlands* (Wiesbaden: Springer-Verlag, 2014), 329. The disadvantage was also aggravated by the fact that Westerners came to occupy elite

positions in the East, and this created a structural blockade for upward mobility for East Germans.

70. Martin Diewald, Heike Solga, and Anne Goedicke, "Old Assets, New Liabilities?: How Did Individual Characteristics Contribute to Labor Market Success or Failure After 1989?," in *After the Fall of the Wall: Life Courses in the Transformation of East Germany*, ed. Martin Diewald, Anne Goedicke, and Karl Ulrich Mayer (Stanford, CA: Stanford University Press, 2006), 65–88, 85, 88. Unskilled workers were particularly exposed to the dangers of downward mobility, even more so after 1995. Individuals in their forties at the time of 1989 also suffered significant losses because they were just a little too young for early retirement. See Martin Diewald, and Mathias Pollmann-Schult, "Erwerbsverläufe in Ostdeutschland–Inklusion und Exklusion seit 1989," in *Inklusion und Exklusion: Analysen zur Sozialstruktur und sozialen Ungleichheit*, ed. Rudolf Stichweh, and Paul Windolf, (Wiesbaden: Springer 2009), 139–156, 142.

71. For health care, see Mary Fulbrook, *The People's State: East German Society from Hitler to Honecker* (New Haven, CT: Yale University Press, 2005). The statistics on policlinics are taken from Philip Manow, "Zerschlagung der Poliklinken und Transfer korporativer Regulierung: Das Gesundheitswesen," in *Transformationspfade in Ostdeutschland. Beiträge zur sektoralen Vereinigungspolitik*, ed. Roland Czada and Gerhard Lembruch, (Frankfurt: Campus, 2008): 165–190, 178.

72. See Solga, "The Rise of Meritocracy?," 161.

73. This is the conclusion by Diewald and Goedicke, "Unusual Turbulences—Unexpected Continuities," 300. As far as the reproduction of the pre-1989 elite is concerned, East Germany stands out from other cases. While old elites did manage to retain advantages after 1989, which was particularly true men for who held upper service-class positions in the GDR. They had a greater chance to enter the new upper-service classes—they did not, on the whole, escape the broader trend of social downward mobility after 1989. In many postsocialist societies, former upper service-class members, in particular, former plant managers, could draw on their knowledge of the firms as well as social capital to thrive after 1989, as detailed by Gil Eyal, Iván Szelényi, and Eleanor Townsley, *Making Capitalism Without Capitalists: Class Formation and Elite Struggles in Post-Communist Central Europe* (London: Verso, 1998). This was, in principle, also true for East Germany. In practice, however, the mechanism was much weaker here than anywhere else in the postsocialist world. East Germany had the "lowest rate of elite reproduction in the region," notes Solga, "The Rise of Meritocracy?," 167. Widespread early retirement, as well as the radical model of privatization, also shaped this outcome.

74. Martin Diewald, "Spirals of Success and Failure?: The Interplay of Control Beliefs and Working Lives in the Transition from Planned to Market Economy," in *After the Fall of the Wall: Life Courses in the Transformation of East Germany*, ed. Martin Diewald, Anne Goedicke, and Karl Ulrich Mayer (Stanford, CA: Stanford University Press, 2006), 214–236.

75. Olaf Struck, *Aufschwung und Unzufriedenheit. Strukturwandel und Lebenssituation in Ostdeutschland*. Working Paper No. 19–2017, University of Bamberg, 2018.

76. Ther, *Europe Since 1989*, 268–270.

77. Goedicke, "A 'Ready-Made State,'" 56. The rate of participation in state-funded trainings increased dramatically during this period. Short-term work was subsidized;

1. HISTORICAL TRAJECTORIES

by April 1991, around 2 million people found themselves in such forms of employment. From 1989 to 1992, around 10 percent of the total labor force was working in subsidized low-wage jobs, as underscored by Diewald and Goedicke, "Unusual Turbulences—Unexpected Continuities," 296. Another million people left the labor market through early retirement, which, until the end of 1992, allowed subsidized transitions into retirement at the age of fifty-five.

78. After 1989 in East Germany, in stark contrast to other cases, the state was by far the most stable—often also the best-paying—employer. Thus, one somewhat ironic outcome of these shifts is that "occupational groups quite close to the former regime, like teachers, did better than others because they profited from begin in the comparably safe haven of the public sector." See Diewald and Goedicke, "Unusual Turbulences—Unexpected Continuities," 302.

79. See Martin Myant, *The Rise and Fall of Czech Capitalism: Economic Development in the Czech Republic Since 1989* (Cheltenham: Edward Elgar 2003), 26.

80. Prices rose steeply—by 56 percent in 1991, by 11 percent in 1992, and by another 20 percent in 1992. Wage increases did not keep up with this trend. The numbers are reported by Lenka Kalinová, *Konec Nadějím* (Prague: Academia, 2012), 339. This was still a moderate development compared to inflation levels in post-Soviet societies.

81. In many ways, Václav Klaus was the opposite of dissident and playwright Václav Havel. Havel was a playwright and an intellectual; Klaus was a technocrat who thought his mission was to execute lawlike economic change in society. Havel was subtle; Klaus was boisterous. On the contrast and the rivalry between the two, see Timothy Barney, " 'A Tale of Two Václavs': Rhetorical History and the Concept of 'Return' in Post-Communist Czech Leadership," *Advances in the History of Rhetoric* 18 (2015): 109–134. Klaus also "won" the personal rivalry: during the 1990s, he "transform[ed] the [Civic Forum] into a right-wing party," thereby consigning Havel's humanistic branch of the former dissident platform to "oblivion." See Krapfl, *Revolution with a Human Face*, 29.

82. Večerník, *Markets and People*, 196–197.

83. This is detailed by Mitchell A. Orenstein, *Out of the Red: Building Capitalism and Democracy in Postcommunist Europe* (Ann Arbor: University of Michigan Press, 2001), 76–79; and by Pieter Vanhuysse, "Czech Exceptionalism?: A Comparative Political Economy Interpretation of Post-Communist Policy Pathways, 1989–2004," *Sociologický časopis/Czech Sociological Review* 42, no. 6 (2006): 1115–1136.

84. The numbers are from Orenstein, *Out of the Red*, 75. The fact that levels of inequality are still comparatively low in the Czech Republic today can be attributed to these social protection mechanisms, as detailed by Nina Bandelj and Matthew Mahutga, "How Socioeconomic Change Shapes Income Inequality in Post-Socialist Europe," *Social Forces* 88, no. 5 (2010): 2133–2162.

85. See Vanhuysse "Czech Exceptionalism?," 1127.

86. Hilary Appel and Mitchell A. Orenstein, *From Triumph to Crisis: Neoliberal Economic Reform in Postcommunist Countries* (Cambridge: Cambridge University Press, 2018), 51, 53.

87. On this issue, see Nina Bandelj, *From Communists to Foreign Capitalists: The Social Foundations of Foreign Direct Investment in Postsocialist Europe* (Princeton, NJ: Princeton University Press, 2008); Myant, *The Rise and Fall of Czech Capitalism*;

1. HISTORICAL TRAJECTORIES

and Jan Drahokoupil, *Globalization and the State in Central and Eastern Europe: The Politics of Foreign Direct Investment* (New York: Routledge, 2008).

88. Jiří Večerník, *Czech Society in the 2000s: A Report on Socio-economic Policies and Structures* (Prague: Alibris 2009), 35.

89. Vanhuysse, "Czech Exceptionalism?," 1125.

90. Večerník, *Markets and People*, 28. Roma communities soon suffered from poverty, social stigma, and the negative effects of residential segregation. In 2016, about a third of Czech Roma were without a job, according to the European Parliament, *Social and Employment Policies in the Czech Republic* (Brussels: Policy Department for Economic, Scientific and Quality of Life Policies, 2018), 21.

91. The quote is taken from Večerník, *Markets and People*, 30. In the mid-1980s, 45 percent of state employees were women. In 1998, this number was 60 percent; in health and education, it was 75 percent. Before 1989, the overwhelmingly male heavy and raw industries was the most prestigious field of employment; after 1989, profits could be generated in the private sector, especially in the predominantly male financial sector. See True, *Gender, Globalization, and Postsocialism*, 82, 86. See also Kalinová, *Konec Nadějím*, 368; and Tomáš Sirovátka and Ondřej Hora. "Public Sector Employment in the Czech Republic After 1989: Old Legacy in New Realities?" *Central European Journal of Public Policy*, no. 7 (2013), on devalued sectors of the economy. After the turn of the century, labor costs in the Czech Republic continued to be among the lowest in the Central European region. See True, *Gender, Globalization, and Postsocialism*, 84.

92. Our World in Data, "Government Health Expenditure as a Share of GDP, 1990 to 2021," accessed December 21, 2022, https://ourworldindata.org/grapher/public-health-expenditure-share-gdp-owid?time=1990..latest&country=DEU~CZE

93. Jiří Večerník and Petr Matějů, *Ten Years of Rebuilding Capitalism: Czech Society After 1989* (Prague: Academia, 1999), 23–26. On entrepreneurship see Ther, *Europe Since 1989*, 124.

94. Ákos Róna-Tas, "The Worm and the Caterpillar: The Small Private Sector in the Czech Republic, Hungary and Slovakia," in *The New Entrepreneurs of Europe and Asia: Patterns of Business Development in Russia, Eastern Europe, and China*, ed. Victoria E. Bonnell and Thomas B. Gold (Armonk, NY: M.E. Sharpe, 2002), 38–65, 59.

95. The outsized role of formal qualifications and skills make the Czech Republic and Germany the Western-most cases of transformation societies. See Diewald et al., "Old Assets, New Liabilities?," 84, Večerník, *Czech Society in the 2000s*, 85–88. Unlike in much of the post-Soviet world, political capital did not constitute a key resource for social upward mobility. Informal networks were less pervasive than in Poland, Hungary, Romania, or Bulgaria. In the Czech Republic and Germany, the implementation of markets was facilitated by the strong industrial profile, bureaucratic traditions, and high levels of education for the general population.

96. Tomáš Katrňák and Petr Fučík, *Návrat k sociálnímu původu* (Prague: CDK, 2010), 87–112. During the 1990s, the significance of income generated from wages decreased, while that generated from entrepreneurial activities, rent, or other financial sources increased. Manual and low-skilled workers' incomes stagnated, and their work lost recognition. See Kalinová, *Konec nadějím*, 366, 367. Unlike in Germany, however, unemployment did not affect the emerging middle class.

Long-term unemployment also remained relatively marginal in the first decade after 1989; see Večerník and Matějů, *Ten Years of Rebuilding Capitalism*, 31.

97. Večerník, *Markets and People*, 266.

98. Večerník and Matějů, *Ten Years of Rebuilding Capitalism*, 165. See also Vladimír Benáček, "The Rise of the 'Grand Entrepreneurs' in the Czech Republic and Their Contest for Capitalism," *Sociologický časopis/Czech Sociological Review* 46, no. 6 (2006): 1151–1170. Some individuals used political connections to reap the benefits of privatization, both by legal and illegal means. The mechanism was described by Gil Eyal et al. in *Making Capitalism Without Capitalists*, 7, as follows: "In a post-communist transition . . . those who are well endowed with cultural capital may be able to convert their former political capital into informal social networks, which can then be usefully deployed to take advantage of new market opportunities." Generally, elite change in the economic domain was greater in the Czech Republic than neighboring Poland and Hungary; see Večerník and Matějů, *Ten Years of Rebuilding Capitalism*, 179.

99. On causality in narrative, see Margaret R. Somers, "The Narrative Constitution of Identity: A Relational and Network Approach," *Theory and Society* 23, no. 5 (1994): 605–649.

100. On the underrepresentation of East Germans in leadership positions, see, for instance, Ronald Gebauer, Axel Salheiser, and Lars Vogel, "Bestandsaufnahme," in *Ostdeutsche Eliten. Träume, Wirklichkeiten und Perspektiven*, ed. Deutsche Gesellschaft E.V. (Berlin: Deutsche Gesellschaft E.V., 2017): 14–34. On the patronizing media discourse, see Thomas Ahbe, "Die Ost-Diskurse als Strukturen der Nobilitierung und Marginalisierung von Wissen: Eine Diskursanalyse zur Konstruktion der Ostdeutschen in den westdeutschen Medien-Diskursen 1989/90 und 1995," in *Die Ostdeutschen in den Medien: Das Bild von den anderen nach 1990*, ed. Thomas Ahbe, Rainer Gries, and Wolfgang Schmale (Leipzig: Leipziger University Press, 2009): 59–112. The "second-class citizens" sentiment has been documented in many studies, quite recently, for instance, by Pew Research Center, "European Public Opinion Three Decades After the Fall of Communism," https://www.pewresearch .org/global/2019/10/15/european-public-opinion-three-decades-after-the-fall-of -communism/, accessed August 7, 2021.

101. Hans-Werner Sinn, "Zehn Jahre deutsche Wiedervereinigung: Ein Kommentar zur Lage der neuen Länder," *IFO-Schnelldienst* 53, no. 26/27 (2000): 10–22, 11; Joachim Ragnitz, "Ostdeutschland heute: Viel erreicht, viel zu tun," *IFO-Schnelldienst* 61, no. 18 (2009): 3–13, 4. Why did German political and economic elites meet little resistance in portraying economic problems in the East as inherent to its people for such a long time? It certainly matters that East Germans rarely had a voice in those institutions. German public discourse about 1989 is, in fact, relatively fragmented. On one side, there is a positive, nationalistic account of the revolutions of 1989; on the other, a negative, blame-laden narrative of economic developments in the East after the fall of the Berlin Wall. For decades, the two strands have existed side by side. Public debate has shifted only very recently, and now East German voices and experiences are moving to the foreground.

102. However, this domestic voice was a nativist voice, excluding minority communities such as the Roma.

103. The quotes are from Veronika Pehe, "The Wild 1990s: 'Transformation Nostalgia' Among the Czech Student Generation of 1989," *East Central Europe* 46, no. 1 (2019): 111–134, 115.

104. This quote is from Krapfl, *Revolution with a Human Face*, 26.

105. Anthropologist Ladislav Holý, in his *Little Czech and the Great Czech Nation: National Identity and the Post-Communist Social Transformation* (Cambridge: Cambridge University Press, 1996), 153, reveals that this was a widely popular theme at the time. He writes, "[T]he return to a market economy was, then, a return to the 'natural' state of society. But the market was also 'natural' because it was an arrangement of economic relations that corresponded to human nature." Analyzing Czech newspapers, Holý finds powerful cultural binaries at play: The market is coded as civilization, development, rationality, and pragmatism; the planned economy is coded as atavistic, irrational, artificial, ideological, and subject to politics. In a similar vein, Gil Eyal analyzes the "post-communist spirit of capitalism" as rooted in the notion that a person must *purge* the socialist past within the self. Eyal argues that neoliberals could easily sidestep their main elite antagonists, intellectuals of the Czechoslovak underground tradition, because they invoked ideas of "sacrifice" and their philosophy seemingly offered a "practical solution" to moral problems in the form of market society. See Gil Eyal, "Anti-Politics and the Spirit of Capitalism: Dissidents, Monetarists, and the Czech Transition to Capitalism," *Theory and Society* 29, no. 1 (2000): 49–92.

106. This quote is taken from Orenstein, *Out of the Red*, 79.

107. See Večerník and Matějů, *Ten Years of Rebuilding Capitalism*, 75.

108. See Martin Babička, "The Future Is in Your Hands: Temporality and the Neoliberal Self the Czech Voucher Privatization," *Journal of Contemporary Central and Eastern Europe* 30, no. 1 (2022): 83–99, 88.

109. Václav Klaus, "Česká transformace byla úspěšná," *Newsletter CEP* 02 (2008): 1–4. We may posit that such narratives locate the root cause of structural weakness after 1989 in the sphere of circulation, not in the realm of production. Macroeconomic problems, in other words, are not blamed on working people in this approach.

110. The ethnography is Eliane S. Weiner, "No (Wo)Man's Land: The Post-Socialist Purgatory of Czech Female Factory Workers," *Social Problems* 52, no 4 (2005): 572–592. For perceptions of "winning" and "losing" in the Czech Republic see Dieter Segert, *Transformationen in Osteuropa im 20: Jahrhundert* (Bonn: Bundeszentrale für Politische Bildung, 2014), 178.

2. REMEMBERING ECONOMIC CHANGE AFTER 1989

1. Edward P. Thompson, *The Making of the English Working Class* (New York: Vintage, 1963), 203.

2. See James Mark, Muriel Blaive, Adam Hudek, Anne Saunders, and Stanislav Tyszka, "1989 After 1989: Remembering the End of State Socialism in East-Central Europe," in *Thinking Through Transition: Liberal Democracy, Authoritarian Pasts, and Intellectual History in East Central Europe After 1989*, ed. Michal Kopeček and Piotr Wciślik (Budapest: Central European University Press, 2015): 463–504.

2. REMEMBERING ECONOMIC CHANGE AFTER 1989

3. A sociological classic on the engineering profession is Robert Zussman, *Mechanics of the Middle Class: Work and Politics Among American engineers* (Berkeley: University of California Press, 1985). On the centrality of the value of individual achievement in U.S.-American engineering and its detrimental effects on gender, see, for instance, Caroll Seron, Susan Silbey, Erin Cech, and Brian Rubineau: "'I Am Not a Feminist, but . . .': Hegemony of a Meritocratic Ideology and the Limits of Critique Among Women in Engineering," *Work and Occupations* 45, no. 2 (2018): 131–167. On care work, see Heidi Bludau, "Hindered Care: Institutional Obstructions to Carework and Professionalism in Czech Nursing," *Anthropology of Work Review* 38, no. 1 (2017): 8–17, 8–9. The idea that care work is purely based on an ethics of altruism is flawed. Individual autonomy, both on the part of the care worker and on the part of the client, is an ethical and professional goal of this type of work.

4. An important collection of perspectives on impoverishment and marginalized groups, including the intersection of poverty with ethnicity and gender, is Rebecca J. Emigh and Iván Szelényi (eds.), *Poverty, Ethnicity, and Gender in Eastern Europe During the Market Transition* (Westport, CT: Praeger, 2001). For an overview of anthropological perspectives on dispossessed and excluded groups, see part IV of Kristen Ghodsee and Mitchell A. Orenstein, *Taking Stock of Shock: The Social Consequences of the 1989 Revolutions* (New York: Oxford University Press, 2021), 155–182.

5. Dolores Augustine, *Red Prometheus. Engineering and Dictatorship in East Germany, 1945–1990* (Cambridge, MA: MIT Press, 2007); Bernd Martens, "East German Economic Elites and Their Companies Two Decades After the Transformation ("Wende"): Still Following the Patterns of the 1990s," *Journal for East European Management Studies* 13, no. 4 (2008): 305–326, 318. During state-socialist times, engineers—although officially relegated to the "intelligentsia"—enjoyed a relatively high status because the regimes placed a high value on modernism, technological advancement, and technical education. Higher education was more or less synonymous with technical education. The technocratic elite, as part of the upper-service class, also maintained close proximity to political power. Leading employees in a firm (those overseeing the production process, acting as "middlemen" for the Communist Party in firms) often had a technical background. In the German Democratic Republic (GDR), engineers had often occupied upper managerial positions in firms. According to Martens, "78 percent of the Fachdirektoren (heads of departments) of selected economic branches of the GDR . . . were engineer and natural-science graduates, while 40 percent had economic qualifications." In 1960s East Germany, the traditional "graduate engineer" degree (*Diplomingenieur*) was supplemented by the so-called technical college engineer (*Fachschulingenieur*), a form of fast-track schooling outside university. This resulted in a considerable expansion of the engineering profession. Of the 370,000 engineers active in the GDR in 1989, around two-thirds had "technical college engineer" degrees. See Barbara Giessmann, "Ostdeutsche Ingenieure im Transformationsprozeß—zwischen Kontinuität und Bruch," in: *Berufsgruppen im Transformationsprozeß Ostdeutschlands: Ingenieure, Meister, Techniker und Ökonomen zwischen Gestern und Übermorgen*, ed. Ingrid Drexel and Barbara Giessmann (Frankfurt: Campus, 1997), 63. This resulted in an oversupply and overqualification of East German engineering personnel. In Czechoslovakia, technical education also expanded considerably

2. REMEMBERING ECONOMIC CHANGE AFTER 1989

throughout the state-socialist period. Here, too, firm managers and their deputies were overwhelmingly educated in technical fields, as noted by Jaroslav Kohout, "Sociology and the Qualifications of Managerial Staff in Czechoslovakia," *International Sociology* 3, no. 4 (1988): 335–342. The problem of an oversupply of technical degrees was, however, less severe in this case.

6. Some East Germans who had lost their jobs in this initial period never managed to get back on their feet. For others, an engineering degree proved a valuable asset in the long run. The German reunification treaty legally recognized GDR titles as an equivalent to a higher education graduate degree. Researchers note that engineers were able to attain privileged positions in German firms after unification: They were less likely to be laid off, received greater responsibility, and were paid better than most other employees, as detailed by Eva-Maria Langen, "Der Fachschulingenieur in den Restrukturierungsprozessen der Ostdeutschen Betriebe—Rationellere Nutzung seines Potentials und Partielle Aufwertung," in *Berufsgruppen im Transformationsprozeß Ostdeutschlands. Ingenieure, Meister, Techniker und Ökonomen zwischen Gestern und Übermorgen*, ed. Ingrid Drexel and Barbara Giessmann (Frankfurt: Campus, 2000), 60. East German engineering associations also remained relatively strong and well organized. This is remarkable because, during the 1990s, most East German professional associations and interest groups lost members and influence. See Steven Padgett, *Organizing Democracy in Eastern Germany: Interest Groups in Post-Communist Society* (Cambridge: Cambridge University Press, 1999), 49.

7. See Jiří Večerník, *Markets and People: The Czech Reform Experience in a Comparative Perspective* (Avebury: Aldershot, 1996). Vladimír Benáček, "The Rise of the 'Grand Entrepreneurs' in the Czech Republic and Their Contest for Capitalism," *Sociologický časopis/Czech Sociological Review* 46, no. 6 (2006): 1161, reports how Czech engineers often could take advantage of their insider knowledge in firms from before the revolution: "Although the technical intelligentsia had delayed access to higher positions, its penetration into the ranks of entrepreneurs accelerated after the mid-1990s." Engineering also enjoyed a high priority among policy planners, who regarded it as the "mother of the Czech industries" and wanted to protect the industry from the negative consequences of privatization, as noted by Jacqui True, *Gender, Globalization, and Postsocialism: The Czech Republic After Communism* (New York: Columbia University Press, 2003), 81. Of course, the Czech model of industrial change was also plagued by structural problems, and because engineers typically work in industry, their economic prospects were closely tied to particular firms. Martin Myant, in *The Rise and Fall of Czech Capitalism: Economic Development in the Czech Republic Since 1989* (Cheltenham: Edward Elgar 2003), 188–189, discusses examples of formerly state-owned Czechoslovak firms undergoing privatization, such as an engineering combine and a steel plant, citing policy failures and limited investments, as well as corruption, as the main problems that bedeviled the transition. Despite fundamental changes in ownership, financing, and the division of labor, however, many structures were retained in Czech manufacturing, thereby securing job prospects for skilled workers. Engineering continues to play a key role in the Czech economy today, especially in the automotive industry and machinery.

8. In the years immediately after the war, health care was still linked to an overarching project of modernizing society (for instance, infant mortality was successfully

2. REMEMBERING ECONOMIC CHANGE AFTER 1989

reduced thanks to this collective effort), but this political valuation of health-care work later disappeared—and with it, the understanding that health care was not an "innately" female profession. See Rosie Read, "Caring Values and the Value of Care: Women, Maternalism, and Caring Work in the Czech Republic," *Contemporary European History* 28 (2019). For Germany, see Barbara Heisig, "Pflege im Transformationsprozess zwischen beruflicher Modernisierung und Professionalisierung," in *Biographische Risiken und neue professionelle Herausforderungen*, ed. Melanie Fabel and Sandra Tiefel (Wiesbaden: Springer, 2004), 193–206; for the Czech Republic, see Tomáš Sirovátka and Ondřej Hora, "Public Sector Employment in the Czech Republic After 1989: Old Legacy in New Realities?," *Central European Journal of Public Policy*, no. 7 (2013): 4–35; as well as Valerie Tóthová and Gabriela Sedláková, "Nursing Education in the Czech Republic," *Nurse Education Today* 28, no. 1 (2008): 33–38. In late socialist Czechoslovakia, nursing was not considered an area of expertise but a mere practical activity; therefore, the Communist leadership saw little reason to invest in the field and to expand it through scientific and educational programs. In the GDR, the situation was similar, although here, as part of an academization of the nursing professions in the 1980s, some were able to obtain a higher education degree in nursing or pediatrics. A specific educational profile for elder care did not exist in either case. Nursing education was relatively uniform across the state-socialist world. Students obtained general secondary education and vocational qualifications simultaneously in nursing schools. Most finished school and started working at around age seventeen or eighteen, when their professional training was considered complete.

9. Scholars disagree on how to evaluate the autonomy of Czechoslovak care workers at work. Tóthová and Sedláková, in "Nursing Education in the Czech Republic," note that the primary role of nurses was to assist doctors. Their knowledge was not considered expertise. They posit that this state of dependency fostered traits such as conformity and lack of empathy. Anthropologist Rosie Read, in "Labour and Love: Competing Constructions of 'Care' in a Czech Nursing Home," *Critique of Anthropology*, 27, no. 2 (2007): 203–222, provides a contrasting interpretation, arguing that nurses did not perceive their detached role as lacking in autonomy. In her view, Czechoslovak nurses were trained to maintain a distance from patients and to establish a neutral, impersonal relationship that was to be informed by medical judgment alone. Nurses consciously avoided acting in a personal, emotionally warm manner toward patients (a kind of behavior that was associated with family ties and therefore inadequate in a medical context). Instead of acting on behalf of the patient, Read argues, they saw themselves as acting on behalf of the institution and its medical goals.

10. The quote is taken from True, *Gender, Globalization, and Postsocialism*, 81; the statistics on labor costs can be found on page 84. The consequences of the partial privatization of the Czech health-care system are discussed by Lenka Kalinová, Konec nadějím a nová očekávání: K dějinám české společnosti 1969–1993 (Prague: Academia, 2012), 345. Pay was very low in comparison to German health-care workers, but also middling compared to neighboring Poland and Hungary. In Czech public opinion, health-care work was (and continues to be) regarded as low in value. Together with other predominantly female professions such as education and accounting, nurses are seen as a "pink-collar" class, ranked as very low in

2. REMEMBERING ECONOMIC CHANGE AFTER 1989

prestige by Czechs. See Jiří Šafr, "Status Homogeneity and Heterogeneity in Social Contacts," *Social Distances and Stratification: Social Space in the Czech Republic. Sociologické studie/Sociological Studies* 8, no. 4 (2008), 53, 55–66.

11. See, for example, Heike Solga, "The Rise of Meritocracy?: Class Mobility in East Germany Before and After 1989," in *After the Fall of the Wall: Life Courses in the Transformation of East Germany*, ed. Martin Diewald, Anne Goedicke, and Karl Ulrich Mayer (Stanford, CA: Stanford University Press). In the long-term, health-care workers struggled with the commodification of their work. Hospitals and health-care facilities were monetized and partly privatized later in the 1990s. Unskilled workers from declining branches of the economy (especially manufacturing and agriculture) were recruited into health-care work, which suppressed wages. Soon, a low-wage sector with an increasing number of migrant workers (often informally employed) developed in elder care.

12. Anna Pollert, surveying Czech engineers in the early 1990s, writes that "the striking interview finding was the spontaneous veering towards employment and labour market concerns, which were far more immediate issues of capitalist change than work process issues . . . [the former] concerns underlined the close identification not only with the survival of the company but with a skilled tradition. The loss of a national asset in manufacturing, and the irresistible lure of the service sector, or better pay across the border or in Western companies were seen as major, regrettable changes." See Anna Pollert, *Transformation at Work in the New Market Economies of Central Eastern Europe* (London: Sage, 1999), 187. Pollert also describes the generational conflict between older employees, whose (higher) wages are still based on a seniority principle, and younger employees who favor individualized pay over tariffed wages and also embrace a new style of management.

13. See, for instance, Petra Schindler-Wisten, "'Pozor, vizita!': Sonda do života zdravotních sester v období tzv. normalizace a transformace," in *Příběhy (ne)obyčejných profesí: Česká společnost v období tvz. normalizace a transformace*, ed. Miroslav Vaněk and Lenka Krátká (Praha: Karolinum, 2014): 419–459.

14. See Anne Goedicke, "A 'Ready-Made State': The Mode of Institutional Transition in East Germany After 1989," in *After the Fall of the Wall: Life Courses in the Transformation of East Germany*, ed. Martin Diewald, Anne Goedicke, and Karl Ulrich Mayer (Stanford, CA: Stanford University Press, 2006), 56.

15. Miroslav Vaněk and Pavel Mücke, *Velvet Revolutions: An Oral History of Czech Society* (Oxford: Oxford University Press, 2016), 137–141, confirm that Czechs profoundly feared unemployment at the time.

16. Joanna Wawrzyniak, describing similar phenomena in her oral history of Polish deindustrialization, refers to these memories as the "nostalgia for sociability, the 'family-like' forms of working life." See Joanna Wawrzyniak, "Hard Times but Our Own: Post-Socialist Nostalgia and the Transformation of Industrial Life in Poland," *Zeithistorische Forschungen/Studies in Contemporary History* 18 (2021): 86.

17. Veronika Pehe, "The Wild 1990s: 'Transformation Nostalgia' Among the Czech Student Generation of 1989," *East Central Europe* 46, no. 1 (2019): 111–134.

18. See Lars Breuer and Anna Delius, "1989 in European Vernacular Memory," *East European Politics and Societies and Cultures* 31, no. 3 (2017): 456–478; Wawrzyniak, "Hard Times but Our Own."

2. REMEMBERING ECONOMIC CHANGE AFTER 1989

19. See the methodological appendix in this book for a discussion of the analysis of biographical segments.

20. For an overview, see Jennie E. Brand, "The Far-Reaching Impact of Job Loss and Unemployment," *Annual Review of Sociology* 41 (2015): 359–375.

21. See Gábor Scheiring, "Left Behind in the Hungarian Rustbelt: The Cultural-Political Economy of Working-Class Neo-Nationalism," *Sociology* 54, no. 6 (2020).

22. One nurse recalls that, before 1989, "we were essentially in charge of everything back then: wiping, dusting, caring, bathing, everything." Nursing also involved exacting physical work. One person remembers how, in winter, nurses had to carry heavy loads of coal to heat hospital ovens every day.

23. With these improvements also came new challenges. Some remember that the introduction of one-way material increased the amount of trash produced by hospitals significantly. Technological improvements did not happen from one day to the next. In the Czech Republic, in particular, health care was (and still is) chronically underfunded, and it often took years, sometimes even decades, for modern technology to arrive in public facilities.

24. Katherine Verdery, *What Was Socialism, and What Comes Next?* (Princeton, NJ: Princeton University Press, 1996).

25. This is the definition given by Brandon J. Griffin et al., "Moral Injury: An Integrative Review," *Journal of Traumatic Stress* 31 (2019): 350–362, 351.

26. On this point, compare Martens, "East German Economic Elites," and Benáček, "The Rise of the 'Grand Entrepreneurs.'"

27. See Pehe, "The Wild 1990s."

28. See Jan Alexa et al., "Czech Republic: Health System Review." *Health Systems in Transition* 17, no. 1 (2015): 1–165; as well as Ulrike Papouschek and Nils Böhlke, *Strukturwandel und Arbeitsbeziehungen im Gesundheitswesen in Tschechien, Deutschland, Polen und Österreich* (Vienna: FORBA, 2008). The shift from a centrally administered system financed by the state toward a decentralized structure paid for by contributions by employees, employers, and the state was intended to depoliticize decision-making processes in health care, to give hospitals and other health facilities as well as regions and districts more autonomy, and to allow private and semiprivate actors to enter the market. In Germany, the principle by which health insurers compensate hospitals according to a flat-rate scheme per patient case (and not, for instance, according to factors such as necessary duration of stay) was a key driver of marketization. Papouschek and Böhlke, *Strukturwandel*, 10, report that, for the country as a whole between 1991 and 2006, the number of hospitals declined by 12.7 percent, the number of available beds declined by 23.3 percent, and the average time a patient spent at a hospital declined by 40 percent, from 14 to 8.5 days. The number of people employed at these institutions, as well as the number of employees on full-time contracts, also declined. However, the private outpatient health-care sector grew after a major reform of public health law in 1995. In this field, a large (informal) subsector of primarily migrant workers emerged, a development that has increased downward pressure on wages in the health-care sector as a whole. During the 1990s, wage disparities within the field grew. Qualified nurses working in state-owned hospitals soon found themselves earning better wages and enjoying better working conditions than elder-care workers in private, outpatient care services. Some East German health-care workers

2. REMEMBERING ECONOMIC CHANGE AFTER 1989

still earn only a little more than the minimum wage today, even if they possess decades of work experience in the field. And some of the educational credentials gained in the GDR, as well as some of the professional vocabulary that had been used in the health-care professions, were trivialized under the new (West) German standards imposed after 1989. In the Czech Republic, elements of marketization had already been introduced into the health-care system before the split with Slovakia in 1993. By enacting a new legal framework that allowed for a plurality of semipublic health insurance providers to operate, policymakers sought to introduce elements of choice, competition, and market efficiency into the field. By the mid-1990s, however, several Czech insurance funds had gone into liquidation after becoming heavily indebted, a fate that also affected many hospitals. See Alexa et al., "Czech Republic." In both cases, nonprofit and charitable organizations operating on a semipublic basis (such as health-care associations that often have a confessional or civic background such as the Red Cross, the Samaritans, or the *Diakonie*) have increasingly played an important role in the field of elder care and mobile care services. See Heisig, "Pflege im Transformationsprozes;" Kalinová, *Konec Nadějím*; Tóthová and Sedláková, "Nursing Education in the Czech Republic."

29. Before 1989, there was scarcity of equipment and labor. After 1989, scarcity was bound to cost efficiency. Health-care workers also remember this shift through the problem of acceleration, in the sense that patients were increasingly being processed instead of being properly taken care of.

30. See Wawrzyniak, "Hard Times but Our Own," 58–88. She notes that this is often circumscribed with the metaphor of the "family," which also resurfaces repeatedly in my interviews. She posits that we can understand it as a form of nostalgia for patriarchal relationships at work, a way of wielding informal power that is also moral power. Some find that the legal and ethical discourse of individual rights goes "too far." An East German midwife in her late fifties, for instance, rejects what she thinks is an "overemphasis" on individual needs, claiming, "The good thing [pre-1989] was, it was a bit of an orderly structure." She feels "sorry" for her young colleagues at times: "they're so idealistic about everything, but really, they don't know how to deal with a situation in which there's something that the patient wants and they can't do it this way . . . You don't try to meet all her demands. I'd say, this is not a spa around here!"

31. On this double role of skills, see Adam Mrozowicki, *Coping with Social Change: Life Strategies of Workers in Poland's New Capitalism* (Leuven: Leuven University Press, 2011), 47–51.

32. On this point, see also Read, "Labour and Love."

33. Biography writing always struggles with creating consistency where there is change. See Michael Bamberg, "Identity and Narration," in *Handbook of Narratology*, ed. Peter Hühn, Wolf Schmid, Jörg Schönert, and Pier John (Berlin: De Gruyter, 2009), 132–143. The problem is aggravated in our context because the state-socialist past is publicly discredited. However, the realms of work, economic achievement, and skills provide a seemingly neutral, uncontested space.

34. Kinga Pozniak, *Nowa Huta: Generations of Change in a Model Socialist Town* (Pittsburgh, PA: University of Pittsburgh Press, 2014).

35. But see Ghodsee and Orenstein, *Taking Stock of Shock*, 120, 126–129, for stark differences between the post-Soviet region and Central Eastern Europe in this respect.

3. DESERVING AND UNDESERVING OTHERS

36. Wawryzniak, "Hard Times but Our Own," discusses the sense of loss in terms of a workplace culture.
37. Gender also factors into this dynamic of competition. Elisabeth, the architect, invokes gender equality as an East German quality and a sign of economic superiority. She has a vivid memory of how, during the 1990s, she had to convince Western business partners of her expertise, often struggling with West German stereotypes about successful women. She argues that this problem did not exist in the GDR, where women were recognized as equal partners. She managed to overcome these stereotypes thanks to her expertise—she invokes reliability, competency, and punctuality—which she associates with her East German education. From research on U.S.-American engineering, we know that the discourse of meritocracy is also used there to downplay the importance of gender disparities. See Seron et al., "I Am Not a Feminist, but . . ."
38. New legal definitions of responsibility at the workplace concentrated authority and decision making at the level of doctors, and enforced a much stronger structure of accountability. These developments were mainly caused by emerging (and ever-shifting) insurance requirements.
39. See Heisig, "Pflege im Transformationsprozess."
40. In fact, we can distinguish two claims here, each with a different relationship to the political meaning of German unity. The first is one of defiance and resistance. Its purpose is to show that East Germans really triumphed over their *brothers and sisters* in the West in economic terms after 1989 because they possessed a deeper, more genuine, and ultimately also more valuable knowledge. The fact that this knowledge has remained hidden and has often been misrecognized in the framework of German market society only serves as further proof that East Germans are excluded, that they do not belong. As a consequence, these qualities are—and will remain—part of an innate East German identity. The second narrative aims at equality. In fact it openly claims it. It holds that East Germans are just as good as West Germans in terms of their work ethic and that they therefore have a right to be fully included into the national community. As long as these qualities continue to be misrecognized or ignored, equality cannot be attained. In order to reject West German superiority in the realm of work and economic expertise, respondents can conjure another legacy of the GDR past: the structure of cooperation in firms, the socialist "collective." See Dorothee Wierling, "Work, Workers, and Politics in the German Democratic Republic," *International Labor and Working-Class History*, 50 (1996). Socialization in a tight-knit collective is regarded as an asset today. Respondents argue that it has provided them with a unique combination of social and practical skills, allowing them to incorporate the fundamental value of team orientation into their work.
41. This is a theme that Pehe, "The Wild 1990s," 127–128, also finds in her interviews, and she argues that it emerged in the late 1990s, when the honeymoon period was over.

3. DESERVING AND UNDESERVING OTHERS

The chapter epigraph quotations are from Adam Smith, *Theory of Moral Sentiments: The Glasgow Edition of the Works and Correspondence of Adam Smith, Vol. I*

3. DESERVING AND UNDESERVING OTHERS

(Oxford: Oxford University Press, 1976), 9; and Richard Sennett and Jonathan Cobb, *The Hidden Injuries of Class* (Cambridge: Cambridge University Press, 1972), 256.

1. We discussed this problem and its links to the moral economy tradition in the introduction. See also Karen A. Hegtvedt and Cathryn Johnson, "Justice Beyond the Individual: A Future with Legitimation," *Social Psychology Quarterly*, 63 no. 8 (2000): 298–311.

2. Compared to Western Europeans or North Americans, citizens in Central Eastern Europe and post-Soviet societies favor state intervention in the economy, support a more active role of the welfare state, and are more critical of economic inequality (in particular of high wages). See Sheri Kunovich and Kazimierz Slomczynski, "Systems of Distribution and a Sense of Equity: A Multilevel Analysis of Meritocratic Attitudes in Post-Industrial Societies," *European Sociological Review* 23, no. 5 (2007): 649–663. One large-scale, cross-national survey finds that egalitarianism is the predominating justice ideology among individuals who grew up in Communist Party–ruled societies because people who were familiarized with those values at a young age also tend to support them later in life. "Living longer under a communist regime," the authors of that study note, "is associated with higher support for welfare state service provision in the post-communist period." See Grigore Pop-Eleches and Joshua A. Tucker, *Communism's Shadow: The Effect of Communist Legacies on Post-Communist Political Attitudes* (Princeton, NY: Princeton University Press, 2017), 198.

3. The authors of that study assert that this was due to the "relative affluence" of these societies. For the Czech Republic, they note that "public opinion . . . has shifted significantly towards less support for basic egalitarian principles, greater opposition to government intervention to promote social welfare, more tolerance of a greater range of inequality, greater perceived general legitimacy of the economic system, and a more favourable view of wealth as due to positive personal qualities." They add that "change in Eastern Germany is somewhat less extensive," but "because the perceived legitimacy of the economic order [market society] was the highest among postcommunist countries by a substantial margin in 1991, the absence of change may here be taken as showing support for market justice." See James R. Kluegel, David S. Mason, and Bernd Wegener, "The Legitimation of Capitalism in the Postcommunist Transition: Public Opinion About Market Justice, 1991–1996," *European Sociological Review* 15, no. 3 (1999): 251–283, 260–261.

4. Hans W. Bierhoff, "Zufriedenheit, Leistungsbereitschaft und Unfairneß in Ost- und Westdeutschland: Zur Psychosozialen Befindlichkeit nach der Wiedervereinigung," in *Gerechtigkeitserleben im Wiedervereinigten Deutschland*, ed. Rudi Schmitt and Leo Montada (Wiesbaden: Springer, 1999), 45–66. These were signs of what Alexis de Tocqueville had called a *revolution of rising expectations*. It should not be equated with support for democracy. But support for market society was certainly closely interlinked with favorable views of democracy and liberalism; it was a sign of open-mindedness and readiness for change. In the early 1990s, most people rejected the political and social standstill that had become characteristic of late socialism and enthusiastically embraced the arrival of the new order.

5. These quotes are taken from Steven Padgett, *Organizing Democracy in Eastern Germany: Interest Groups in Post-Communist Society* (Cambridge: Cambridge University Press, 1999), 110.

3. DESERVING AND UNDESERVING OTHERS

6. Soon after reunification, a decreasing share of East Germans thought of income differences as a legitimate way to encourage individual effort in market society. By the mid-1990s, support for this idea had dropped significantly relative to 1989, as noted by Heinz-Herbert Noll and Bernhard Christoph, "Akzeptanz und Legitimität sozialer Ungleichheit," in *Sozialer und Politischer Wandel in Deutschland. Analysen mit Allbus-Daten aus Zwei Jahrzehnten*, ed. Rüdiger Schmitt-Beck, Martina Wasmer, and Achim Koch (Wiesbaden: VS Verlag, 2004), 97–125, 107–110. Immediately after the fall of the Berlin Wall, around 59 percent of East Germans saw income differences as legitimate, but only 44 percent did so in 1994, and then again 49 percent around the turn of the century. Noll and Christoph note that the uptick in 2000 likely represents a new, younger cohort entering the survey, not a reversal of the trend. A comparable shift occurred with regard to the question of whether status differences legitimately reflect a structure of opportunities that individuals could have taken advantage of—a question that measured whether a person believed equality of opportunity was given after 1989. This was positively affirmed by 46 percent right after the fall of the Berlin Wall but by a mere 27 percent in 1998. During the 1990s, more and more East Germans felt they were being cheated on, and the share of East Germans who thought that social upward mobility and wealth could be attained only by illegitimate means was sharply rising. For the purpose of our discussion, West German trends after 1989 provide a useful negative case, as described by Ann S. Orloff, *The Politics of Pensions: A Comparative Analysis of Britain, Canada, and the United States, 1880–1940* (Madison: University of Wisconsin Press, 1993). Two decades after 1989, East Germans were less satisfied with their material situation and with their living situation than West Germans, notes Petra Böhnke, "Ost-Glück versus West-Glück?," in *Leben in Ost-und Westdeutschland: Eine Sozialwissenschaftliche Bilanz der Deutschen Einheit 1990–2010*, ed. Peter Krause and Ilona Ostner (Frankfurt: Campus, 2010), 695–708. They felt they earned less than their West German peers and thus less than they deserved. East Germans showed less support for individualistic beliefs and more support for egalitarian views than their West German counterparts. See Jean-Yves Gerlitz, Kai Mühleck, Percy Scheller, and Markus Schrenker, "Justice Perceptions in Times of Transition: Trends in Germany, 1991–2006," *European Sociological Review* 28, no. 2 (2012): 263–282. In terms of order-related justice beliefs, the period between 1991 and 2000 in fact saw the two Germanies growing apart instead of together, assert Noll and Christoph, *Akzeptanz*. The return of egalitarianism is similarly documented by Bernd Wegener and Stefan Liebig, "Gerechtigkeitsvorstellungen in Ost-und Westdeutschland im Wandel: Sozialisation, Interessen, Lebenslauf," in *Leben in Ost-und Westdeutschland: Eine Sozialwissenschaftliche Bilanz der Deutschen Einheit 1990–2010*, ed. Peter Krause and Ilona Ostner (Frankfurt: Campus, 2010), 90.

7. See Kluegel et al., "The Legitimation of Capitalism." Between 1991 and 1995, the view that income differences expressed differences in effort and merit declined among Czechs. In 1991, 19 percent of respondents found disparities in income too small and 59 percent found them to be too large, but in 1995, only 5 percent thought they were too small and 81 percent thought they were too large. During the same period, support for the statement that "large profits for entrepreneurs are beneficial to everyone" declined from 67 percent to only 31 percent, according to Jiří Večerník,

3. DESERVING AND UNDESERVING OTHERS

Markets and People: The Czech Reform Experience in a Comparative Perspective (Avebury: Aldershot, 1996), 59, 60.

8. See Dieter Segert, *Transformationen in Osteuropa im 20: Jahrhundert* (Bonn: Bundeszentrale für Politische Bildung, 2014), 178; as well as Večerník, *Markets and People*, 52, 229. In comparison, in Poland, Hungary, or Slovakia, a majority of households reported that it was more difficult to make ends meet in 1995 than in 1989. In the Czech Republic, only about one-third of the population interpreted these changes to mean a deterioration of their status and in the financial means of their family. A sense of loss no doubt did exist. But in the Czech Republic, it was particularly acute among the elderly and those with low levels of education. A sense of gain, in turn, was most strongly felt by entrepreneurs, those with higher education, and young people. See Klára Vlachová and Blanka Řeháková, "Subjective Mobility After 1989: Do People Feel a Social and Economic Improvement or Relative Deprivation?," *Sociologický časopis/Czech Sociological Review* 3, no. 1 (1995): 137–155, 146–149.

9. Already in 1994, around half the population was skeptical about the course of privatization, expressing the belief that property is moving into the "wrong hands." See Večerník, *Markets and People*, 156.

10. See Ladislav Holy, in his *Little Czech and the Great Czech Nation: National Identity and the Post-Communist Social Transformation* (Cambridge: Cambridge University Press, 1996), 153; and Michael L. Smith, "Perceived Corruption, Distributive Justice, and the Legitimacy of the System of Social Stratification in the Czech Republic," *Communist and Post-Communist Studies* 43, no. 4 (2010): 439–451, on perceptions of corruption.

11. Kristen Ghodsee and Mitchell A. Orenstein, *Taking Stock of Shock: The Social Consequences of the 1989 Revolutions* (New York: Oxford University Press, 2021), 119–120.

12. Johanna Kallio and Mikko Niemelä, "Who Blames the Poor?: Multilevel Evidence of Support for and Determinants of Individualistic Explanation of Poverty in Europe," *European Societies* 16, no. 1 (2014): 112–135, 178, 122.

13. See Simone M. Schneider and Juan C. Castillo, "Poverty Attributions and the Perceived Justice of Income Inequality: A Comparison of East and West Germany," *Social Psychology Quarterly* 78, no. 3 (2015): 263–282, 273, 278. A critical issue seems to be that East Germans tend to regard matters of economic justice as linked to West German political dominance. The authors note that their measure of external attributions ("failure of the economic system") might be read by East German respondents as an "indicator of system disapproval." It is known that system disapproval and internal attributions can go hand in hand. See James Kluegel and Eliot R. Smith, *Beliefs About Inequality: Americans' Views of What Is and What Ought to Be* (Boulder, CO: Transaction, 1986).

14. Gerlitz et al., "Justice Perceptions in Times of Transition;" and Michael L. Smith and Petr Matějů, "Two Decades of Value Change: The Crystallization of Meritocratic and Egalitarian Beliefs in the Czech Republic," *Social Justice Research* 25, no. 4 (2012): 421–439, provide evidence for this position. On the "extraordinary mentality,, see Stefan Liebig and Ronald Verwiebe, "Einstellungen zur Sozialen Ungleichheit in Ostdeutschland," *Zeitschrift für Soziologie* 29, no. 1(2000): 3–26, 21; as well as Schneider and Castillo, "Poverty Attributions," 267. On East Germans evaluating

3. DESERVING AND UNDESERVING OTHERS

the collective plight, see Leo Montada and Anne Dieter, "Gewinn-und Verluster-fahrungen in den Neuen Bundesländern: Nicht die Kaufkraft der Einkommen, sondern Politische Bewertungen sind entscheidend," in *Gerechtigkeitserleben im Wiedervereinigten Deutschland*, ed. Rudi Schmitt and Leo Montada (Wiesbaden: Springer, 1999), 19–44. On Czech perceptions, see Martin Kreidl, "Perceptions of Poverty and Wealth in Western and Post-Communist Countries," *Social Justice Research* 13, no. 2 (2000): 151–176, 171.

15. Researchers note that, when people compare themselves to others, the act of choosing the targets of comparison is part of the process of reasoning about justice. Motives to compare can vary. Individuals might draw comparisons to generate information, or to take and affirm a moral stance, but they might also do so for purely affective reasons such as "feeling better about oneself." See Abraham P. Buunk and Frederick X. Gibbons, "Social Comparison: The End of a Theory and the Emergence of a Field," *Organizational Behavior and Human Decision Processes* 102, no. 1 (2007): 3–21, 7–8.

16. There are two ways in which this can happen. First, respondents may bring up deservingness accounts as part of their biographical narrative. Second, in the focused part of the interview, respondents were prompted to talk about others. The wording of the two particularly relevant questions asked was as follows: 'Some people think that those who did not manage to 'get back on their feet' after 1989 economically were responsible for themselves. Do you agree?' And "In turn, some people think that some had generated 'undeserved wealth' after 1989. Do you agree?"

17. For analyzing boundaries, I draw on Michèle Lamont and Virag Molnár, "The Study of Boundaries in the Social Sciences," *Annual Review of Sociology* (2002): 167–195; as well as Luis Presser, "Violent Offenders, Moral Selves: Constructing Identities and Accounts in the Research Interview," *Social Problems* 51, no. 1 (2004): 82–101. From a subfield of social justice research, further valuable insights that lend support to the proposition that the post-1989 period serves as a framework of both social and temporal references can be gleaned: In temporal comparison theory, as developed by Stuart Albert, "Temporal Comparison Theory," *Psychological Review* 84, no. 6 (1977): 485–503, comparisons are defined as an act of comparing at least two points in time of a personal trajectory. Individuals look back to an earlier stage in their lives, juxtapose the "then" and the "now," and derive a positive or a negative difference from this. This creates a sense of coherence, stability, and sameness. Temporal comparisons can also be drawn at the group level.

18. Herbert M. Lefcourt, "Locus of Control and the Response to Aversive Events," *Canadian Psychological Review/Psychologie Canadienne* 17, no. 3 (1976): 202–209, calls this the "locus of control." I draw specifically on Daniel Miller, *Social Justice* (Oxford: Oxford University Press, 1979), 83–114, to understand what justice principles are invoked when someone's choices are evaluated. Deservingness accounts are informed by justice principles. As discussed in the introduction, the principle of merit rests on the notion of individual responsibility; it highlights inner dispositions such as effort, convictions, or psychological traits; the principle of need foregrounds environmental factors such as beneficial or disadvantageous conditions, resources, relationships, and available cultural tools. The principle of equality looks beyond this distinction and argues that a different standard of evaluation

altogether must be applied: it regards the resulting disparity to be illegitimate and claims that equality of outcomes must be guaranteed.

19. Because the prompt invites respondents to evaluate unequal outcomes and asks for personalized stories, the primary focus is on the tension between merit and need. Prior studies have identified this tension as key to the problem of responsibility attributions, for instance, Schneider and Castillo, "Poverty Attributions," 265. People make inferences about the inputs that are necessary to achieve something by first considering outcomes, as classically formulated by Melvin J. Lerner, "The Justice Motive in Social Behavior," *Journal of Social Issues* 31, no. 3 (1975): 1–19. The analysis thus begins by schematically distinguishing between "positive" and "negative" outcomes as narrated by respondents. Stories with a positive result are usually concerned with how someone managed to cope with economic hardship and difficulties, such as unemployment. Here, hardship is located in the middle part of the story. Most stories with a negative result are concerned with how someone is stuck in a negative economic plight (not managing to cope), or how someone has amassed wealth (including welfare benefits) by illegitimate means. Scholars note that more than one justice principle can be held by the same person and one can be introduced to relativize the other. See Kluegel and Smith, *Beliefs About Inequality*; as well as Wim Van Oorschot, "Making the Difference in Social Europe: Deservingness Perceptions Among Citizens of European Welfare States," *Journal of European Social Policy* 16, no. 1 (2006). Acknowledging disadvantages of age and sickness, for instance, makes economic failure likely to be understood as partly beyond control and therefore less likely to be regarded as deserved. It is normal to relativize a principle when generating a story or an account, something that survey questionnaires usually miss when forcing an either/or decision. One strength of the narrative method and analysis is that it can distinguish between relativizing a principle to some degree and abandoning it altogether.

20. Respondents don't share a single definition of "economic success." Given the economic challenges of the post-1989 years in East Germany and the Czech Republic, economic success does not signify becoming wealthy; rather, it means getting through the time with a sense of autonomy, achievement, the notion of a "decent" outcome in terms of a middle-class ideal of having a steady job, being able to provide for one's family, being able to travel, and to "stay true to oneself."

21. Czech proverb: *Bez práce nejsou koláče*.

22. See Van Oorschot, "Making the Difference in Social Europe."

23. See Lenka Kissová, "The Production of (Un)Deserving and (Un)Acceptable: Shifting Representations of Migrants within Political Discourse in Slovakia," *East European Politics and Societies* 32, no. 4 (2018): 743–766, and Bernadette Nadya Jaworsky & Jan Krotký, "'A brother is more than a neighbour': Symbolic boundary work in Czech pro-migration discourse," *European Journal of Cultural and Political Sociology* 8, no. 3 (2021): 329–354.

24. As shown in table 3.1, accounts of undeserved success are the only type that do not revolve around overcoming economic hardship. In the others, the acting subject faces a troubling moral choice (a "dilemma") and is forced to live with the consequences. The fundamental narrative structure is that of a potentially tragic choice, which, according to Philip Smith, "is marked by a strong sense of character movement. . . . The essence of tragedy is the futility of human striving, the fall from

3. DESERVING AND UNDESERVING OTHERS

grace, the missed opportunity and the horror of suffering, the disintegration of society, and the movement from social integration to social isolation and atomization." See Philip Smith, *Why War?: The Cultural Logic of Iraq, the Gulf War, and Suez* (Chicago: University of Chicago Press, 2005), 25. In accounts of "deserved success," these dangers are avoided. Tragedy is averted, and elements of heroism become visible. One can vividly relate to the tragic narrative structure but less so to examples of undeserved success, which have more of a cynical (or fatalistic, but perhaps also comical) element to them.

25. For East Germany, see, for instance, Martin Diewald, "Spirals of Success and Failure?: The Interplay of Control Beliefs and Working Lives in the Transition from Planned to Market Economy," in *After the Fall of the Wall: Life Courses in the Transformation of East Germany*, ed. Martin Diewald, Anne Goedicke, and Karl Ulrich Mayer (Stanford, CA: Stanford University Press, 2006), 214–236. For the Czech Republic, see Petr Matějů, "From Equality to Equity?: The Czech Republic Between Two Ideologies of Distributive Justice." *Czech Sociological Review* 1, no. 3 (1993): 251–275, 272. Kreidl, "Perceptions of Poverty and Wealth," 176, confirms the association between unemployment and egalitarian beliefs. The longer a person was unemployed, the stronger this person's inclination to explain wealth by structural causes. The problem of "value crystallization" is further explored in a longitudinal perspective by Smith and Matějů, "Two Decades of Value Change," 432. Between 1991 and 2009, the authors find, certain social groups favor egalitarian beliefs: those with low social status, those with experiences of unemployment, and those with low levels of education. In contrast, those with high levels of education and high status lean toward the merit principle. From this, they conclude that beliefs have "now [in 2012] reached a value structure similar to that of . . . Western countries." At the same time, however, Czechs, similar to citizens in other postsocialist societies, "tend to be highly sensitive to the presence of economic inequality," as highlighted by Smith, "Perceived Corruption," 442. In an earlier study, Vlachová and Řeháková, "Subjective Mobility After 1989," 146–149, note that the sense of loss in the Czech Republic after 1989 was moderate compared to other postsocialist societies. It was acute only among the elderly and those with low levels of education. A sense of gain, in turn, could be found among entrepreneurs, those with higher education, and young people.

26. In chapter 2, we encountered the phenomenon that experiences of joblessness in the past can be differently interpreted. For some, these episodes serve as an illustration that there are forces in society far beyond an individual's control; others, emphasizing the fact that they managed to cope successfully, draw the lesson from it that persistence and individual commitment matter above all.

27. The deservingness accounts considered here are in fact narratives about the *degree* to which the merit principle can be applied or not. They do not rest on a binary opposition but really on a different extent to which people are ready to *relativize* the principle of merit: Engineers do so less, health-care workers more strongly.

28. The burden of proof lies with the principle of need.

29. Hannah Arendt, *The Life of the Mind* (Boston: Houghton Mifflin Harcourt, 1978), remarks that there can be no conception of individual responsibility, of willpower as intervening in time, without the idea of a given order of time. Willpower structures time into a *before* and *after*, without which humans would be deprived of

agency, trapped in historical determinism. In what she calls the "wonder of beginnings," a person anchors the idea of agency in a larger horizon of meaning. The idea of autonomy and responsibility is also imbued with human dignity.

30. See Leslie McCall, *The Undeserving Rich: American Beliefs About Inequality, Opportunity, and Redistribution* (Cambridge: Cambridge University Press, 2013); Kreidl, "Perceptions of Poverty and Wealth," 171.

31. With Pierre Nora's concept, there's an association with nationalism. But that actually also makes sense if we understand the post-1989 period as potentially the source of nationalist feelings. Pierre Nora, "Between Memory and History: Les Lieux de Mémoire," *Representations* 26 (1989): 7–24.

32. Smith, *Theory of Moral Sentiments*, 10.

4. THE SOCIAL EXPERIENCE OF THE
TRANSFORMATION PERIOD

The quotes in the chapter epigraph are from Svetlana Alexievich, *Second Hand Time: The Last of the Soviets* (New York: Random House, 2016), 159; and Didier Eribon, *Returning to Reims* (Cambridge, MA: MIT Press, 2013), 172.

1. As outlined in the introduction, this discussion draws on a combination of moral economy approaches, social memory studies, and relational sociology. Classic works such as Glen H. Elder, *Children of the Great Depression: Social Change in Life Experience* (Boulder, CO: Westview Press, 1999), or Katherine S. Newman, *Falling from Grace: The Experience of Downward Mobility in the American Middle Class* (New York: Free Press, 1988), illustrate how economic crises and times of economic hardship affect interpersonal relations. Ways of coping with economic hardship, which become part of family memory, also shape the memory of these episodes in the long run.

2. For the estimate of East German migration flows between 1989 and 2017, see Die ZEIT, "Ost-West-Wanderung," May 5 2019, www.zeit.de/politik/deutschland /2019-05/ost-west-wanderung-abwanderung-ostdeutschland-umzug.

3. Ivan Krastev and Stephen Holmes, *The Light That Failed: A Reckoning* (London: Allen Lane, 2019), 37.

4. Dušan Drbohlav, "Patterns of Immigration in the Czech Republic, Hungary and Poland," in *European Immigrations: Trends, Structures and Policy Implication*, ed. Marek Okólski (Amsterdam: Amsterdam University Press, 2012), 179–209.

5. The classic formulation of foci-theory is Scott L. Feld, "The Focused Organization of Social Ties," *American Journal of Sociology* 86, no. 5 (1981): 1015–1035.

6. Ronald S. Burt, "Decay Functions," *Social Networks* 22, no. 1 (2000): 1–28. On the various structural reasons for why ties dissolve, see also Claire Bidart and Daniel Lavenu, "Evolutions of Personal Networks and Life Events," *Social Networks* 27, no. 4 (2005): 359–376; Jacob Habinek, John Levi Martin, and Benjamin D. Zablocki, "Double-Embeddedness: Spatial and Relational Contexts of Tie Persistence and Re-Formation," *Social Networks* 42 (2015): 27–41; and Barry Wellman, Renita Yuklin Wong, David Tindall, and Nancy Nazer, "A Decade of Network Change: Turnover, Persistence and Stability in Personal Communities," *Social Networks* 19, no. 1 (1997): 27–50.

4. THE SOCIAL EXPERIENCE OF THE TRANSFORMATION PERIOD

7. Richard Sennett and Jonathan Cobb, *The Hidden Injuries of Class* (Cambridge: Cambridge University Press, 1972).
8. For discussions of the concept of homophily, see Miller McPherson, Lynn Smith-Lovin, and James M. Cook, "Birds of a Feather: Homophily in Social Networks," *Annual Review of Sociology* 27 (2001): 415–444; and Mark T. Rivera, Sara B. Soderstrom, and Brian Uzzi, "Dynamics of Dyads in Social Networks: Assortative, Relational, and Proximity Mechanisms," *Annual Review of Sociology* 36 (2010): 91–115.
9. For a global comparison of informal ties and their salience in CEE societies, see Florian Pichler and Claire Wallace, "Patterns of Formal and Informal Social Capital in Europe," *European Sociological Review* 23, no. 4 (2007): 423–435. An exemplary examination of this subject in Russia is provided by Alena Ledeneva, *Russia's Economy of Favours: Blat, Networking, and Informal Exchanges* (Cambridge: Cambridge University Press, 1998).
10. For social capital among East Germans after the fall of the Berlin Wall, see Peter Boenisch and Lutz Schneider, "The Social Capital Legacy of Communism: Results from the Berlin Wall Experiment," *European Journal of Political Economy* 32 (2013): 391–411; and Paul Schmelzer, "Netzwerkveränderung als Folge der Transformation?," *Berliner Journal für Soziologie* 15, no. 1 (2005): 73–86. In the Czech case, findings are less representative for the wider population but instead are focused on the question of elite reproduction and change after 1989. Social capital was a critical determinant of upward mobility, as described by Vladimír Benáček, "The Rise of the 'Grand Entrepreneurs' in the Czech Republic and Their Contest for Capitalism," *Sociologický časopis/Czech Sociological Review* 46, no. 6 (2006). An early survey conducted in 1993 already revealed that social capital positively affected income and status, as noted by Petr Matějů and Nelson Lim, "Who Has Gotten Ahead After the Fall of Communism?," *Czech Sociological Review* 3, no. 2 (1995): 117–136. A study examining the 2001 *International Social Survey Programme* results for the Czech Republic confirmed this association, noting that "the higher a respondent's prestige, the greater the participation in exchange networks." See Petr Matějů and Anna Vitásková, "Interpersonal Trust and Mutually Beneficial Exchanges: Measuring Social Capital for Comparative Analyses," *Sociologický časopis/Czech Sociological Review* 42, no. 3 (2006): 493–516. Individuals who were socially upward mobile managed to develop more extensive networks of weak ties than the socially stagnant or downward mobile. What is more, former cadres of the Communist nomenklatura had excellent opportunities to become private entrepreneurs and to advance socially after the revolution. They managed to convert their pre-1989 political capital efficiently into post-1989 social capital. Mobilizing existing networks, in particular, constituted a success strategy, as demonstrated by Ed Clark, "The Role of Social Capital in Developing Czech Private Business," *Work, Employment and Society* 14, no. 3 (2000): 439–458. Clark, who interviewed the same entrepreneurs at various points in time during the 1990s, finds that the most successful among them had ties to the former nomenklatura. The primary significance of existing networks challenges the idea that an entrepreneurial attitude was by itself decisive for economic success after 1989; Clark writes: "On the surface, they may appear to be individualistic, risk-taking 'entrepreneurs,' but these founders could not have exploited these opportunities by themselves. Indeed, their ability to draw on the help of trustworthy contacts in extensive networks built up before 1990 went some

4. THE SOCIAL EXPERIENCE OF THE TRANSFORMATION PERIOD

way to dissipate the risks." Social capital also compensated for a lack of economic capital. Most people could draw on few financial resources after the system transition, and banks had little incentive to give out loans; those who could mobilize existing resources in the form of information and networks used them to enter the entrepreneurial sector. The fact that most people viewed former firm managers and high-ranking members of the service class with great suspicion inadvertently contributed to the formation of stronger bonds among those in this elite class.

11. The quotes are taken from Marc M. Howard, *The Weakness of Civil Society in Post-Communist Europe* (Cambridge: Cambridge University Press, 2003), 72, 163.

12. See Corinna Kausmann et al., "Zivilgesellschaftliches Engagement," in *Datenreport Zivilgesellschaft*, ed. Holger Krimmer (Wiesbaden: VS Verlag 2019): 55–92, 65–67.

13. See Kalinová, *Konec Nadějím*, 347.

14. Tereza Pospíšilová, "Dobrovolnictví v České republice před rokem 1989: diskurzy, definice, aktualizace," *Sociologický časopis/Czech Sociological Review* 47, no. 5 (2011): 887–910, 892–893, argues that there is much more continuity in voluntary activities than there are breaks. See also the volume by Marek Skovajsa et al., *Občanský sektor: Organizovaná občanská společnost v České Republice* (Praha: Portál 2010), which provides an overview of the rich landscape of civil society organizations and their history in the Czech Republic. On nongovernmental organizations (NGOs), see Petra Rakušanová, *Povaha občanské společnosti v České Republice v kontextu střední Evropy* (Praha: Sociologický ústav AV ČR, 2007), 68–71.

15. Skovajsa et al., *Občanský sector*.

16. The quote is taken from Markéta Sedláčková and Jiří Šafr, "Legitimacy and Civic Culture: Trust in Democracy in the Czech Republic after EU Accession (2004–2014)," *Comparative Sociology* 17, no. 3–4 (2018): 318–353, 336.

17. See https://ourworldindata.org/covid-vaccinations (accessed July 7, 2022). By November 2021, a mere roughly 60 percent of the population in Saxony had received basic immunization. In the northwestern state of Schleswig-Holstein, this number was around 75 percent at the time; see Robert Koch Institut, *Epidemiologisches Bulletin* 27/2022, https://www.rki.de/DE/Content/Infekt/EpidBull/Archiv/2022/Ausgaben/27_2022.pdf.

18. On generalized trust, see Christian Bjørnskov, "Determinants of Generalized Trust: A Cross-Country Comparison," *Public Choice* 130, no. 1–2 (2007): 1–21. On privatization and perceptions of unfairness, see James Kluegel, and David S. Mason, "Fairness Matters: Social Justice and Political Legitimacy in Post-Communist Europe," *Europe-Asia Studies* 56, no. 6 (2004): 813–834. Eric M. Uslaner and Gabriel Badescu, "Honesty, Trust, and Legal Norms in the Transition to Democracy: Why Bo Rothstein Is Better Able to Explain Sweden Than Romania," in *Creating Social Trust in Post-Socialist Transition*, ed. Janos Kornai, Bo Rothstein, and Susan Rose-Ackerman (New York: Palgrave MacMillan, 2004), 31–51, offer a differentiated view of the problem of corruption. They note that high levels of corruption after 1989 did not damage generalized trust as much as is generally assumed. Relying on indexes of corruption diverts our attention away from more profound, cultural dimensions of trust in postsocialist societies. Their argument (derived mainly from the case of Romania) is that the continuing importance of small-scale economic favors and norms of reciprocity after 1989 makes many of the practices in question, such as paying a small bribe at the doctor's office, appear as more natural. The fact

4. THE SOCIAL EXPERIENCE OF THE TRANSFORMATION PERIOD

that confidence in institutions and official ways of obtaining things is low does not necessarily imply that people distrust each other. On this point, see also Nina Bandelj, "On Postsocialist Capitalism," *Theory and Society* 45, no. 1 (2016): 89–106; and Richard Rose, *Understanding Post-Communist Transformation: A Bottom Up Approach* (London: Routledge, 2009), 63, who confirms this view, asserting that in postsocialist societies, "trust in people you know" and "trust in most people" is dissociated from trust in institutions: "Trust in people you know" is generally high, "trust in most people" is relatively high, but trust in institutions is extremely low. Unlike in Western Europe, there is also no correlation between generalized trust and gross domestic product (GDP) growth in Central Eastern European societies, as noted by Matějů and Vitasková, "Interpersonal Trust and Mutually Beneficial Exchanges," 500.

19. The quote is taken from Sedláčková and Šafr, "Legitimacy and Civic Culture," 335; see also Matějů and Vitásková, "Interpersonal Trust and Mutually Beneficial Exchanges," 500.

20. The first study for East Germany is Rüdiger Schmitt-Beck and Robert Rohrschneider, "Soziales Kapital und Vertrauen in die Institutionen der Demokratie," in *Sozialer und Politischer Wandel in Deutschland. Analysen mit Allbus-Daten aus zwei Jahrzehnten*, ed. Rüdiger Schmitt-Beck, Martina Wasmer, and Achim Koch (Wiesbaden: VS Verlag, 2004), 235–260; the second study, from which the quote is taken, is Markus Freitag and Richard Traunmüller, "Spheres of Trust: An Empirical Analysis of the Foundations of Particularised and Generalised Trust," *European Journal of Political Research* 48, no. 6 (2009): 782–803, 795.

21. On Croatia see Dražen Cepić, *Class Cultures in Post-Socialist Eastern Europe* (New York: Routledge, 2018); on Poland, see Zbigniew Karpiński, "Social Association and Social Inequality in Poland, 1988–2013," *International Journal of Sociology* 46, no. 4 (2016): 288–319.

22. Bernhard Nauck and Otto G. Schwenk, "Did Societal Transformation Destroy the Social Networks of Families in East Germany?," *American Behavioral Scientist* 44, no. 11 (2001): 1864–1878.

23. Birgit Becker, "Der Einfluss der Bezugsgruppenmeinung auf die Einstellung gegenüber Ausländern in Ost- und Westdeutschland/The Impact of the Reference Group on Attitudes Toward Foreigners in East and West Germany," *Zeitschrift für Soziologie* 34, no. 1 (2005): 40–59, 43, claimed that findings were "contradictory." The "niche" is discussed by Beate Volker and Henk Flap, "Weak Ties as a Liability: The Case of East Germany," *Rationality and Society* 13, no. 4 (2001): 419. The niche is defined as strong ties under state-socialist rule, ties that could be entrusted with political views, "a shelter from the meddling by the government and the party into . . . private lives." But it is also important to keep in mind that workplace ties often defied the private/public opposition, as argued by social historian Martin Kohli, "DDR als Arbeitsgesellschaft?," 31–61. The second study on changing ties mentioned is Martin Diewald and Jörg Lüdicke, "Community Lost or Freedom Gained?: Changes of Social Networks After 1989," in *After the Fall of the Wall: Life Courses in the Transformation of East Germany*, ed. Martin Diewald, Anne Goedicke, and Karl-Ulrich Mayer (Stanford, CA: Stanford University Press, 2006), 191–213. The authors differentiate types of ties and types of support. Relative to the "time before 1989," in 1993, 35 percent report "less emotional closeness" toward friends,

4. THE SOCIAL EXPERIENCE OF THE TRANSFORMATION PERIOD

only 5 percent report greater closeness, the rest reported unchanged feelings of closeness. In contrast, there is marked stability, even deepening, of core family ties. These ties, which were already close before the revolution, "became emotionally even closer, . . . more important for personal recognition, and provided more information about the new environment." An important caveat, however, is that respondents in the sample used in this study remained in the East; thus, the experience of those who left is not represented. Still, the findings are corroborated by two further studies. The first is Christine Posner, *Die Bedeutung sozialer Einbindung für die Entwicklung von Individualisierungsprozessen: Eine theoretische Annäherung an das Phänomen der Individualisierung sowie eine empirische Analyse der sozialen Bindungen unter den Bedingungen des sozialen Umbruchs in Deutschland* (Frankfurt Peter Lang, 2002); the second is Johannes Schaub, "Freundschaftsnetzwerke in den neuen Bundesländern," *Gruppe. Interaktion. Organisation. Zeitschrift für Angewandte Organisationspsychologie (GIO)* 33, no. 3 (2002): 295–310. The latter is a regional case study specifically focusing on East German friendship networks after the fall of the Berlin Wall. Schaub documents both continuity and change, observing that the intensity of single ties weakened significantly, but networks grew overall.

24. Nauck and Schwenk, "Did Societal Transformation Destroy?," draw on the dataset *Familiensurvey des Deutschen Jugendinstituts (DJI)*. A critical discussion of this measure can be found in Rainer Diaz-Bone, *Ego-Zentrierte Netzwerkanalyse und Familiale Beziehungssysteme* (Wiesbaden: Deutscher Universitätsverlag, 1997), 171–173. The quote is taken from Nauck and Schwenk, "Did Societal Transformation Destroy?," 1871. The interpretation of the time after 1989 as a time of insecurity experienced in one's interpersonal network is also corroborated by the finding that East Germans tend to have fewer weak ties and also value strong ties more than West Germans; see, for instance, Becker, "Der Einfluss der Bezugsgruppenmeinung," 43.

25. On the lack of Czech longitudinal measures (and the quote), see Julia Häuberer, *Social Capital Theory. Towards a Methodological Foundation* (Wiesbaden: Springer Verlag 2010), 31. Czech divorce rates are described by Tomáš Sobotka, "Fertility in Central and Eastern Europe After 1989: Collapse and Gradual Recovery," *Historical Social Research/Historische Sozialforschung* 36, no. 2 (2011): 246–296. Most of these processes peaked at some point during the mid-1990s and returned to a gradual trajectory afterward. While some have interpreted these (ongoing) developments in a rather fatalistic fashion—as the harbingers of the decline of the traditional family—there is evidence that they indicate new patterns of family cohesion. See Marcel Tomášek, "Naše blízké vztahy a společenské demokratizační změny: K novému chápání zdrojů integrace a reprodukce společnosti po roce 1989," *Gender rovné příležitosti výzkum* 8, no. 2 (2007): 1–6. Labor market change after 1989 had an effect on Czech marriages. A panel study conducted from 1994 to 1996 documented a sense of economic stress and irritation as well as effects of economic anxiety on family cohesion. According to the authors, it was not the "objective economic conditions" of these families, however, but rather husbands' cultural struggles with gendered "breadwinner" expectations (or in other words, coping styles) that regularly engendered marital stress and led to divorce, as documented in Joseph Hraba, Frederick O. Lorenz, and Zdeňka Pechačová, "Family Stress During the Czech

4. THE SOCIAL EXPERIENCE OF THE TRANSFORMATION PERIOD

Transformation," *Journal of Marriage and Family* 62, no. 2 (2000): 520–531. For Czech data on friendship after 1989, see, for instance, Klára Vlachová and Blanka Řeháková, "Subjective Mobility After 1989: Do People Feel a Social and Economic Improvement or Relative Deprivation?," *Sociologický časopis/Czech Sociological Review* 3, no. 1 (1995): 137–155. In this early study, the authors use data from a 1993 survey asking respondents about their friends. They document a tendency toward social closure (individuals befriending those who are very similar to them) that can be explained primarily by level of education. Thus, soon after the transition, a pattern of two distinct groups—each with great homogeneity in their respective circle of friends—became evident: individuals with at least a high school degree and individuals without this level of education. The two were separated by an "imaginary boundary," as they write. They also note that people with higher levels of education interact more regularly with friends and acquaintances. This is further confirmed by Blanka Řeháková, "Vzorce přátelství v české společnosti/Friendship Patterns in Czech Society," *Sociologický časopis/Czech Sociological Review* 39, no. 4 (2003): 509–528. In her assessment of Czech friendship patterns based on the 2001 *International Social Survey Programme* measure, Řeháková documents a strong tendency toward homophily in friendship ties with regard to level of education, gender, and age for Czech respondents in 2001. Those with higher educational credentials tend to have more friends, and, unlike those with lower levels of education, they also tend to make friends at work. She documents that friendship is regarded as distinct from family and kinship. Only a little more than one-quarter of respondents in this study name as their closest friend someone they are related to; the majority does not. Jiří Šafr, "Status Homogeneity and Heterogeneity in Social Contacts," in *Social Distances and Stratification: Social Space in the Czech Republic*, ed. Jiří Šafr and Julia Häuberer, (Prague: Sociologický ústav AV ČR, 2008), 55–66, uses a position-generator survey implemented in 2007 to study social distance, stratification, and friendship ties. He surmises that, given the history of Communist Party rule, making friends in one's neighborhood could potentially bring social diversity to one's circle of affiliates, as "in the Czech Republic, which had forty years of socialist housing policy bringing together people of different social background, we can still generally consider neighbourhood composition and consequently, elementary school, as a more status heterogeneous environment." However, he finds that (in 2007 at least), the workplace is much more important for getting to know people who could potentially become friends. In line with Řeháková, he also corroborates the finding that those with lower levels of education tend to embed their friendship ties strongly in a neighborhood context. In general, Šafr confirms the significant role of educational boundaries in Czech friendship networks, concluding that education homogeneity appears "very stable over time." There are indicators that these patterns were already present before the system transition. Citing research conducted in the 1960s that found a similar pattern of social closure (although based on a sample limited to males), Šafr remarks, "[S]ince the end of the 1960s there is virtually no change in the extent of homogeneity. . . . Closeness seems to be a more or less stable characteristic of Czech society."

26. Avshalom Caspi and Terrie E. Moffitt, "When Do Individual Differences Matter?: A Paradoxical Theory of Personality Coherence," *Psychological Inquiry* 4, no. 4 (1993): 247–271, 247.

4. THE SOCIAL EXPERIENCE OF THE TRANSFORMATION PERIOD

27. In the survey, East German and Czech respondents both report that it is important to them that their friends can relate to their views on the transformation time. The question reads: "With regard to the developments in the aftermath of the revolution: How important is it to you personally that your friends are able to relate to your views on the aftermath of the revolution?" Answers are on a scale from 0 to 10 (0 = not important, 10 = very important). In the results, East Germans are slightly more insistent that others share their views (with a mean of 6.1 and a median of 7) than Czechs (with a mean of 5.1 and a median of 6). The results indicate that this constitutes an important and meaningful issue for respondents (given the fact that there is a general tendency to choose middle categories when answering survey questions like this). Another question posed in the survey corroborates the notion that people went through the post-1989 period *together with others*. Asked to report the share of close friends that respondents have known since 1989, most report having known the majority of them for that length. The question reads, "How many of your close friends today have you known since the time of the revolution 1989/90 (including people you've known before the revolution)?" From sixty-one responses, answer categories and responses are as follows: "all" (7), "the majority" (35), "some" (15), "none" (3), "no answer" (1). The results are roughly the same for East Germans and Czechs. These findings speak to earlier, statistically representative findings on East German support networks that demonstrate that the time after 1989 was perceived as a challenge, as in Diewald and Lüdicke, "Community Lost or Freedom Gained?," 204.

28. For instance, Diane Vaughan's classic *Uncoupling: Turning Points in Intimate Relationships* (New York: Vintage, 1990), provides a rich qualitative study of relationship endings.

29. For a succinct overview of the literature on tie formation, see Mario L. Small, *Unanticipated Gains: Origins of Network Inequality in Everyday Life* (New York: Oxford University Press, 2009), 11–20. For the consequences of negative affect, see Giuseppe Labianca and Daniel J. Brass, "Exploring the Social Ledger: Negative Relationships and Negative Asymmetry in Social Networks in Organizations," *Academy of Management Review* 31, no. 3 (2006): 596–614, and Giuseppe Labianca, "Negative Ties in Organizational Networks," *Contemporary Perspectives on Organizational Social Networks* (Bingley, UK: Emerald Group Publishing, 2014), 239–259.

30. See the discussion above, and especially Burt, "Decay Functions," on natural tie dissolution.

31. The "broken tie" is a relation of animosity that is formed by moral tie dissolution in the past. It is a former strong relation turned negative. Hence, the broken tie could also be understood as a type of what network researchers have called "negative ties": relationships based on sentiments of animosity, see Labianca and Brass, "Exploring the Social Ledger," and Labianca, "Negative Ties in Organizational Networks." The moment of breaking nourishes negative sentiments. For this reason, the broken tie is not merely a thing of the past; it still affects the present. We can scrutinize this systematically, using concepts from social psychology. Viewing the broken tie as a negative tie, it is possible to distinguish three elements: negative affect, cognitive judgment, and behavioral intention. The first, negative affect, reveals a violation of a formerly positive bond and is articulated either with reference to a single event as a breach of trust, or as a description of negative character

4. THE SOCIAL EXPERIENCE OF THE TRANSFORMATION PERIOD

traits from which the respondent wishes to disassociate the self. In the latter case, traits such as envy, laziness, arrogance, or competitiveness are frequently referenced. Perceived "incompatibility" of self and former friend, described in Deborah M. Casper and Noel A. Card, "We Were Best Friends, But . . .": Two Studies of Antipathetic Relationships Emerging from Broken Friendships," *Journal of Adolescent Research* 25, no. 4 (2010): 499–526, 511, is based on affective evaluations of another person's character, including the feelings about another person's feeling. In Maria's account, negative affect is tied to the moment when her friend showed up at the birthday party, revealing her new, corrupted self. In this very moment, the former friend had performed a breach (carrying money into a sphere of intimacy), which is why she unfriends her—she does so by removing her from the circle of *genuine* friends, stating, "She occupied my guests, my friends, in this way!" Second, cognitive judgments concern the other person's agency with respect to breaking the tie. The act of developing unpleasant character traits or attitudes is regarded as a choice; it thus becomes an object of cognitive evaluation. Because a person is aware of the quality of the common bond in the past, he or she is also cognizant of the fact that the outcome could be different. This insight into the contingency of the mutual bond only enables moral judgment about another person's agency. Cognitive judgment is concerned with the possible trajectory of the relation. In Maria's story, this is exemplified by the moment in which the former friend showed up at the reunion, disappointing her one more time by confirming her transgressive attitude and signaling her unwillingness to return to her older self. The third attribute, behavioral intention, is revealed in strategies of avoiding someone and withdrawing from the relation. These strategies include reducing the formerly strong tie to a weak tie, as well as retrospectively reclassifying the relationship. When Maria asserts that she does not want her "around anymore," she underscores her intention to avoid her former friend in the future.

32. In the survey, respondents were asked to report on breaks in response to the following question: "In each case in which contact to someone broke off after 1989: did, in these cases, contact between this person and at least one friend of yours also break off?" Answer categories and number of responses are as follows: "generally yes" (24), "generally less so" (15), "no such case" (11), "no answer" (11). If we take the first and the second answer category to indicate breaks, then around 66 percent of East German respondents and around 59 percent of Czech respondents report breaks in the survey. However, there are ambiguities. The question asks for triadic breaks (meaning breaks among three not between two people). There is also no way to distinguish justified and unjustified breaks in the responses. We can read the results as substantiating the assumption that breaks *did play a role* after 1989—which is a relevant finding—but further inferences should not be drawn. Respondents were also asked to evaluate the role of moving away as a cause of tie dissolution. Moving away, as we have seen, counts as a "natural" factor, as in Burt, "Decay Functions." Overall, respondents tend to reject it as a major cause. The question reads: "In each case in which contact to someone broke off after 1989: what role, in your opinion, did moving away play in it?" On a scale of 11 (from 0 to 10, 0 = different causes than moving away, 1 0 =moving away as the main cause), the average score for sixty-one respondents is 4.1, the median is 4 (for East Germans, the mean is 4.18, the median is 4.5; for Czechs, the mean is 3.9, the median

is 3). Given that Czechs have not experienced much emigration after 1989, it is less surprising that they do not deem it all that important—yet it is arguably noteworthy that East Germans, who have experienced a massive population exodus after 1989, do not either. Again, these numbers must be treated with caution. As network researchers have demonstrated, there are possibly many more structural causes of tie dissolution besides relocating one's residence.

33. This estimate is taken from Catherine Epstein, "The Stasi: New Research on the East German Ministry of State Security," *Kritika: Explorations in Russian and Eurasian History* 5, no. 2 (2004): 341.

34. See Jens Gieseke, "The Stasi and East German Society: Some Remarks on Current Research," *GHI Bulletin Supplement* 9 (2014): 59–72.

35. On transitional justice and access to former secret police files, good overviews are provided by Gary Bruce, "Access to Secret Police Files, Justice, and Vetting in East Germany Since 1989," *German Politics and Society* 26, no. 1 (2008): 82–111, and by Katherine Verdery in "Postsocialist Cleansing in Eastern Europe: Purity and Danger in Transitional Justice," *Socialism Vanquished, Socialism Challenged: Eastern Europe and China, 1989-2009,* ed. Nina Bandelj and Dorothy J. Solinger (Oxford: Oxford University Press, 2012), 63–82.

36. Some respondents remark that they decided against accessing the files for fear that this might hurt some relationships even today. The quote is taken from Marci Shore, "(The End of) Communism as a Generational History: Some Thoughts on Czechoslovakia and Poland," *Contemporary European History* 18, no 3 (2009): 327.

37. The quote is taken from Nina Bandelj, "Thinking About Social Relations in Economy as Relational Work," in *Re-Imagining Economic Sociology,* ed. Patrik Aspers and Nigel Dodd (Oxford: Oxford University Press), 233–234.

38. Michèle Lamont, *The Dignity of Working Men: Morality and the Boundaries of Race, Class, and Immigration* (Cambridge, MA: Harvard University Press, 2000).

39. Andrew R. Sayer, *The Moral Significance of Class* (Cambridge: Cambridge University Press, 2005), 148–149.

40. Pierre Bourdieu, *Outline of a Theory of Practice* (New York: Cambridge University Press, 1977). For an expansion of this view and the discussion of moral economic sentiments, see Sayer, *The Moral Significance of Class.* For relational perspectives in economic sociology see Bandelj, "Thinking About Social Relations."

41. The quote is taken from Sayer, *The Moral Significance of Class,* 56.

42. Viviana A. Zelizer, *The Social Meaning of Money* (New York: Basic Books, 1998).

43. Allison J. Pugh, *The Tumbleweed Society: Working and Caring in an Age of Insecurity* (Oxford: Oxford University Press, 2015).

44. For the notion of "acting on behalf," see Julia P. Adams, "1-800-How-Am-I-Driving?," *Social Science History* 35, no. 1 (2011): 1–17. Solidarity in remembering is a form of *speaking* on behalf. This can also happen by incorporating someone else's story into a generalized, collective account of economic hardship after 1989. Social memory is performed through acts of recounting economic experiences in the form of a *we* instead of an *I*. It matters greatly that the relation to the person in question is maintained over time. For similar arguments, see also Francesca Polletta, *Inventing the Ties That Bind: Imagined Relationships in Moral and Political Life* (Chicago: Chicago University Press, 2020).

4. THE SOCIAL EXPERIENCE OF THE TRANSFORMATION PERIOD

45. On the decline in East Germany, see Howard, *The Weakness of Civil Society*, 73, 163. The succinct title is David Ost, *The Defeat of Solidarity* (Ithaca, NY: Cornell University Press, 2005).
46. The literature on this topic is unsurprisingly vast. Very informative contributions are Harry Blatterer, *Everyday Friendships: Intimacy as Freedom in a Complex World* (New York: Palgrave MacMillan, 2015), and Lois M. Verbrugge, "The Structure of Adult Friendship Choices," *Social Forces* 56, no. 2 (1977): 576–597.
47. The quote is taken from Blatterer, *Everyday Friendships*, 94.
48. See Avishai Margalit, *On Betrayal* (Cambridge, MA: Harvard University Press, 2017), 74, 110.
49. These concepts and social semiotics of surrender are offered by Robin Wagner Pacifici, *The Art of Surrender: Decomposing Sovereignty at Conflict's End* (Chicago: University of Chicago Press, 2005).
50. The quote is taken from Margalit, *On Betrayal*, 112. On the fragility of social relations see also Gabriella Turnaturi, *Betrayals: The Unpredictability of Human Relations* (Chicago: University of Chicago Press, 2005).
51. The first quote is taken from Avishai Margalit, *The Ethics of Memory* (Cambridge, MA: Harvard University Press, 2004), 30; the problem of betrayal as "replacement" is discussed in Margalit, *On Betrayal*, 93, 110. On the reevaluation of the very meaning of a relationship see also Vaughan, *Uncoupling*.
52. These are the findings by Diewald and Lüdicke, "Community Lost or Freedom Gained?," 210–212.
53. For instance, Cepić, *Class Cultures*, and Karpiński, "Social Association."
54. See Pierre Bourdieu, *Distinction: A Social Critique of the Judgement of Taste* (Cambridge, MA: Harvard University Press, 1984). For "thick" moral concepts, see Gabriel Abend, *The Moral Background: An Inquiry into the History of Business Ethics* (Princeton, NJ: Princeton University Press, 2014), 38, 39.
55. Margalit, *On Betrayal*, 93.
56. We may find the idea of equality as something rooted in character dispositions to be odd. After all, we like to think of equality as a social condition, a structural, external feature of the world that grants each and every individual access to resources. But there are different ways of conceiving of it. In fact, a venerable school of thought has for centuries promoted notions of equality that rely *exclusively* on images of a person's intrinsic characteristics: the conservative, moralistic tradition. Here, the cosmology of legitimate and illegitimate inequality—in particular, the question of what counts as acceptable social mobility—is predicated on the notion of personal virtue. As the philosopher Pierre Rosanvallon notes in *The Society of Equals* (Cambridge, MA: Harvard University Press, 2013), 109, nineteenth-century scholars who promoted this doctrine defined equality "by the (theoretical) possibility that anyone might join the elite rather than by any index of progress for the average person." Anyone could rise to the top, but only if he or she had the proper virtues and talents. This implies, first, that a person's inner qualities are the *only* legitimate source of economic success. This element of the conservative tradition seems outdated from the standpoint of our contemporary meritocratic understanding: we value action, the sense that a person did something in order to credit them with the rewards for their achievements; we reject the

4. THE SOCIAL EXPERIENCE OF THE TRANSFORMATION PERIOD

claim that someone deserves a particular social status just because they were born into the right place and family. And this is how respondents in this study, who value individual agency, think about the matter, too. But there is another dimension to the conservative tradition that still has traction today: the belief that moral integrity makes status differences *acceptable*. According to this view, it is legitimate for someone to ascend the social ladder as long as this person's inner life is not corrupted by it. As we have seen, this latter way of reasoning about inequality and justice is widespread after 1989. The conviction that there must be some type of moral symmetry between a person's inner qualities and their status in society emerges as an important motif of the transformation experience. It is arguably the default position—a set of beliefs that seem so natural, so obvious to everyone, that they need no justification. We could see how numerous respondents treat social differences as a matter of character: In refusing to criticize others in material and financial terms, specifically, they resort to a moral critique of inequality. In this way, perceptions of structural disparities are translated into judgments about individual persons.

57. This quote is taken from Joseph E. Davis, "Victim Narratives and Victim Selves: False Memory Syndrome and the Power of Accounts," *Social Forces* 52, no. 4 (2005): 529–548, 532.

58. The quote is taken from Sayer, *The Moral Significance of Class*, 114. The idea of working class "respectability" is elaborated by Sennett and Cobb, *The Hidden Injuries of Class*, as well by Lamont, *The Dignity of Working Men*.

EPILOGUE: HOW RIGHT-WING POPULISTS CAPTURE DESERVINGNESS

1. See Robin Wagner Pacifici. *What Is an Event?* (Chicago: University of Chicago Press, 2017).

2. See Ron Eyerman, *Memory, Trauma, and Identity* (New York: Palgrave, 2019), 5; Jeffrey C. Alexander, *Trauma: A Social Theory* (Hoboken, NJ: John Wiley, 2012).

3. Ivan Krastev and Stephen Holmes, *The Light That Failed: A Reckoning* (London: Allen Lane, 2019),; Timothy Snyder, *The Road to Unfreedom: Russia, Europe, America* (New York: Tim Duggan Books, 2018).

4. See, for instance, Diana C. Mutz, "Status Threat, Not Economic Hardship, Explains the 2016 Presidential Vote, *Proceedings of the National Academy of Sciences*, 115 (2018): E4330–E4339, and Stephen L. Morgan, "Status Threat, Material Interests, and the 2016 Presidential Vote," *Socius* 4 (2018): 1–17.

5. Noam Gidron and Peter A. Hall, "Populism as a Problem of Social Integration," *Comparative Political Studies* 53, no. 7 (2020): 1027–1059.

6. Michael J. Sandel, *The Tyranny of Merit: What's Become of the Common Good?* (New York: Penguin Classics, 2020).

7. On this point, see the insightful analysis by Melinda Cooper, *Family Values: Between Neoliberalism and the New Social Conservatism* (New York: Zone Books, 2017). For postsocialist Hungary, Chris Hann demonstrates this for the example of Hungarian *workfare* programs in rural towns. These are public funds; however, they are widely accepted as long as they are successfully symbolically framed within what Hann

calls the "government's edifying philosophy of a 'work-based society,'" see Chris Hann, "Moral(ity) and Economy: Work, Workfare and Fairness in Provincial Hungary," *European Journal of Sociology* 59, no. 29 (2018): 244. Compare also Arlie Russel Hochschild's notion of the "deep story" of felt injustices from her ethnography of Louisiana Tea Party supporters, Arlie Russel Hochschild, *Strangers in their Own Land: Anger and Mourning on the American right* (New York, New Press, 2016).

8. On the latter point, see Christopher J. Bickerton and Carlo Invernizzi Accetti, *Technopopulism: The New Logic of Democratic Politics* (New York: Oxford University Press, 2021). Building on this argument, I would say that *moral* articulations of technical competence—rooted in economic memories, as I have described in this book—are truly central to this style of politics.

9. Jonathan Olsen, "The Left Party and the AfD: Populist Competitors in Eastern Germany," *German Politics and Society* 36 1 (2018): 70–83, 82. Germany's Alternative for Germany Party (AfD) lacks a single *charismatic* leader, and in its short time of existence, it already underwent major personnel shifts in its inner circles of power. At the time of its founding in 2013, AfD was headed by West German senior academics with a strong footing in the economics profession. Initially, the party's signature political position was its "Euroscepticism." See Kai Arzheimer "The AfD: Finally a Successful Right-Wing Populist Eurosceptic Party for Germany?," *West European Politics* 38, no. 3 (2015): 535–556, for a criticism of the common currency and discontent with European Union monetary politics—German conservatives (well beyond this party) regarded any relaxation of member states' debt burden in the wake of the 2010 Eurocrisis as unconstitutional.

10. Sean Hanley and Milada A. Vachudova, "Understanding the Illiberal Turn: Democratic Backsliding in the Czech Republic," *East European Politics* 34, no. 3 (2018): 276–296; Vladimir Havlík, "Technocratic Populism and Political Illiberalism in Central Europe," *Problems of Post-Communism* 66, no. 6, (2019): 369–384. Scholars label the Association of Dissatisfied Citizens Party (ANO) an "entrepreneurial party" operating in a framework of "technocratic populism" or "managerial populism." See Havlík, "Technocratic Populism." ANO's quick ascent to power was facilitated by a deep crisis of political trust and by the financial crisis in the late 2000s.

11. AfD Thuringia "Meine Heimat, mein Thüringen: Wahlprogramm der Alternative für Deutschland für die Landtagswahl Tührungen 2019," accessed August 10, 2020, https://cdn.afd.tools/wp-content/uploads/sites/178/2019/09/Wahlprogramm _AfD-Thu%CC%88ringen_2019_Online-Fassung-final_gesichert.pdf, 88. Quotes by Babiš are taken from Havlík, "Technocratic Populism," 375, and from ANO's website: ANO, "Můj příběh," accessed July 20, 2020, https://www.anobudelip.cz/cs/o-nas /andrej-babis/.

12. The Eastern branches of AfD engage in the politics of memory around 1989 and its aftermath. The party promises to "finish the revolution" ("Vollende die Wende"), a slogan that is ambiguous but speaks to a trope popular among some East Germans who believe that the fight against Communist Party rule before 1989 is equivalent to the struggle against "decadent," "corrupt" West German elites today (who are regarded to have "stolen" East German sovereignty after 1989). In 2020, AfD launched a campaign to investigate the *Treuhand* privatization and its economic fallout in the federal parliament.

236

EPILOGUE

13. Robert E. Lane, "Market Justice, Political Justice," *American Political Science Review* 80, no. 2, (1986): 383–402.
14. See Hann, "Moral(ity and) Economy."

METHODOLOGICAL APPENDIX

1. Marci Shore, *The Taste of Ashes: The Afterlife of Totalitarianism in Eastern Europe* (New York: Random House, 2013), xi.
2. Most individuals contacted were in their early twenties at the onset of the transformation. At around this age, memory formation is known to be particularly consequential. In this phase, "long-term goals and plans are formulated, the individual becomes integrated with society and with an immediate social group." See Martin A. Conway and Christopher W. Pleydell-Pearce, "The Construction of Autobiographical Memories in the Self-Memory System," *Psychological Review* 107, no. 2 (2000), 261–288, 280. Individuals are likely to form episodic memories of significant events that become critical elements of autobiographical identity. See also Lynn Abrams, *Oral History Theory* (London: Routledge, 2016), 90. Beyond the individual level, Howard Schumann and Amy Corning, "The Conversion of Generational Effects into Collective Memory," *International Journal of Public Opinion Research* 29, no. 3 (2016): 520–532. suggest that the "critical years" condition also shapes generational memory.
3. Michael Bamberg, "Identity and Narration," in *Handbook of Narratology*, edited by Peter Hühn, Wolf Schmid, Jörg Schönert, and Pier John (Berlin: De Gruyter, 2009), 132.
4. Narrative-biographical interviews start with a broad question that allows the respondent to create a thread that structures the entire conversation. The role of the interviewer is to encourage narration, not to ask for evaluations. I draw on biographical methodologies that build on Fritz Schütze's paradigmatic approach to tracing biographical agency; see Markieta Domecka and Adam Mrozowicki, "Linking Structural and Agential Powers: A Realist Approach to Biographies, Careers and Reflexivity," in *Realist Biography and European Policy: An Innovative Approach to European Policy Studies*, edited by Jeffrey D. Turk and Adam Mrozowicki (Ithaca, NY: Cornell University Press, 2013), 191–213. Unlike classical narrative interview methodologies, however, I do not situate biographical narratives in an overarching meaning structure, such as family history, habitus, generation, or social milieu. Examples of important narrative interview studies in this context are Peter Alheit, Kerstin Bast-Haider, and Petra Drauschke, *Die zögernde Ankunft im Westen: Biographien und Mentalitäten in Ostdeutschland* (Frankfurt: Campus, 2004); and Monika Wohlrab-Sahr, Uta Karstein, and Thomas Schmidt-Lux, *Forcierte Säkularität: Religiöser Wandel und Generationendynamik im Osten Deutschlands* (Frankfurt: Campus, 2009).
5. Confronting one's choices in the past—narrating personal agency—also means constructing those choices from the standpoint of the present. See Domecka and Mrozowicki, "Linking Structural and Agential Powers."
6. As with any methodological choice, this is a trade-off. Because time and energy are limited in an interview context, any combination of approaches means that some richness of detail will be lost.

METHODOLOGICAL APPENDIX

7. Alexandra Leyk and Joanna Wawrzyniak, *Cięcia: Mówiona historia transformacji* (Warsaw: Wydawnictwo Krytyki Politycznej, 2020).

8. See Uwe Flick, "Episodic Interviewing," in *Qualitative Researching with Text, Image and Sound*, edited by Martin W. Bauer and George Gaskell (Thousand Oaks, CA: Sage, 2000), 75–92; and Sabina Misoch, *Qualitative Interviews* (Berlin: Walter de Gruyter, 2014), 57–64. For the analysis of the interview material, I draw on Herbert J. Rubin and Irene S. Rubin, *Qualitative Interviewing: The Art of Hearing Data* (Thousand Oaks, CA: Sage, 2012); Rubin and Rubin also advocate a combined approach.

9. This implies that, here, the interviewer assumes a more active role than in the biographical interview. See Misoch, *Qualitative Interviews*, 57ff.

10. For a similar approach, see the illuminating study by Luis Presser, "Violent Offenders, Moral Selves: Constructing Identities and Accounts in the Research Interview," *Social Problems* 51, no. 1 (2004): 82–101. I asked respondents, first, to assess how (and if) people had changed in general after 1989. Here, they could introduce stories from their wider network of acquaintances. I then prompted them to share episodes of change from their trusted environment, such as their circle of friends. These are not fully standardized questions (they are part of a dynamically developing conversation); however, the segments generated in response to topical questions can be used for systematic comparison, which is particularly useful for exploring group-specific accounts. See Michèle Lamont and Ann Swidler, "Methodological Pluralism and the Possibilities and Limits of Interviewing." *Qualitative Sociology* 34, no 2 (2014): 153–171.

11. Mario L. Small, *Unanticipated Gains: Origins of Network Inequality in Everyday Life* (New York: Oxford University Press, 2009); Matthew Desmond, "Relational Ethnography," *Theory and Society* 43, (2014), 547–579.

12. Oral history practitioners emphasize that there is no evidence that respondents, in most interview studies, are consciously misrepresenting the past. The quality, vividness, and depth of the information provided will instead depend "upon the specific encoding that happened at the time and the circumstances in which the remembering is taking place," notes Abrams, *Oral History Theory*, 86. It is known that, in recall bias, however, the present circumstances unintentionally shape what, and how, people remember (as well as what and how they forget). Social psychological research has shown that events defined as "important" tend to be recalled somewhat more reliably than others. See William Glick, George P. Huber, C. Chet Miller, Harold D. Doty, and Kathleen M. Suttcliffe, "Studying Changes in Organizational Design and Effectiveness: Retrospective Event Histories and Periodic Assessments," *Organization Science* 1, no. 3 (1990): 293–312, 302. There is evidence that negative events are remembered in greater detail than positive ones. See Elizabeth A. Kensinger, "Negative Emotion Enhances Memory Accuracy: Behavioral and Neuroimaging Evidence," *Current Directions in Psychological Science* 16, no. 4 (2007): 213–218. Memories of significant events shape autobiographical identity and can be accessed via episodic memories. In this study, I selected respondents from an age group that, around the time after 1989, was most likely to form these kinds of episodic memories (the period from late adolescence to around thirty years of age). See Abrams, *Oral History Thory*, 90; Conway and Pleydell-Pearce, "The Construction of Autobiographical Memories," 280.

METHODOLOGICAL APPENDIX

13. Glick et al., "Studying Changes in Organizational Design and Effectiveness," 297.
14. Wagner Pacifici, *What Is an Event?*
15. Compare the reflections of anthropologists Gail Kligman and Katherine Verdery on this point, who observe a "politicized silence" when it comes to collective meaning making of life under state socialism. Gail Kligman and Katherine Verdery, *Peasants Under Siege: The Collectivization of Romanian Agriculture 1949–1962* (Princeton, NJ: Princeton University Press 2011), 469–470.

BIBLIOGRAPHY

Abend, Gabriel. *The Moral Background: An Inquiry Into the History of Business Ethics.* Princeton, NJ: Princeton University Press, 2014.

Abrams, Bradley F. *The Struggle for the Soul of the Nation: Czech Culture and the Rise of Communism.* Lanham, MD: Rowman & Littlefield, 2005.

Adams, Julia P. "1-800-How-Am-I-Driving?" *Social Science History* 35, no. 1 (2011): 1–17.

Adams, J. Stacy. "Inequity in Social Exchange." *Advances in Experimental Social Psychology* 2 (1965): 267–299.

AfD Thuringia. "Meine Heimat, mein Thüringen. Wahlprogramm der Alternative für Deutschland für die Landtagswahl Tührungen 2019." Accessed 10 August 2020. https://cdn.afd.tools/wp-content/uploads/sites/178/2019/09/Wahlprogramm_AfD -Thu%CC%88ringen_2019_Online-Fassung-final_gesichert.pdf.

Ahbe, Thomas, "Die Ost-Diskurse als Strukturen der Nobilitierung und Marginalisierung von Wissen. Eine Diskursanalyse zur Konstruktion der Ostdeutschen in den westdeutschen Medien-Diskursen 1989/90 und 1995." *Die Ostdeutschen in den Medien: Das Bild von den anderen nach 1990*, ed. Thomas Ahbe, Rainer Gries und Wolfgang Schmale, 59–112. Leipzig: Leipziger University-Verlag, 2009.

Albert, Stuart, "Temporal Comparison Theory." *Psychological Review* 84, no. 6 (1977): 485–503.

Alexa, Jan, et al. "Czech Republic: Health System Review." *Health Systems in Transition* 17, no. 1 (2015): 1–165.

Alexander, Jeffrey C. "Market as Narrative and Character: For a Cultural Sociology of Economic Life." *Journal of Cultural Economy* 4, no. 4 (2011): 477–488.

——. *The Meanings of Social Life. A Cultural Sociology.* Oxford: Oxford University Press, 2003.

——. *Trauma: A Social Theory.* Hoboken, NJ: John Wiley, 2012.

Alexievich, Svetlana. *Second Hand Time: The Last of the Soviets*. New York: Random House, 2016.

Alheit, Peter, Kerstin Bast-Haider, and Petra Drauschke. *Die zögernde Ankunft im Westen. Biographien und Mentalitäten in Ostdeutschland*. Frankfurt: Campus, 2004.

ANO. "Můj příběh." Accessed 20 July 2020. https://www.anobudelip.cz/cs/o-nas/andrej -babis/

Appel, Hilary and Mitchell A. Orenstein. *From Triumph to Crisis. Neoliberal Economic Reform in Postcommunist Countries*. Cambridge: Cambridge University Press, 2018.

Arendt, Hannah. *The Life of the Mind*. Boston: Houghton Mifflin Harcourt, 1978.

Arnold, Thomas C., "Rethinking Moral Economy." *American Political Science Review* 96, no. 1 (2001): 85–95.

Arzheimer, Kai. "The AfD: Finally a Successful Right-Wing Populist Eurosceptic Party for Germany?" *West European Politics* 38, no. 3 (2015): 535–556.

Augustine, Dolores. *Red Prometheus. Engineering and Dictatorship in East Germany, 1945–1990*. Cambridge, MA: MIT Press, 2007.

Babička, Martin, "The Future Is in Your Hands: Temporality and the Neoliberal Self and the Czech Voucher Privatization." *Journal of Contemporary Central and Eastern Europe* 30, no. 1 (2022): 83–99.

Bamberg, Michael. "Identity and Narration." In *Handbook of Narratology*, ed. Peter Hühn, Wolf Schmid, Jörg Schönert, and Pier John, 132–143. Berlin: De Gruyter, 2009.

Bandelj, Nina. *From Communists to Foreign Capitalists. The Social Foundations of Foreign Direct Investment in Postsocialist Europe*. Princeton, NJ: Princeton University Press, 2008.

——. "On Postsocialist Capitalism." *Theory and Society* 45, no. 1 (2016): 89–106.

——. "Thinking About Social Relations in Economy as Relational Work." In *Re-Imagining Economic Sociology*, ed. Patrik Aspers and Nigel Dodd, 227–251. Oxford: Oxford University Press, 2015.

Bandelj, Nina, and Christopher W. Gibson. "Contextualizing Anti-Immigrant Attitudes of East Europeans." *Review of European Studies* 12, no. 3 (2020): 32–49.

Bandelj, Nina, and Matthew Mahutga. "How Socioeconomic Change Shapes Income Inequality in Post-Socialist Europe." *Social Forces* 88, no. 5 (2010): 2133–2162.

Barney, Timothy. " 'A Tale of Two Václavs': Rhetorical History and the Concept of 'Return' in Post-Communist Czech Leadership." *Advances in the History of Rhetoric* 18 (2015): 109–134.

Bartha, Estzer. *Alienating Labour: Workers on the Road from Socialism to Capitalism in East Germany and Hungary*. Oxford: Berghahn, 2013.

Bauerkämper, Arnd. *Die Sozialgeschichte der DDR*. Munich: Oldenbourg Wissenschaftsverlag, 2005.

Becker, Birgit. "Der Einfluss der Bezugsgruppenmeinung auf die Einstellung gegenüber Ausländern in Ost- und Westdeutschland/The Impact of the Reference Group on Attitudes Toward Foreigners in East and West Germany." *Zeitschrift für Soziologie* 34, no. 1 (2005): 40–59.

Benáček, Vladimír. "The Rise of the 'Grand Entrepreneurs' in the Czech Republic and Their Contest for Capitalism." *Sociologický časopis/Czech Sociological Review* 46, no. 6 (2006): 1151–1170.

Berend, Ivan T. *From the Soviet Bloc to the European Union: The Economic and Social Transformation of Central and Eastern Europe Since 1973*. Cambridge: Cambridge University Press, 2009.

BIBLIOGRAPHY

Berezin, Mabel. "Events as Templates of Possibility: An Analytic Typology of Political Facts." In *The Oxford Handbook of Cultural Sociology*, ed. Jeffrey C. Alexander, Ronald Jacobs, and Philip Smith, 613–635. New York: Oxford University Press, 2012.

Bernhard, Michael H., and Jan Kubik. "A Theory of the Politics of Memory." In *Twenty Years After Communism: The Politics of Memory and Commemoration*, ed. Michael H. Bernhard and Jan Kubik, 7–34. New York: Oxford University Press, 2014.

Bickerton, Christopher J., and Carlo Invernizzi Accetti. *Technopopulism: The New Logic of Democratic Politics*. New York: Oxford University Press, 2021.

Bidart, Claire, and Daniel Lavenu. "Evolutions of Personal Networks and Life Events." *Social Networks* 27, no. 4 (2005): 359–376.

Bierhoff, Hans W., "Zufriedenheit, Leistungsbereitschaft und Unfairneß in Ost-und Westdeutschland: Zur Psychosozialen Befindlichkeit nach der Wiedervereinigung." In *Gerechtigkeitserleben im Wiedervereinigten Deutschland*, ed. Rudi Schmitt and Leo Montada, 45–66. Wiesbaden: Springer, 1999.

Bjørnskov, Christian. "Determinants of Generalized Trust: A Cross-Country Comparison." *Public Choice* 130, no. 1–2 (2007): 1–21.

Blatterer, Harry. *Everyday Friendships: Intimacy as Freedom in a Complex World*. New York: Palgrave MacMillan, 2015.

Bludau, Heidi. "Hindered Care: Institutional Obstructions to Carework and Professionalism in Czech Nursing." *Anthropology of Work Review* 38, no. 1 (2017): 8–17.

Boenisch, Peter, and Lutz Schneider. "The Social Capital Legacy of Communism: Results from the Berlin Wall Experiment." *European Journal of Political Economy* 32 (2013): 391–411.

Böhnke, Petra. "Ost-Glück versus West-Glück?" In *Leben in Ost-und Westdeutschland. Eine Sozialwissenschaftliche Bilanz der Deutschen Einheit 1990–2010*, ed. Peter Krause and Ilona Ostner, 695–708. Frankfurt: Campus, 2010.

Bourdieu, Pierre. *Distinction. A Social Critique of the Judgement of Taste*. Cambridge, MA: Harvard University Press, 1984.

——. *Outline of a Theory of Practice*. New York: Cambridge University Press, 1977.

Boyer, Christoph. "Sozialgeschichte der Arbeiterschaft und Staatssozialistische Entwicklungspfade: Konzeptionelle Überlegungen und eine Erklärungsskizze." In *Arbeiter im Staatssozialismus: Ideologischer Anspruch und Soziale Wirklichkeit*, ed. Peter Hübner, Christoph Kleßmann, and Klaus Tenfelde, 71–86. Cologne: Böhlau Verlag 2005.

Boym, Svetlana. *The Future of Nostalgia*. New York: Basic Books, 2008.

Brand, Jennie E. "The Far-Reaching Impact of Job Loss and Unemployment." *Annual Review of Sociology* 41 (2015): 359–375.

Bren, Paulina. *The Greengrocer and His TV: The Culture of Communism After the 1968 Prague Spring*. Ithaca, NY: Cornell University Press, 2010.

Breuer, Lars, and Anna Delius. "1989 in European Vernacular Memory." *East European Politics and Societies and Cultures* 31, no. 3 (2017): 456–478.

Brie, Michael. "Staatssozialistische Länder Europas im Vergleich. Alternative Herrschaftsstrategien und divergente Typen." In *Einheit als Privileg. Vergleichende Perspektiven auf die Transformation Ostdeutschlands*, ed. Helmut Wiesenthal, 39–104. Frankfurt: Campus, 1996.

Brown, Wendy. *In the Ruins of Neoliberalism: The Rise of Antidemocratic Politics in the West*. New York: Columbia University Press, 2019.

BIBLIOGRAPHY

Bruce, Gary. "Access to Secret Police Files, Justice, and Vetting in East Germany Since 1989." *German Politics and Society* 26, no. 1 (2008): 82–111.

Brückweh, Kerstin, Clemens Villinger and Kathrin Zöller. *Die lange Geschichte der Wende: Geschichtswissenschaft im Dialog*. Berlin: Ch. Links Verlag, 2020.

Buchowski, Michal. "Property Relations, Class, and Labour in Rural Poland." In *Postsocialist Europe: Anthropological Perspectives from Home*, ed. Peter Skalnik and Lázló Kurti, 51–75. New York: Berghahn, 2009.

Burt, Ronald S. "Decay Functions." *Social Networks* 22, no. 1 (2000): 1–28.

Buunk, Abraham P., and Frederick X. Gibbons. "Social Comparison: The End of a Theory and the Emergence of a Field." *Organizational Behavior and Human Decision Processes* 102, no. 1 (2007): 3–21.

Casper, Deborah M., and Noel A. Card. "We Were Best Friends, But . . .": Two Studies of Antipathetic Relationships Emerging from Broken Friendships." *Journal of Adolescent Research* 25, no. 4 (2010): 499–526.

Caspi, Avshalom, and Terrie E. Moffitt, "When Do Individual Differences Matter?: A Paradoxical Theory of Personality Coherence." *Psychological Inquiry* 4, no. 4 (1993): 247–271.

Cepić, Dražen. *Class Cultures in Post-Socialist Eastern Europe*. New York: Routledge, 2018.

Clark, Andrew, and Claudia Senik. "Who Compares to Whom? The Anatomy of Income Comparisons in Europe." *The Economic Journal* 120 (2010): 573–594.

Clark, Ed. "The Role of Social Capital in Developing Czech Private Business." *Work, Employment and Society* 14, no. 3 (2000): 439–458.

Conway, Martin A., and Christopher W. Pleydell-Pearce, "The Construction of Autobiographical Memories in the Self-memory System." *Psychological Review* 107, no. 2 (2000): 261–288

Cooper, Melinda. *Family Values: Between Neoliberalism and the New Social Conservatism*. New York: Zone Books, 2017.

Davis, Joseph E. "Victim Narratives and Victim Selves: False Memory Syndrome and the Power of Accounts." *Social Forces* 52, no 4 (2005): 529–548.

Della Porta, Donatella. *Mobilizing for Democracy: Comparing 1989 and 2011*. Oxford: Oxford University Press, 2014.

Desmond, Matthew. "Relational Ethnography." *Theory and Society* 43 (2014): 547–579.

Deutsch, Morton. "Equity, Equality, and Need: What Determines Which Value Will Be Used as the Basis of Distributive Justice?" *Journal of Social Issues* 31, no. 3 (1975): 137–149.

Diaz-Bone, Rainer. *Ego-Zentrierte Netzwerkanalyse und Familiale Beziehungssysteme*. Wiesbaden: Deutscher Universitätsverlag, 1997.

Diewald, Martin. "Spirals of Success and Failure?: The Interplay of Control Beliefs and Working Lives in the Transition from Planned to Market Economy." In *After the Fall of the Wall: Life Courses in the Transformation of East Germany*, ed. Martin Diewald, Anne Goedicke, and Karl Ulrich Mayer, 214-236. Stanford, CA: Stanford University Press, 2006.

Diewald, Martin, and Anne Goedicke. "Unusual Turbulences—Unexpected Continuities. Transformation Life Courses in Retrospective." In *After the Fall of the Wall: Life Courses in the Transformation of East Germany*, ed. Martin Diewald, Anne Goedicke, and Karl Ulrich Mayer, 293-318. Stanford, CA: Stanford University Press, 2006.

BIBLIOGRAPHY

Diewald, Martin, and Jörg Lüdicke. "Community Lost or Freedom Gained?: Changes of Social Networks After 1989." In *After the Fall of the Wall: Life Courses in the Transformation of East Germany*, ed. Martin Diewald, Anne Goedicke, and Karl-Ulrich Mayer, 191–213. Stanford, CA: Stanford University Press, 2006.

Diewald, Martin, and Mathias Pollmann-Schult. "Erwerbsverläufe in Ostdeutschland–Inklusion und Exklusion seit 1989." In *Inklusion und Exklusion: Analysen zur Sozialstruktur und sozialen Ungleichheit*, ed. Rudolf Stichweh and Paul Windolf, 139–156. Wiesbaden: Springer, 2009.

Diewald, Martin, Heike Solga, and Anne Goedicke. "Old Assets, New Liabilities?: How Did Individual Characteristics Contribute to Labor Market Success or Failure After 1989?" In *After the Fall of the Wall: Life Courses in the Transformation of East Germany*, ed. Martin Diewald, Anne Goedicke, and Karl Ulrich Mayer, 65–88. Stanford, CA: Stanford University Press, 2006.

Die ZEIT. "Ost-West-Wanderung." May 5 2019. www.zeit.de/politik/deutschland/2019-05/ost-west-wanderung-abwanderung-ostdeutschland-umzug.

Domecka, Markieta, and Adam Mrozowicki, "Linking Structural and Agential Powers: A Realist Approach to Biographies, Careers and Reflexivity." In *Realist Biography and European Policy: An Innovative Approach to European Policy Studies*, ed. Jeffrey D. Turk and Adam Mrozowicki, 191–213. Ithaca, NY: Cornell University Press, 2013.

Drahokoupil, Jan. *Globalization and the State in Central and Eastern Europe: The Politics of Foreign Direct Investment*. New York: Routledge, 2008.

Drbohlav, Dušan. "Patterns of Immigration in the Czech Republic, Hungary and Poland." In *European Immigrations: Trends, Structures and Policy Implication*, ed. Marek Okólski, 179–209. Amsterdam: Amsterdam University Press, 2012.

Dunn, Elisabeth C. *Privatizing Poland: Baby Food, Big Business, and the Remaking of Labor*. Ithaca, NY: Cornell University Press, 2004.

Durkheim, Emile. *The Division of Labor in Society*. New York: Simon and Schuster, 1997.

Duru-Bellat, Marie, and Elise Tenret. "Who's for Meritocracy?: Individual and Contextual Variations in the Faith." *Comparative Education Review* 56, no. 2 (2012): 223–247.

Elder, Glen H, *Children of the Great Depression: Social Change in Life Experience*. Boulder, CO: Westview Press, 1999.

Elster, Jon, Claus Offe, and Ulrich K. Preuss. *Institutional Design in Post-Communist Societies: Rebuilding the Ship at Sea*. Cambridge: Cambridge University Press, 1998.

Emigh, Rebecca J., and Iván Szelényi, eds. *Poverty, Ethnicity, and Gender in Eastern Europe During the Market Transition*. Westport, CT: Praeger, 2001.

Emirbayer, Mustafa. "Manifesto for a Relational Sociology." *American Journal of Sociology* 103, no. 2 (1997): 281–317.

Epstein, Catherine. "The Stasi: New Research on the East German Ministry of State Security." *Kritika: Explorations in Russian and Eurasian History* 5, no. 2 (2004): 321–348.

Eribon, Didier. Returning to Reims. Cambridge, MA: MIT Press, 2013.

European Parliament. *Social and Employment Policies in the Czech Republic*. Brussels: Policy Department for Economic, Scientific and Quality of Life Policies, 2018.

Evans, Jennifer V. "The Moral State. Men, Mining, and Masculinity in the Early GDR." *German History* 23, no. 3 (2005): 355–370.

Evanson, Richard K. "Regime and Working Class in Czechoslovakia 1948–1968." *Soviet Studies* 37, no. 2 (1985): 248–268.

BIBLIOGRAPHY

Eyal, Gil. "Anti-Politics and the Spirit of Capitalism: Dissidents, Monetarists, and the Czech Transition to Capitalism." *Theory and Society* 29, no. 1 (2000): 49–92.

Eyal, Gil, Iván Szelényi, and Eleanor Townsley. *Making Capitalism Without Capitalists: Class Formation and Elite Struggles in Post-Communist Central Europe*. London: Verso, 1998.

Eyerman, Ron. *Memory, Trauma, and Identity*. New York: Palgrave, 2019.

Fassin, Didier. "Moral Economies Revisited." *Annales. Histoires, Science Sociales* 64 (2009): 1237–1266.

Feld, Scott L. "The Focused Organization of Social Ties." *American Journal of Sociology* 86, no. 5 (1981): 1015–1035.

Flick, Uwe. "Episodic Interviewing." In *Qualitative Researching with Text, Image and Sound*, ed. Martin W. Bauer and George Gaskell, 75–92. Thousand Oaks, CA: Sage, 2000.

Fourcade, Marion, and Kieran Healy. "Moral Views of Market Society." *Annual Review of Sociology* 33 (2007): 285–311.

Fraser, Nancy, and Axel Honneth. *Redistribution or Recognition? A Political Philosophical Exchange*. London: Verso, 2003.

Fulbrook, Mary. *The People's State. East German Society from Hitler to Honecker*. New Haven, CT: Yale University Press, 2005.

Gebauer, Ronald, Axel Salheiser, and Lars Vogel. "Bestandsaufnahme." In *Ostdeutsche Eliten. Träume, Wirklichkeiten und Perspektiven*, ed. Deutsche Gesellschaft E.V., 14–33. Berlin: Deutsche Gesellschaft E.V., 2017.

Geißler, Rainer. *Die Sozialstruktur Deutschlands*. Wiesbaden: Springer-Verlag, 2014.

Gensburger, Sarah. "Halbwachs' Studies in Collective Memory. A Founding Text for Contemporary 'Memory Studies'"? *Journal of Classical Sociology* 16, no. 4 (2016): 396–413.

Gerlitz, Jean-Yves, Kai Mühleck, Percy Scheller, and Markus Schrenker, "Justice Perceptions in Times of Transition: Trends in Germany, 1991–2006." *European Sociological Review* 28, no. 2 (2012): 263–282.

Ghodsee, Kristen, and Mitchell A. Orenstein. *Taking Stock of Shock: The Social Consequences of the 1989 Revolutions*. New York: Oxford University Press, 2021.

Gidron, Noam, and Peter A. Hall, "Populism as a Problem of Social Integration." *Comparative Political Studies* 53, no. 7 (2020): 1027–1059.

Gieseke, Jens. "The Stasi and East German Society: Some Remarks on Current Research." *GHI Bulletin Supplement* 9 (2014): 59–72.

Giessmann, Barbara. "Ostdeutsche Ingenieure im Transformationsprozeß—zwischen Kontinuität und Bruch." In *Berufsgruppen im Transformationsprozeß Ostdeutschlands: Ingenieure, Meister, Techniker und Ökonomen zwischen Gestern und Übermorgen*, ed. Ingrid Drexel and Barbara Giessmann, 63–90. Frankfurt: Campus, 1997.

Glaeser, Andreas. *Divided in Unity. Identity, Germany, and the Berlin Police*. Chicago: University of Chicago Press, 2000.

Glick, William, George P. Huber, C. Chet Miller, Harold D. Doty, and Kathleen M. Suttcliffe. "Studying Changes in Organizational Design and Effectiveness: Retrospective Event Histories and Periodic Assessments." *Organization Science* 1, no. 3 (1990): 293–312.

Goedicke, Anne. "A 'Ready-Made State': The Mode of Institutional Transition in East Germany After 1989." In *After the Fall of the Wall: Life Courses in the Transformation of East Germany*, ed. Martin Diewald, Anne Goedicke, and Karl Ulrich Mayer, 44–64. Stanford, CA: Stanford University Press, 2006.

Griffin, Brandon J., et al. "Moral Injury: An Integrative Review." *Journal of Traumatic Stress* 31, (2019): 350–362.

Grünert, Holle. "Das Beschäftigungssystem der DDR." In *Arbeit, Arbeitsmarkt und Betriebe*, ed. Lutz Burkhardt, 19–68. Opladen: Leske & Budrich 1996.

Gudeman, Stephen, and Chris Hann. *Economy and Ritual: Studies in Postsocialist Transformations*. New York: Berghahn, 2017.

Habinek, Jacob, John Levi Martin, and Benjamin D. Zablocki. "Double-Embeddedness: Spatial and Relational Contexts of Tie Persistence and Re-Formation." *Social Networks* 42 (2015): 27–41.

Halbwachs, Maurice. *On Collective Memory*. Chicago: University of Chicago Press, 1992.

Hanley, Sean, and Milada A. Vachudova. "Understanding the Illiberal Turn: Democratic Backsliding in the Czech Republic." *East European Politics* 34, no. 3 (2018): 276–296.

Hann, Chris. "Moral(ity) and Economy: Work, Workfare and Fairness in Provincial Hungary." *European Journal of Sociology* 59, no. 29 (2018): 225–254.

Häuberer, Julia. *Social Capital Theory: Towards a Methodological Foundation*. Wiesbaden: Springer Verlag, 2010.

Havlík, Vladimir. "Technocratic Populism and Political Illiberalism in Central Europe." *Problems of Post-Communism* 66, no. 6 (2019): 369–384.

Hegewisch, Ariane, Chris Brewster, and Josef Koubek. "Different Roads. Changes in Industrial and Employee Relations in the Czech Republic and East Germany Since 1989." *Industrial Relations Journal* 27, no. 1 (1996): 50–64.

Hegtvedt, Karen A., and Cathryn Johnson. "Justice Beyond the Individual: A Future with Legitimation." *Social Psychology Quarterly* 63 no 8 (2000): 298–311.

Hegtvedt, Karen, and Deena Isom. "Inequality: A Matter of Justice?" In *Handbook of the Social Psychology of Inequality*, ed. Jane McLeod, Edward J. Lawler, and Michael Schwalbe, 65–94. Dordrecht: Springer, 2014.

Heimann, Mary. *Czechoslovakia: The State That Failed*. New Haven, CT: Yale University Press, 2011.

Hoffmann, Dierk. "Leistungsprinzip und Versorgungsprinzip. Widersprüche der DDR-Arbeitsgesellschaft." In *Sozialstaatlichkeit in der DDR: sozialpolitische Entwicklungen im Spannungsfeld von Diktatur und Gesellschaft 1945/49-1989*, ed. Dierk Hoffmann and Michael Schwartz, 89–113. Munich: Oldenbourg Verlag, 2005.

Heisig, Barbara. "Pflege im Transformationsprozess zwischen beruflicher Modernisierung und Professionalisierung." In *Biographische Risiken und neue professionelle Herausforderungen*, ed. Melanie Fabel and Sandra Tiefel, 193–206. Wiesbaden: Springer, 2004.

Hochschild, Arlie R. *Strangers in their Own Land: Anger and Mourning on the American right* (New York, The New Press, 2016).

Holý, Ladislav. The *Little Czech and the Great Czech Nation: National Identity and the Post-Communist Social Transformation*. Cambridge: Cambridge University Press, 1996.

Homans, George C. *Social Behavior: Its Elementary Forms*. New York: Harcourt, Brace and World, 1974.

Honneth, Axel. *The I in We: Studies in the Theory of Recognition*. Cambridge: Polity, 2012.

BIBLIOGRAPHY

Howard, Marc M. *The Weakness of Civil Society in Post-Communist Europe*. Cambridge: Cambridge University Press, 2003.

Hraba, Joseph, Frederick O. Lorenz, and Zdeňka Pechačová. "Family Stress During the Czech Transformation." *Journal of Marriage and Family* 62, no. 2 (2000): 520–531.

Innes, Abby. *Czechoslovakia. The Short Goodbye*. New Haven, CT: Yale University Press, 2001.

Jarausch, Konrad H. "Care and Coercion: The GDR as Welfare Dictatorship." In *Dictatorship as Experience: Towards a Socio-Cultural History of the GDR*, ed. Konrad H. Jarausch, 47–69. New York: Berghahn, 1999.

Jaworsky, B. Nadya and Jan Krotký. "'A Brother Is More Than a Neighbour': Symbolic Boundary Work in Czech Pro-Migration Discourse." *European Journal of Cultural and Political Sociology* 8, no. 3 (2021): 329–354.

Judt, Tony, with Timothy Snyder. *Thinking the Twentieth Century*. New York: Penguin Press, 2012.

Kalinová, Lenka. Konec nadějím a nová očekávání: K dějinám české společnosti 1969–1993. Prague: Academia, 2012.

Kalinová, Lenka. "Mythos und Realität des Arbeiterstaates in der Tschechoslowakei." *Arbeiter im Staatssozialismus: Ideologischer Anspruch und Soziale Wirklichkeit*, ed. Peter Hübner, Christoph Kleßmann, and Klaus Tenfelde, 87–107. Cologne: Böhlau Verlag, 2005.

Kallio, Johanna, and Mikko Niemelä. "Who Blames the Poor?: Multilevel Evidence of Support for and Determinants of Individualistic Explanation of Poverty in Europe." *European Societies* 16, no. 1 (2014): 112–135.

Karpiński, Zbigniew. "Social Association and Social Inequality in Poland, 1988–2013." *International Journal of Sociology* 46, no. 4 (2016): 288–319.

Katrňák, Tomáš, and Petr Fučík. *Návrat k sociálnímu původu*. Prague: CDK, 2010.

Kausmann, Corinna, et al. "Zivilgesellschaftliches Engagement." In *Datenreport Zivilgesellschaft*, ed. Holger Krimmer, 55–92. Wiesbaden: VS Verlag 2019.

Kaźmierska, Kaja, and Katarzyna Waniek. *Telling the Great Change: The Process of the Systemic Transformation in Poland in Biographical Perspective*. Łódź: Wydawnictwo Uniwersytetu Łódzkiego, 2020.

Kensinger, Elizabeth A. "Negative Emotion Enhances Memory Accuracy: Behavioral and Neuroimaging Evidence." *Current Directions in Psychological Science* 16, no. 4 (2007): 213–218.

King, Lawrence, Gábor Scheiring, and Elias Nosrati. "Deaths of Despair in Comparative Perspective." *Annual Review of Sociology* 48 (2022): 299–322.

Kissová, Lenka. "The Production of (Un)Deserving and (Un)Acceptable Shifting Representations of Migrants within Political Discourse in Slovakia." *East European Politics and Societies* 32, no 4 (2018): 743–766.

Kligman, Gail, and Katherine Verdery. *Peasants Under Siege: The Collectivization of Romanian Agriculture 1949–1962*. Princeton, NJ: Princeton University Press 2011.

Kluegel, James R., David S. Mason, and Bernd Wegener. "The Legitimation of Capitalism in the Postcommunist Transition: Public Opinion about Market Justice, 1991–1996." *European Sociological Review* 15, no. 3 (1999): 251–283.

Kluegel, James R., and David S. Mason, "Fairness Matters: Social Justice and Political Legitimacy in Post-Communist Europe." *Europe-Asia Studies* 56, no. 6 (2004): 813–834.

BIBLIOGRAPHY

Kluegel James R., and Eliot R. Smith. *Beliefs About Inequality: Americans' Views of What Is and What Ought to Be*. Boulder, CO: Transaction Publishers, 1986.

Kohli, Martin. "Die DDR als Arbeitsgesellschaft?: Arbeit, Lebenslauf und Soziale Differenzierung." In *Sozialgeschichte der DDR*, ed. Hartmut Kaelble, Jürgen Kocka, and Helmut Zwahr, 31–61. Stuttgart: Klett-Cola, 1994.

Kohout, Jaroslav. "Sociology and the Qualifications of Managerial Staff in Czechoslovakia." *International Sociology* 3, no. 4 (1988): 335–342.

Kotkin, Stephen. *Magnetic Mountain: Stalinism as a Civilization*. Berkeley: University of California Press, 1997.

Krapfl, James. *Revolution with a Human Face: Politics, Culture, and Community in Czechoslovakia, 1989–1992*. Ithaca, NY: Cornell University Press, 2013.

Krastev, Ivan, and Stephen Holmes. *The Light That Failed: A Reckoning*. London: Allen Lane, 2019.

Kreidl, Martin. "Perceptions of Poverty and Wealth in Western and Post-communist Countries." *Social Justice Research* 13, no. 2 (2000): 151–176.

——. "Socialist Egalitarian Policies and Educational Inequality in Central Europe After World War II." *Sociologia/Slovak Sociological Review* 38, no. 3 (2006): 199–221.

Krejčí, Jaroslav, and Pavel Machonin. *Czechoslovakia 1918–92: A Laboratory for Social Change*. New York: St. Martin's Press, 1996.

Kunovich, Sheri, and Kazimierz Slomczynski, "Systems of Distribution and a Sense of Equity: A Multilevel Analysis of Meritocratic Attitudes in Post-Industrial Societies." *European Sociological Review* 23, no. 5 (2007): 649–663.

Labianca, Giuseppe. "Negative Ties in Organizational Networks." In *Contemporary Perspectives on Organizational Social Networks*, 239–259. Bingley, UK: Emerald, 2014.

Labianca, Giuseppe, and Daniel J. Brass. "Exploring the Social Ledger: Negative Relationships and Negative Asymmetry in Social Networks in Organizations." *Academy of Management Review* 31, no. 3 (2006): 596–614.

Lane, Robert E. "Market Justice, Political Justice." *American Political Science Review* 80, no 2, (1986): 383–402.

Langen, Eva-Maria. "Der Fachschulingenieur in den Restrukturierungsprozessen der Ostdeutschen Betriebe—Rationellere Nutzung seines Potentials und Partielle Aufwertung." In *Berufsgruppen im Transformationsprozeß Ostdeutschlands: Ingenieure, Meister, Techniker und Ökonomen zwischen Gestern und Übermorgen*, ed. Ingrid Drexel and Barbara Giessmann, 45–62. Frankfurt: Campus, 2000.

Lamont, Michèle. *The Dignity of Working Men: Morality and the Boundaries of Race, Class, and Immigration*. Cambridge, MA: Harvard University Press, 2000.

Lamont, Michèle, and Virag Molnár. "The Study of Boundaries in the Social Sciences." *Annual Review of Sociology* (2002): 167–195.

Lamont, Michèle, and Ann Swidler. "Methodological Pluralism and the Possibilities and Limits of Interviewing." *Qualitative Sociology* 34, no. 2 (2014): 153–171.

Lampland, Martha. *The Object of Labor: Commodification in Socialist Hungary*. Chicago: University of Chicago Press, 1995.

Ledeneva, Alena. *Russia's Economy of Favours: Blat, Networking, and Informal Exchanges*. Cambridge: Cambridge University Press, 1998.

Lefcourt, Herbert M. "Locus of Control and the Response to Aversive Events." *Canadian Psychological Review/Psychologie Canadienne* 17, no 3 (1976), 202–209.

BIBLIOGRAPHY

Lerner, Melvin J. "The Justice Motive in Social Behavior." *Journal of Social Issues* 31, no 3 (1975), 1–19.

Leyk, Aleksandra, and Joanna Wawrzyniak, *Cięcia: Mówiona historia transformacji.* Warsaw: Wydawnictwo Krytyki Politycznej, 2020.

Liebig, Stefan, and Carsten Sauer. "Sociology of Justice." In *Handbook of Social Justice Theory and Research*, ed. Clara Sabbagh and Manfred Schmitt, 37–59. New York: Springer, 2016.

Liebig, Stefan, and Ronald Verwiebe. "Einstellungen zur Sozialen Ungleichheit in Ostdeutschland." *Zeitschrift für Soziologie* 29, no. 1 (2000): 3–26.

Lindenberger, Thomas. "'Asoziale Lebensweise': Herrschaftslegitimation, Sozialdisziplinierung und die Konstruktion eines 'Negativen Milieus' in der SED-Diktatur." *Geschichte und Gesellschaft* 31, no. 2 (2005): 227–254.

Lutz, Burkart, and Holle Grünert, "Der Zerfall der Beschäftigungsstrukturen der DDR 1989–1993." In *Arbeit, Arbeitsmarkt und Betriebe. Berichte der Kommission für die Erforschung des sozialen und politischen Wandels in den neuen Bundesländern*, ed. Burkart Lutz, Hildegard M. Nickel, Rudi Schmidt, and Arndt Sorge, 69–120. Wiesbaden: VS Verlag für Sozialwissenschaften, 1996.

Macura, Vladmír. *The Mystifications of a Nation: "The Potato Bug" and Other Essays on Czech Culture.* Madison: University of Wisconsin Press, 2010.

Maier, Charles. *Dissolution: The Crisis of Communism and the End of East Germany.* Princeton, NJ: Princeton University Press, 1999.

Major, Brenda. "From Social Inequality to Personal Entitlement: The Role of Social Comparisons, Legitimacy Appraisals, and Group Membership." *Advances in Experimental Social Psychology* 26 (1994): 293–355.

Manow, Philip. "Zerschlagung der Poliklinken und Transfer korporativer Regulierung: Das Gesundheitswesen." In *Transformationspfade in Ostdeutschland. Beiträge zur sektoralen Vereinigungspolitik*, ed. Roland Czada and Gerhard Lembruch, 165–190. Frankfurt: Campus, 2008.

Margalit, Avishai, *On Betrayal.* Cambridge, MA: Harvard University Press, 2017.

——. *The Ethics of Memory.* Cambridge, MA: Harvard University Press, 2004.

Mark, James, Muriel Blaive, Adam Hudek, Anne Saunders, and Stanislav Tyszka. "1989 After 1989: Remembering the End of State Socialism in East-Central Europe." In *Thinking Through Transition: Liberal Democracy, Authoritarian Pasts, and Intellectual History in East Central Europe After 1989*, ed. Michal Kopeček and Piotr Wciślik, 463–504. Budapest: Central European University Press, 2015.

Martens, Bernd. "East German Economic Elites and Their Companies Two Decades After the Transformation ("Wende"): Still Following the Patterns of the 1990s." *Journal for East European Management Studies* 13, no. 4 (2008): 305–326.

Maškarinec, Pavel. "Komparace systémových projevů totalitního panství NDR a Československa v letech 1953–1968 v rovině politického pluralismu a způsobů jeho potírání." *Slovenská politologická revue* 1 (2010): 39–58.

Massino, Jill. *Ambiguous Transitions: Gender, Everyday Life, and the State in Socialist and Postsocialist Romania.* New York: Berghahn, 2019.

Matějů, Petr. "From Equality to Equity?: The Czech Republic Between Two Ideologies of Distributive Justice." *Czech Sociological Review* 1, no. 3 (1993): 251–275.

Matějů, Petr, and Nelson Lim. "Who Has Gotten Ahead After the Fall of Communism?" *Sociologický časopis/Czech Sociological Review* 3, no. 2 (1995): 117–136.

BIBLIOGRAPHY

Matějů, Petr. and Anna Vitásková. "Interpersonal Trust and Mutually Beneficial Exchanges: Measuring Social Capital for Comparative Analyses." *Sociologický časopis/ Czech Sociological Review* 42, no. 3 (2006): 493–516.

Mau, Steffen. *Lütten-Klein: Leben in der ostdeutschen Transformationsgesellschaft.* Berlin: Suhrkamp, 2019.

McCall, Leslie. *The Undeserving Rich: American Beliefs about Inequality, Opportunity, and Redistribution.* Cambridge: Cambridge University Press, 2013.

McDermott, Kevin. *Communist Czechoslovakia, 1945–89: A Political and Social History.* New York: Macmillan International Higher Education, 2015.

McPherson, Miller, Lynn Smith-Lovin, and James M. Cook. "Birds of a Feather: Homophily in Social Networks." *Annual Review of Sociology* 27 (2001): 415–444.

Meuleman, Bart, Femke Roosma, and Koen Abts. "Welfare Deservingness Opinions from Heuristic to Measurable Concept: The CARIN Deservingness Principles Scale." *Social Science Research* 85 (2020): 102352.

Mijs, Jonathan B. "The Paradox of Inequality: Income Inequality and Belief in Meritocracy Go Hand in Hand." *Socio-Economic Review* 19, no. 1 (2021): 7–35.

Miller, Daniel. *Principles of Social Justice.* Cambridge, MA: Harvard University Press, 1999.

——. *Social Justice.* Oxford: Oxford University Press, 1979.

Mische, Ann. "Relational Sociology, Culture, and Agency." In *The Sage Handbook of Social Network Analysis*, ed. Joan Scott and Peter J. Carrington, 80–97. Los Angeles: Sage, 2011.

Misoch, Sabina. *Qualitative Interviews.* Berlin: de Gruyter, 2014.

Mohr, John, et. al. *Measuring Culture.* New York: Columbia University Press, 2020.

Montada, Leo, and Anne Dieter. "Gewinn-und Verlusterfahrungen in den Neuen Bundesländern: Nicht die Kaufkraft der Einkommen, sondern Politische Bewertungen sind entscheidend." In *Gerechtigkeitserleben im Wiedervereinigten Deutschland*, ed. Rudi Schmitt and Leo Montada, 19–44. Wiesbaden: Springer, 1999.

Morgan, Stephen L. "Status Threat, Material Interests, and the 2016 Presidential Vote." *Socius* 4 (2018): 1–17.

Mrozowicki, Adam. *Coping with Social Change: Life Strategies of Workers in Poland's New Capitalism.* Leuven: Leuven University Press, 2011.

Mueller, Carol. "Claim 'Radicalization'?: The 1989 Protest Cycle in the GDR." *Social Problems* 46, no. 4 (1999): 528–546.

Murdock, Caitlin. *Changing Places: Society, Culture, and Territory in the Saxon-Bohemian Borderlands, 1870–1946.* Ann Arbor: University of Michigan Press, 2010.

Mutz, Diana C. "Status Threat, Not Economic Hardship, Explains the 2016 Presidential Vote." *Proceedings of the National Academy of Sciences* 115 (2018): E4330–E4339.

Myant, Martin. *The Rise and Fall of Czech Capitalism: Economic Development in the Czech Republic Since 1989.* Cheltenham, UK: Edward Elgar, 2003.

Nauck, Bernhard, and Otto G. Schwenk. "Did Societal Transformation Destroy the Social Networks of Families in East Germany?" *American Behavioral Scientist* 44, no. 11 (2001): 1864–1878.

Newman, Katherine S. *Falling from Grace: The Experience of Downward Mobility in the American Middle Class.* New York: Free Press, 1988.

Noll, Heinz-Herbert, and Bernhard Christoph. "Akzeptanz und Legitimität sozialer Ungleichheit." In *Sozialer und Politischer Wandel in Deutschland. Analysen mit*

Allbus-Daten aus Zwei Jahrzehnten, ed. Rüdiger Schmitt-Beck, Martina Wasmer, and Achim Koch, 97–125. Wiesbaden: VS Verlag, 2004.

Nora, Pierre. "Between Memory and History: Les Lieux de Mémoire." *Representations* 26 (1989): 7–24.

Offe, Claus. *Varieties of Transition: The East European and East German Experience.* Cambridge: Polity Press, 1996.

Olick, Jeffrey K. "Collective Memory: The Two Cultures." *Sociological Theory* 17, no. 3 (2000): 333–348.

Olsen, Jonathan. "The Left Party and the AfD: Populist Competitors in Eastern Germany." *German Politics and Society* 36, no. 1 (2018): 70–83.

Orenstein, Mitchell A. *Out of the Red: Building Capitalism and Democracy in Postcommunist Europe.* Ann Arbor: University of Michigan Press, 2001.

Orloff, Ann S. *The Politics of Pensions: A Comparative Analysis of Britain, Canada, and the United States, 1880–1940.* Madison: University of Wisconsin Press, 1993.

Ost, David. *The Defeat of Solidarity.* Ithaca, NY: Cornell University Press, 2005.

Padgett, Stephen. *Organizing Democracy in Eastern Germany: Interest Groups in Post-Communist Society.* Cambridge: Cambridge University Press, 1999.

Papouschek, Ulrike, and Nils Böhlke, *Strukturwandel und Arbeitsbeziehungen im Gesundheitswesen in Tschechien, Deutschland, Polen und Österreich.* Vienna: FORBA, 2008.

Patico, Jennifer. "Spinning the Market: The Moral Alchemy of Everyday Talk in Postsocialist Russia." *Critique of Anthropology* 29, no. 2 (2009): 205–224.

Pehe, Veronika. *Velvet Retro: Postsocialist Nostalgia and the Politics of Heroism in Czech Popular Culture.* New York: Berghahn, 2020.

——. "The Wild 1990s: 'Transformation Nostalgia' Among the Czech Student Generation of 1989." *East Central Europe* 46, no. 1 (2019): 111–134.

Pew Research Center. "European Public Opinion Three Decades After the Fall of Communism." https://www.pewresearch.org/global/2019/10/15/european-public-opinion -three-decades-after-the-fall-of-communism/.

Pichler, Florian, and Claire Wallace. "Patterns of Formal and Informal Social Capital in Europe." *European Sociological Review* 23, no. 4 (2007): 423–435.

Pokorny, Jiří, "Die Betriebsklubs in der Tschechoslowakei 1945–1968: Zur Organisation sozialistischer Erziehung, Kultur und Erholung der Arbeiterschaft." In *Sozialgeschichtliche Kommunismusforschung: Tschechoslowakei, Polen, Ungarn und die DDR 1945–1968*, ed. Christiane Brenner and Peter Heumos, 263–275. Munich: Oldenbourg Verlag, 2005.

Polanyi, Karl. *The Great Transformation: The Political and Economic Origins of Our Time.* Boston: Beacon Press, 2001.

Pollak, Reinhard, and Walter Müller. "Soziale Mobilität in Ost-und Westdeutschland im ersten Jahrzehnt nach der Wiedervereinigung." In *Sozialer und politischer Wandel in Deutschland*, ed. Rüdiger Schmitt-Beck, Martina Wasmer, and Achim Koch, 69–95. Wiesbaden: Springer, 2004.

Pollert, Anna. *Transformation at Work in the New Market Economies of Central Eastern Europe.* London: Sage, 1999.

Polletta, Francesca. *Inventing the Ties That Bind: Imagined Relationships in Moral and Political Life.* Chicago: Chicago University Press, 2020.

BIBLIOGRAPHY

Pop-Eleches, Grigore, and Joshua A. Tucker. *Communism's Shadow: The Effect of Communist Legacies on Post-Communist Political Attitudes.* Princeton, NJ: Princeton University Press, 2017.

Posner, Christine. *Die Bedeutung sozialer Einbindung für die Entwicklung von Individualisierungsprozessen: Eine theoretische Annäherung an das Phänomen der Individualisierung sowie eine empirische Analyse der sozialen Bindungen unter den Bedingungen des sozialen Umbruchs in Deutschland.* Frankfurt: Peter Lang, 2002.

Pospíšilová, Tereza. "Dobrovolnictví v České republice před rokem 1989: diskurzy, definice, aktualizace." *Sociologický časopis/Czech Sociological Review* 47, no. 5 (2011): 887–910.

Pozniak, Kinga, and Nowa Huta. *Generations of Change in a Model Socialist Town.* Pittsburgh, PA: University of Pittsburgh Press, 2014.

Presser, Luis. "Violent Offenders, Moral Selves: Constructing Identities and Accounts in the Research Interview." *Social Problems* 51, no 1 (2004): 82–101.

Pugh, Allison J. *The Tumbleweed Society: Working and Caring in an Age of Insecurity.* Oxford: Oxford University Press, 2015.

Pullmann, Michal. *Konec experimentu: Přestavba a pád komunismu v Československu.* Prague: Scriptorium, 2011.

——. "'Ruhige Arbeit' und Einhegung der Gewalt. Ideologie und Gesellschaftlicher Konsens in der Spätsozialistischen Tschechoslowakei." In *Ordnung und Sicherheit, Devianz und Kriminalität im Staatssozialismus. Tschechoslowakei und DDR 1948/49–1989,* ed. Volker Zimmermann and Michal Pullman, 39–59. Göttingen: Vandenhoeck & Ruprecht, 2014.

Ragnitz, Joachim. "Ostdeutschland heute: Viel erreicht, viel zu tun." *IFO-Schnelldienst* 61, no. 18 (2009): 3–13.

Rakušanová, Petra. *Povaha občanské společnosti v České Republice v kontextu střední Evropy.* Praha: Sociologický ústav AV ČR, 2007.

Read, Rosie. "Caring Values and the Value of Care: Women, Maternalism, and Caring Work in the Czech Republic." *Contemporary European History* 28, (2019): 500–511.

——. "Labour and Love: Competing Constructions of 'Care' in a Czech Nursing Home." *Critique of Anthropology,* 27, no. 2 (2007): 203–222.

Reed, Isaac A. *Power in Modernity: Agency Relations and the Creative Destruction of the King's Two Bodies.* Chicago: University of Chicago Press, 2020.

Reed, Isaac A., and Julia P. Adams. "Culture in the Transitions to Modernity: Seven Pillars of a New Research Agenda." *Theory and Society* 40, no. 3 (2011): 247–272.

Řeháková, Blanka. "Vzorce přátelství v české společnosti/Friendship Patterns in Czech Society." *Sociologický časopis/Czech Sociological Review* 39, no. 4 (2003): 509–528.

Rivera, Mark T., Sara B. Soderstrom, and Brian Uzzi. "Dynamics of Dyads in Social Networks: Assortative, Relational, and Proximity Mechanisms." *Annual Review of Sociology* 36, (2010): 91–115.

Robert Koch Institut. *Epidemiologisches Bulletin* 27/2022, https://www.rki.de/DE/Content /Infekt/EpidBull/Archiv/2022/Ausgaben/27_2022.pdf?__blob=publicationFile (accessed December 18, 2022).

Róna-Tas, Ákos. "The Worm and the Caterpillar: The Small Private Sector in the Czech Republic, Hungary and Slovakia." In *The New Entrepreneurs of Europe and Asia: Patterns of Business Development in Russia, Eastern Europe, and China,* ed. Victoria E. Bonnell and Thomas B. Gold, 38–65. Armonk, NY: M.E. Sharpe, 2002.

Rosanvillon, Pierre. *The Society of Equals*. Cambridge, MA: Harvard University Press, 2013.

Rose, Richard. *Understanding Post-Communist Transformation: A Bottom Up Approach*. London: Routledge, 2009.

Rubin, Herbert, and Irene S. Rubin. *Qualitative Interviewing: The Art of Hearing Data*. Thousand Oaks, CA: Sage, 2012.

Sachweh, Patrick, and Sebastian Koos. "The Moral Economies of Market Societies: Popular Attitudes Towards Market Competition, Redistribution and Reciprocity in Comparative Perspective." *Socio-Economic Review* 17, no. 4 (2019): 793–821.

Šafr, Jiří. "Status Homogeneity and Heterogeneity in Social Contacts." In *Social Distances and Stratification: Social Space in the Czech Republic*, ed. Jiří Šafr and Julia Häuberer, 55–66. Prague: Sociologický ústav AV ČR, 2008.

Sandel, Michael J. *The Tyranny of Merit: What's Become of the Common Good?* New York: Penguin Classics, 2020.

Savage, Mike. *The Return of Inequality: Social Change and the Weight of the Past*. Cambridge, MA: Harvard University Press, 2021.

Saxonberg, Steve. "Eastern Europe." In *The Routledge Handbook of the Welfare State*, ed. Bent Greve, 171–182. London: Routledge, 2012.

Sayer, Andrew R. *The Moral Significance of Class*. Cambridge: Cambridge University Press, 2005.

Schaub, Johannes. "Freundschaftsnetzwerke in den neuen Bundesländern." *Gruppe Interaktion Organisation: Zeitschrift für Angewandte Organisationspsychologie (GIO)* 33, no. 3 (2002): 295–310.

Scheiring, Gábor. "Left Behind in the Hungarian Rustbelt: The Cultural-Political Economy of Working-Class Neo-Nationalism." *Sociology* 54, no. 6 (2020): 1159–1177.

Schindler-Wisten, Petra. " 'Pozor, vizita!' Sonda do života zdravotních sester v období tzv. normalizace a transformace," In *Příběhy (ne)obyčejných profesí. Česká společnost v období tvz. normalizace a transformace*, ed. Miroslav Vaněk and Lenka Krátká, 419–459. Praha: Karolinum, 2014.

Schlegelmilch, Cordula. "Zwischen Kollektiv und Individualisierung-Gemeinschaftserfahrungen im Umbruch." In *Vergesellschaftung und Frauenerwerbsarbeit im Ost-West-Vergleich*, ed. Sabine Gensior, 27–49. Berlin: Edition Sigma, 1995.

Schmelzer, Paul. "Netzwerkveränderung als Folge der Transformation?" *Berliner Journal für Soziologie* 15, no. 1 (2005): 73–86.

Schmitt-Beck, Rüdiger, and Robert Rohrschneider. "Soziales Kapital und Vertrauen in die Institutionen der Demokratie." In *Sozialer und Politischer Wandel in Deutschland: Analysen mit Allbus-Daten aus zwei Jahrzehnten*, ed. Rüdiger Schmitt-Beck, Martina Wasmer, and Achim Koch, 235–260. Wiesbaden: VS Verlag, 2004.

Schneider, Simone M., and Juan C. Castillo. "Poverty Attributions and the Perceived Justice of Income Inequality: A Comparison of East and West Germany." *Social Psychology Quarterly* 78, no 3 (2015): 263–282.

Schumann, Howard, and Amy Corning. "The Conversion of Generational Effects into Collective Memory." *International Journal of Public Opinion Research* 29, no. 3 (2016): 520–532.

Sedláčková, Markéta, and Jiří Šafr. "Legitimacy and Civic Culture: Trust in Democracy in the Czech Republic After EU Accession (2004–2014)." *Comparative Sociology* 17, no. 3–4 (2018): 318–353.

BIBLIOGRAPHY

Segert, Dieter. *Das 41. Jahr. Eine andere Geschichte der DDR.* Cologne: Böhlau Verlag, 2008.

——. *Transformationen in Osteuropa im 20: Jahrhundert.* Bonn: Bundeszentrale für Politische Bildung, 2014.

Sekula, Allan. *Photography Against the Grain: Essays and Photo Works, 1973–1983.* Halifax: Nova Scotia College of Arts and Design, 1984.

Sennett, Richard, and Jonathan Cobb. *The Hidden Injuries of Class.* Cambridge: Cambridge University Press, 1972.

Seron, Caroll, Susan Silbey, Erin Cech, and Brian Rubineau. "'I Am Not a Feminist, but . . .': Hegemony of a Meritocratic Ideology and the Limits of Critique Among Women in Engineering." *Work and Occupations* 45, no. 2 (2018): 131–167.

Sewell, William H. "Three Temporalities: Toward an Eventful Sociology." In *The Historic Turn in the Human Sciences,* ed. Terrence McDonnell, 245–280. Ann Arbor: University of Michigan Press, 1996.

Shiller, Robert J. *Narrative Economics: How Stories Go Viral & Drive Major Economic Events.* Princeton, NJ: Princeton University Press, 2019.

Shore, Marci. "(The End of) Communism as a Generational History: Some Thoughts on Czechoslovakia and Poland." *Contemporary European History* 18, no. 3 (2009): 303–329.

——. *The Taste of Ashes: The Afterlife of Totalitarianism in Eastern Europe.* New York: Random House, 2013.

Simko, Christina. "Forgetting to Remember: The Present Neglect and Future Prospects of Collective Memory in Sociological Theory." In *Handbook of Contemporary Sociological Theory,* ed. Seth Abrutyn, 457–475. New York: Springer, 2016.

Sinn, Hans-Werner. "Zehn Jahre deutsche Wiedervereinigung. Ein Kommentar zur Lage der neuen Länder." *IFO-Schnelldienst* 53, no. 26/27 (2000): 10–22.

Sirovátka, Tomáš, and Ondřej Hora. "Public Sector Employment in the Czech Republic After 1989: Old Legacy in New Realities?" *Central European Journal of Public Policy,* no. 7 (2013): 4–35.

Skovajsa, Marek, et al. *Občanský sektor: Organizovaná občanská společnost v České republice.* Praha: Portál, 2010.

Small, Mario L. *Unanticipated Gains: Origins of Network Inequality in Everyday Life.* New York: Oxford University Press, 2009.

Smith, Adam. *Theory of Moral Sentiments: The Glasgow Edition of the Works and Correspondence of Adam Smith, Vol. I.* Oxford: Oxford University Press, 1976.

Smith, Michael L. "Perceived Corruption, Distributive Justice, and the Legitimacy of the System of Social Stratification in the Czech Republic." *Communist and Post-Communist Studies* 43, no. 4 (2010): 439–451.

Smith, Michael L., and Petr Matějů. "Two Decades of Value Change: The Crystallization of Meritocratic and Egalitarian Beliefs in the Czech Republic." *Social Justice Research* 25, no. 4 (2012): 421–439.

Smith, Philip. *Why War?: The Cultural Logic of Iraq, the Gulf War, and Suez.* Chicago: University of Chicago Press, 2005.

Snyder, Timothy. *The Road to Unfreedom: Russia, Europe, America.* New York: Tim Duggan Books, 2018.

Sobotka, Tomáš. "Fertility in Central and Eastern Europe After 1989: Collapse and Gradual Recovery." *Historical Social Research/Historische Sozialforschung* 36, no. 2 (2011): 246–296.

BIBLIOGRAPHY

Solga, Heike. "The Rise of -Meritocracy?: Class Mobility in East Germany Before and After 1989." In *After the Fall of the Wall: Life Courses in the Transformation of East Germany*, ed. Martin Diewald, Anne Goedicke, and Karl Ulrich Mayer, 140–169. Stanford, CA: Stanford University Press.

Somers, Margaret R. "The Narrative Constitution of Identity: A Relational and Network Approach." *Theory and Society* 23, no. 5 (1994): 605–649.

Špiláčková, Martina. *Soziale Arbeit im Sozialismus: Ein Beispiel aus der Tschechoslowakei (1968–1989)*. Wiesbaden: Springer-Verlag, 2014.

Struck, Olaf. "Aufschwung und Unzufriedenheit. Strukturwandel und Lebenssituation in Ostdeutschland." Working Paper No. 19-2017, University of Bamberg, 2018

Swidler, Ann. "Culture in Action: Symbols and Strategies." *American Sociological Review* 51, no. 2 (1986): 273–286.

Tavits, Margit, and Natalia Letki. "When Left Is Right: Party Ideology and Policy in Post-Communist Europe." *American Political Science Review* 103, no 4 (2009): 555–569.

Ther, Philip. *Europe Since 1989: A History*. Princeton, NJ: Princeton University Press, 2016.

Thompson, Edward P. *The Making of the English Working Class*. New York: Vintage Books, 1963.

Tomášek, Marcel. "Naše blízké vztahy a společenské demokratizační změny. K novému chápání zdrojů integrace a reprodukce společnosti po roce 1989." *Gender rovné příležitosti výzkum* 8, no. 2 (2007): 1–6.

Tóthová, Valerie, and Gabriela Sedláková. "Nursing Education in the Czech Republic." *Nurse Education Today* 28, no. 1 (2008): 33–38.

Traunmüller, Richard. "Spheres of Trust: An Empirical Analysis of the Foundations of Particularised and Generalised Trust." *European Journal of Political Research* 48, no. 6 (2009): 782–803.

True, Jacqui. *Gender, Globalization, and Postsocialism: The Czech Republic After Communism*. New York: Columbia University Press, 2003.

Tucker, Aviezer. *The Legacies of Totalitarianism: A Theoretical Framework*. Cambridge: Cambridge University Press, 2015.

Turnaturi, Gabriella. *Betrayals: The Unpredictability of Human Relations*. Chicago: University of Chicago Press, 2005.

Uslaner, Eric M., and Gabriel Badescu. "Honesty, Trust, and Legal Norms in the Transition to Democracy: Why Bo Rothstein Is Better Able to Explain Sweden Than Romania." In *Creating Social Trust in Post-Socialist Transition*, ed. Janos Kornai, Bo Rothstein, and Susan Rose-Ackerman, 31–51. New York: Palgrave MacMillan, 2004.

Vaněk, Miroslav, and Pavel Mücke. *Velvet Revolutions: An Oral History of Czech Society*. Oxford: Oxford University Press, 2016.

Vanhuysse, Pieter. "Czech Exceptionalism?: A Comparative Political Economy Interpretation of Post-Communist Policy Pathways, 1989–2004." *Sociologický časopis/Czech Sociological Review* 42, no. 6 (2006): 1115–1136.

Van Oorschot, Wim. "Making the Difference in Social Europe: Deservingness Perceptions Among Citizens of European Welfare States." *Journal of European Social Policy* 16, no. 1 (2006): 23–42.

Vaughan, Diane. *Uncoupling: Turning Points in Intimate Relationships*. New York: Vintage, 1990.

BIBLIOGRAPHY

Večerník, Jiří. *Czech Society in the 2000s: A Report on Socio-Economic Policies and Structures*. Prague: Alibris, 2009.

——. *Markets and People: The Czech Reform Experience in a Comparative Perspective*. Avebury: Aldershot, 1996.

Večerník, Jiří, and Petr Matějů. *Ten Years of Rebuilding Capitalism: Czech Society After 1989*. Prague: Academia, 1999.

Verbrugge, Lois M. "The Structure of Adult Friendship Choices." *Social Forces* 56, no. 2 (1977): 576–597.

Verdery, Katherine. "Postsocialist Cleansing in Eastern Europe: Purity and Danger in Transitional Justice." In *Socialism Vanquished, Socialism Challenged: Eastern Europe and China, 1989–2009*, ed. Nina Bandelj and Dorothy J. Solinger, 63–82. Oxford: Oxford University Press, 2012.

——. *What Was Socialism, and What Comes Next?* Princeton, NJ: Princeton University Press, 1996.

Vlachová, Klára, and Blanka Řeháková. "Subjective Mobility After 1989: Do People Feel a Social and Economic Improvement or Relative Deprivation?" *Sociologický časopis/ Czech Sociological Review* 3, no. 1 (1995): 137–155.

Volker, Beate, and Henk Flap. "Weak Ties as a Liability: The Case of East Germany." *Rationality and Society* 13, no. 4 (2001): 397–428.

Wagner-Pacifici, Robin. *The Art of Surrender: Decomposing Sovereignty at Conflict's End*. Chicago: University of Chicago Press, 2005.

——. *What Is an Event?* Chicago: University of Chicago Press, 2017.

Walter, Stefan. " 'Arbeit und Fleiß, das sind die Flügel . . .': Die Thematisierung von Arbeit und Leistung in Poesialben der DDR und der Bundesrepublik zwischen 1945 und 1989." *AIS-Studien* 11, no. 2 (2018): 7–24.

Wanner, Catherine. "Money, Morality and New Forms of Exchange in Postsocialist Ukraine." *Ethnos* 70, no. 4 (2005): 515–537.

Watkins-Hayes, Celeste, and Elyse G. Kovalsky. "The Discourse of Deservingness." In *The Oxford Handbook of the Social Science of Poverty*, ed. David Brady and Linda M. Burton, 193–220. Oxford: Oxford University Press, 2016.

Wawrzyniak, Joanna. "Hard Times but Our Own: Post-Socialist Nostalgia and the Transformation of Industrial Life in Poland." *Zeithistorische Forschungen/Studies in Contemporary History* 18 (2021): 73–92.

Wegener, Bernd, and Stefan Liebig. "Gerechtigkeitsvorstellungen in Ost-und West-deutschland im Wandel: Sozialisation, Interessen, Lebenslauf." In *Leben in Ost-und Westdeutschland. Eine Sozialwissenschaftliche Bilanz der Deutschen Einheit, 1990–2010*, ed. Peter Krause and Ilona Ostner, 83–102. Frankfurt: Campus, 2010.

Weiner, Eliane S. "No (Wo) Man's Land: The Post-Socialist Purgatory of Czech Female Factory Workers." *Social Problems* 52, no. 4 (2005): 572–592.

Wellman, Barry, Renita Yuklin Wong, David Tindall, and Nancy Nazer. "A Decade of Network Change: Turnover, Persistence and Stability in Personal Communities." *Social Networks* 19, no. 1 (1997): 27–50.

Wherry, Fred F. *The Culture of Markets*. Cambridge: Polity, 2012.

Wierling, Dorothee. "Work, Workers, and Politics in the German Democratic Republic." *International Labor and Working-Class History* 50 (1996): 44–63.

Winant, Gabriel. *The Next Shift: The Fall of Industry and the Rise of Health Care in Rustbelt America*. Cambridge, MA: Harvard University Press, 2021.

Windolf, Paul. "Die Wirtschaftliche Transformation. Politische und Ökonomische Systemrationalitäten." In *Der Vereinigungsschock. Vergleichende Betrachtungen Zehn Jahre danach*, ed. Wolfgang Schluchter and Peter Quint, 392–413. Weilerswist: Velbrück Wissenschaft, 2001.

Wohlrab-Sahr, Monika, Uta Karstein, and Thomas Schmidt-Lux. *Forcierte Säkularität. Religiöser Wandel und Generationendymaik im Osten Deutschlands*. Frankfurt: Campus, 2009.

Xu, Bin. "Intragenerational Variations in Autobiographical Memory: China's 'Sent-Down Youth' Generation." *Social Psychology Quarterly* 82, no. 2 (2019): 134–157.

Yagan, Danny. "Employment Hysteresis from the Great Recession." *Journal of Political Economy* 127, no. 5 (2019): 2505–2558.

Yurchak, Alexei. *Everything Was Forever, Until It Was No More: The Last Soviet Generation*. Princeton, NJ: Princeton University Press, 2006.

Zatlin, Jonathan R. "Scarcity and Resentment. Economic Sources of Xenophobia in the GDR, 1971–1989." *Central European History* 40, no. 4 (2007): 683–720.

Zelizer, Viviana A. *The Social Meaning of Money*. New York: Basic Books, 1998.

Zussman, Robert. *Mechanics of the Middle Class: Work and Politics Among American Engineers*. Berkeley: University of California Press, 1985.

INDEX

Abend, Gabriel, 30
agency: and eventfulness, 20;
    biographical, 70, 73, 84, 118, 178;
    economic, 57, 167; individual and
    structural, 56, 109, 111, 116, 143; moral
    evaluation of, 11, 25–27, 92, 93, 97–98,
    102, 106, 131, 133, 134, 160, 164
agriculture, 7, 30, 52
Alexander, Jeffrey, 26, 168
Alexievich, Svetlana, 111
Alternative for Germany (AfD), 169, 170
anticommunism, 58
anti-intellectualism, 43
Association of Dissatisfied Citizens
    (ANO), 170
attributions of responsibility, 102. *See also*
    principles of distributive justice
Augustine, Dolores, 64
Austria, 90, 177; border to communist-
    ruled Hungary, 47
Austro-Hungarian Empire, 34

Babiš, Andrej, 170
Balkans, 48
Bandelj, Nina, 5, 142
Bavaria, 115, 117

Belarus, 6
Berezin, Mabel, 20
Berlin, 9, 36, 46, 47
Berlin Wall: erection of the, 40; fall of
    the, 4, 10, 47, 50, 51, 57, 68, 71, 72, 83,
    88, 109, 113, 118, 120, 126, 128, 132, 143,
    144, 150
betrayal, 95, 158–60
Black Sea, 133
Blaive, Muriel, 62
Bohemia: industrialization, 37, 175
Bohemian, Moravian, and Silesian lands
    (Czech lands), 34
Bourdieu, Pierre, 29, 140, 145, 152, 162
"breaching experiment," 132
breadwinner model, 28, 154
Britain, 94
Brno, 48
broken tie, 132–35
"Brussels bureaucracy," 60
Bulgaria, 114
Burt, Ronald, 116

California, 1
car industry, 66, 74
Caspi, Avshalom, 129

Center for Economics and Politics
(CEP), 60
Central Eastern Europe, 15, 17, 65, 80, 114,
161, 168, 180
child care, 41, 154; and privatization, 55
China, 19
Christianity, 22
Cibulka's list, 137
Civic Forum, 47
climate crisis, 2, 16
Cobb, Jonathan, 92, 117
Cold War, 35, 43
collective (organizational unit), 41, 42,
85, 143
Communist Party, 13, 130, 155; elite, 5, 7,
43, 46, 56; functionaries, 40, 103; rule,
36, 39, 95, 121, 132, 135, 170, 174
Communist Party of Czechoslovakia
(KSČ), 35, 39, 43, 44
corruption, 5, 61, 95, 122, 123; and
privatization, 53, 54, 60, 103, 108,
124; and right-wing populism, 170;
perceptions of, 10, 79, 109, 124, 171
COVID-19 pandemic, 63, 78, 123
"critical years hypothesis," 19
Croatia, 125
cultural trauma, 26, 168

Das Leben der Anderen (movie), 136
"deaths of despair," 8
defiance, 45, 96, 153
deindustrialization, 4, 8, 15, 86, 114, 171
demographic trends after 1989, 127;
population decline, 114
Desmond, Matthew, 179
Diaz-Bone, Rainer, 126
Diewald, Martin, 51, 126
disassociating, 132, 134, 142, 143, 164, 165.
See also broken tie
dissidents, 5, 43, 46, 122
distributive justice: popular ideas of,
23–27; principles of, 9, 24, 31, 97
divorce, 29, 116, 125, 127, 132
Dunn, Elizabeth, 9
Durkheim, Emile, 17, 18, 157, 168
duty to work, 40, 104

East German Communist Party (SED),
36, 39, 44, 47, 170
economic integration, 37
economic nationalism, 49, 59, 60
economic think tanks, 57, 58, 60
economic victimhood, 27, 93, 108,
109, 167
economy of shortage, 88, 119
egalitarianism, 10, 93–96, 105, 163; as
a justice ideology, 94, 161; in state-
socialist societies, 40, 43
Eight Party Congress of 1971 (GDR), 44
emigration, 113
engineering, 63, 170; and acceleration,
76; and entrepreneurial activities,
69–70; and gender, 63; and job
security, 67; and legal frameworks of
regulation, 81; and monetization, 78;
and notions of distributive justice, 93,
103, 105; and recognition of skills after
1989, 64, 65, 68, 74, 84, 87–88; and
Soviet economy, 38; and technological
advances, 74; and unemployment, 65;
construction engineering, 74, 78, 87,
109, 131, 136; status in state-socialist
societies, 64
entrepreneurship, 51, 55, 69, 70, 76,
79, 139, 140, 142; and social
capital, 120
envy, 99, 144, 145, 152
equality, 43, 97, 113, 142–46, 143, 162–63;
of opportunity, 102, 106–8
Eribon, Didier, 111
European Bank for Reconstruction and
Development (EBRD), 6
European Union (EU), 8, 60, 90
eventful sociology, 20, 21
"extraordinary mentality," 96
Eyerman, Ron, 168

Flap, Henryk, 126
forced labor, 139
foreign direct investments, 54
France, 18
friendship, 3, 12, 18, 32, 111, 115, 132, 161;
and betrayal, 158–62; and patterns of

change after 1989, 126, 127; and tie decay, 116; as a "thick moral" concept, 30; episodes of broken ties, 132–54; workplace and friendship relations in state-socialist societies, 127

Garfinkel, Harold, 132
gender, 4, 63, 92, 118, 161, 176, 177; and economic nationalism, 14; and engineering, 15; and health care, 65; and homophily, 132; and ideas about work, 155; and social downward mobility, 28; and social position in notions of deservingness, 105; and state-socialist labor policies, 40; and styles of network attachment, 155; and support networks, 28; and unemployment, 54; and wage disparities after 1989, 55
Ghodsee, Kristen, 8
Gibson, Christopher, 5
Gidron, Noam, 168
Glaeser, Andreas, 9
Great Depression, 4

Habsburg Parliament, 59
Halbwachs, Maurice, 18
Hall, Peter, 168
Hann, Chris, 9
Havel, Václav, 47
health care, 6, 65; and acceleration, 77; and coercive measures before 1989, 83; and gender inequality, 40, 54, 65; and improved working conditions after 1989, 75; and insurance level classification, 82; and labor costs, 65; and loss of autonomy, 82; and monetization after 1989, 65; and rise of bureaucratization, 81–82; and sectoral shifts, 15; and state-socialist welfare, 41, 65; and the rise of medical ethics, 82–83; and underinvestment, 55; inferior value in state-socialism, 64–66. See also privatization, of hospitals
heavy military industry, 74

higher education: and social mobility after 1989, 65; in state-socialism, 40, 42
Hitler, Adolf, 35
Holmes, Stephen, 11, 114, 168
Holy, Ladislav, 95
homophily, 118, 132
Honecker, Erich, 44, 47
Honneth, Axel, 18, 27, 146
hospitals, 83, 115, 177; and bed occupancy, 80; and privatization, 51, 67, 77, 79; and working conditions in state-socialism, 82; working conditions in state-socialism, 75
Hungary, 7, 8, 36, 38, 120, 168
Husák, Gustav, 44, 47

individualization, 12, 128
Industrial Age, 37
industrial politics, 37–38
informal economy of state-socialist societies, 28, 41
Institute for Economic Research (IFO), 58
intelligentsia, 42
International Monetary Fund (IMF), 6

job loss, 67–69; and long-term unemployment, 72; and negative ramifications, 71; fear of, 68. See also unemployment
Judt, Tony, 33

Kaźmierska, Kaja, 179
kinship ties, 119, 127, 158; and patterns of change after 1989, 126, 130
Klaus, Václav, 48, 53, 58, 59, 60, 90
Kohli, Martin, 39
Krastev, Ivan, 11, 114, 168
Kreidl, Martin, 107

labor force, 7, 14, 40, 43, 50, 52, 66, 67
labor market: and discrimination of ethnic minorities, 54; and gender inequality, 55, 155; and life chances after 1989, 15, 25, 63, 105, 109, 154, 175;

labor force (*continued*)
and perceptions of change, 96, 97,
100, 106, 124, 155, 156; and reforms
of the 1990s, 52, 53, 68; and reforms
of the 2000s, 150; and skills, 84; and
social capital, 120; and valuation of
skills, 64; crisis, 51, 60, 68, 71, 72, 93,
113, 125, 175
labor office, 68, 71, 104
labor policies, 6, 52, 54; paternalistic
policies in state-socialism, 39–41
Lamont, Michèle, 142
Lampland, Martha, 9
Lane, Robert, 171
Latvia, 114
Leyk, Alexsandra, 179
LGBQT+ rights, 168
liberalization of prices, 6, 52
lieux de mémoire, 108
life expectancy, 8
Lithuania, 114
"living in truth," 122
Lockheed Martin, 1
Lüdicke, Jörg, 126

Margalit, Avishai, 158, 159, 160, 162
market justice, 95, 100, 103, 171. *See also*
meritocratic ideology
market society, 12, 57, 61, 88, 92, 96,
109, 134, 174; and gender inequality,
154; and social capital, 120, 124;
enthusiasm for, 94; promise of, 9, 52,
90, 91; transition to, 11, 32, 66, 148
Marx, Karl, 21, 108
Matějů, Petr, 56
Mau, Steffen, 43
McCall, Leslie, 107
Mead, George Herbert, 27
Mečiar, Vladimír, 48
meritocratic ideology, 2, 10, 12, 24, 30, 32,
55, 94, 96, 105, 107, 163, 164, 169
Merton, Robert, 179
"mezzogiorno problem," 58
migration, 177
Miller, Daniel, 24
Moffitt, Terrie E., 129

monetary union of Germany, 50, 58
Moore, Barrington, 46
moral economy: macro level, 20–23;
micro level, 23–27
moral framework, 12, 14, 16, 17–31, 34,
38, 56, 97, 165; and justice ideas,
23–27; and memory, 19–22; and social
relations, 27–31
Moscow, 36, 44, 47
Mrozowicki, Adam, 15, 178
Mücke, Pavel, 179
Munich Agreement of 1938, 35

nativism, 46; and violence, 48
Nauck, Bernhard, 126
Nazi occupation of Czechoslovakia, 35
Nazi past, of Germany, 36
Nazism, 173
neo-Nazi groups, 48
network density, 116
New Russians, 30
Newman, Katherine, 28
niche, 28, 126. *See also* informal economy
of state-socialist societies
nomenklatura, 124. *See also* Communist
Party
Nora, Pierre, 108
normal distribution, 116
normalization, 44
nostalgia, 10, 70, 85, 86, 156; for informal
workplace hierarchies, 83; of the late-
socialist period, 47; red nostalgia, 95
Nowa Huta, 85

Offe, Claus, 13, 37
oral history, 15, 62, 174, 178
Orenstein, Mitchell, 8
Organization for Economic Co-operation
and Development (OECD), 54

Pehe, Veronika, 70
people's property, 108
personality coherence, 129
Poland, 5, 7, 8, 15, 36, 38, 53, 120, 125, 168,
169, 173, 179
Polanyi, Karl, 21, 22, 23, 24

polarization, 5
policlinic, 51, 67
Pollert, Anna, 38
poverty, 4, 53
Pozniak, Kinga, 85
Prague, 35, 36, 46, 47, 53, 62, 173
Prague Spring, 36, 43, 44
privatization, 8, 9, 49–56, 51, 56, 58, 60,
    68, 83, 124, 170; and its association
    with corruption, 95, 103, 108; and
    social structure, 92; Czech model,
    52–56; German model, 49–52;
    narrative by right-wing populists, 170;
    of hospitals, 79
productive labor, 13, 42, 44, 46, 54, 85, 86,
    91, 163
propaganda, 5, 46, 47, 48, 135, 180; and
    economic virtues in state-socialism,
    38
Prussia, 34, 35
public sector: and wage inequalities, 50,
    54, 65
public sphere, 57–58
Pugh, Allison, 155
Putnam, Robert, 121

Red Army, 35
refugee crisis of 2015, 177
retraining, 68, 71, 72, 74, 98, 128, 152
Rieger, František Ladislav, 59
Roma, minority group, 46, 54, 104
Romania, 120
Rona-Tas, Akos, 55
Rostock, 43
Russia, 5, 49, 95, 119, 173, 180
rust belt, 8

Saxony, 139; industrialization, 37, 175
Sayer, Andrew, 145, 146, 165
Scheiring, Gábor, 46
Schwenk, Otto G., 126
secret police, 100, 121, 123, 136;
    informants, 36, 103, 135, 136, 137, 138.
    See also Stasi
Sekula, Allan, 1, 2
Sennett, Richard, 92, 117

shame, 2, 28, 145, 148, 151, 153
shock therapy, 6, 7, 31, 49, 52, 58
Shore, Marci, 5, 139, 173
Simmel, Georg, 134
Sinn, Hans-Werner, 58
skills, 11, 31, 83–91; and labor market
    outcomes, 51, 55; and mismatch
    between wages, 91; revaluation of,
    14; ruptures in the recognition of, 87;
    value of engineering skills, 64; value
    of health-care workers' skills, 64
Škoda (firm), 54
Slovakia, 7, 35, 37, 38, 48, 53, 114, 174, 175
small businesses, 53, 55, 132
Small, Mario, 179
Smith, Adam, 92, 109
Snyder, Timothy, 168
social capital, 4, 97, 120, 127
social closure, 127, 162
social cohesion, 18, 121; and solidarity,
    129, 155, 156, 157; and trust, 125. See
    also solidarity
social cohesion: and trust, 125
social comparison, 93, 107
social conservatism, 39, 44, 45, 181
social contract, 13, 14, 15, 22, 46, 64, 175.
    See also moral economy
social entitlements, 41
social integration through work,
    39–47, 163
social mobility, 52, 117; and broken
    friendship ties, 146; in state-socialist
    societies, 39, 42–43; perceptions of, 32;
    promise of, 9, 43
social recognition, 3, 24, 31, 146,
    162; and equality, 146; and moral
    evaluation of agency, 113; and
    right-wing populism, 168; and
    social connections, 27; and social
    inclusion, 17–18, 167; methods to
    study, 179. See also Honneth, Axel
"socially deviant behavior," 45
solidarity, 130, 155–58
Soviet Russia, 161
Soviet Union, 5, 8, 113, 133, 139
Soviet-occupied zone of Germany, 35

split of Czechoslovakia, 49, 53. *See also* Velvet Divorce

Sportprojekt (firm), 69

St. Petersburg, 30

Stalin, Joseph, 35

Stasi (East German secret police), 33, 136; file, 137

state-owned companies, 38, 39, 50, 68, 69, 71, 72, 132, 155; and identity, 41–42; and privatization, 50, 53, 66

state-owned property, 50

strong ties, 29, 30, 31, 130, 146, 162; and patterns of change after 1989, 125–28

structural embeddedness, 116

support networks, 28, 130; after 1989, 27, 28

symbolic boundaries, 30, 97; and race, 104

technological advances, 74–76; computerization, 74; improved hygiene in health care, 75; new medical equipment, 75; specialization, 75

temporality, 10–11, 107; and betrayal, 159; and biographical ruptures, 70; and justice ideas, 20–22, 26, 93, 106–10; and shift from one temporal regime to another, 47

The Engineer's Odyssey (TV series), 38

Ther, Philip, 50

Thompson, Edward Palmer, 21, 23, 63

Thuringia, 170

tie dissolution, 133–35, 180

Treuhandanstalt, 66, 67, 109. *See also* privatization

True, Jacqui, 65

Trump, Donald, 168, 169

trust, 118–25; and informal relations, 119; and secret police activities, 137; and social capital, 120; civic trust and associationism, 121; generalized trust, 123, 124; particularistic trust, 124. *See also* secret police informants; social capital

Turkmenistan, 6

turncoat (opportunist), 103, 108, 109

U.S. Americans: gendered ideas about work, 155; memories of 9-11, 19; social mobility, 28; views of inequality, 10, 107

Ukraine, 5, 28, 95, 114, 119, 120, 161, 180

unemployment, 51, 52, 54, 60, 65, 68, 71, 72, 96, 98, 101, 105, 108, 128, 130, 132, 139, 150, 155; and entrepreneurship, 51; and long-term unemployment, 70; and memory of, 70; and social capital, 130; and welfare attitudes, 25; in state-socialist societies, 40, 67; rates after 1989, 7, 14, 49, 50. *See also* job loss

unification, of Germany, 14, 47, 48, 49, 58, 86, 89, 104, 124, 139, 142, 170

United States, 4, 19, 41, 94, 168

Vaněk, Miroslav, 179

Večerník, Jiří, 54, 56

Velvet Divorce, 48

Velvet Revolution, 4, 59, 62, 69, 109, 138, 154, 157

Verdery, Katherine, 76

vernacular memories, 62, 70

Vienna, 59, 173

Vietnamese, minority group, 46

Villa Tugendhat, 48

Visegrad (region), 8

Volker, Beate, 126

Volkswagen (firm), 54

voucher privatization, 50, 53, 60. *See also* privatization

Wagner-Pacifici, Robin, 20, 180

Waniek, Katerina, 179

Warsaw, 47

Washington Consensus, 6, 54

Wawrzyniak, Joanna, 83, 179

weak ties, 120, 141

wealth, 2, 10, 23, 24, 30, 56, 94, 104, 108, 150, 162, 169; and corruption, 5, 95, 103

welfare dictatorship, 33, 46

Western Europe, 41, 90, 122

INDEX

Winant, Gabriel, 15
window of opportunity, 52, 106
Wismut (firm), 139
working class, 65
working-class people, 142; and cross-class
    friendships, 161; and demand for care,
    15; in state-socialist societies. *See also*
    social mobility

World Bank (WB), 6
World War I, 35

Xu, Bin, 19

Yugoslavia, 36, 48

Zelizer, Viviana, 148